"WELCOME"
A Foreigner's Guide
to
Successful Living
in the
Southern United States

By
Irva Hayward
and
David W. Coombs

"WELCOME"
A Foreigner's Guide
to Successful Living
in the Southern United States

By: Irva Hayward
and David W. Coombs

The Best of Times, Inc.
P.O. Box 1360
Pelham, Alabama 35124

Book Design: Lori Smith & Shannon Ritchie
Cover Design & Illustration: Scott Camp

Exclusive distribution:
Southern Publishers Group
147 Corporate Way
Pelham, Alabama 35124
205/664-6980 • 800/628-0903

ISBN 0-9624032-7-X
Printed and bound in the United States of America
0 9 8 7 6 5 4 3 2 1

About the Authors

Irva R. Hayward, B.A., M.S., is employed in the Orlean Bullard Beeson School of Education, Samford University, Birmingham, Alabama, and is a part-time instructor in the Department of Family and Consumer Economics. Ms. Hayward is a naturalized American who was born and brought up in South Africa. She emigrated with her husband and three children from South Africa and has lived in four different cultures. She has had wide experience in counselling and teaching internationals.

David W. Coombs, Ph.D., MPH, is an associate professor in the School of Public Health and Senior Academic Officer in the Sparkman Center for International Public Health Education, University of Alabama at Birmingham. Dr. Coombs is a native of Florida, and has lived and taught extensively in South and Central America. Dr. Coombs has had extensive experience teaching and counselling foreign newcomers in the United States. He currently teaches international students in the School of Public Health.

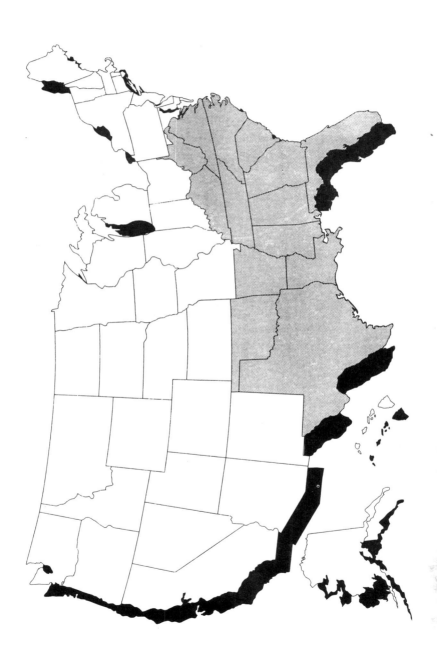

Introduction

This book is for Foreign Newcomers (Internationals)

We have written this book to help foreign newcomers: Students, business people, professionals, or immigrants. We hope the information herein will help the reader to understand this country and to adjust to everyday living in the United States. Some of the information is only relevant to the South, but most is also applicable to the rest of the United States as well.

This book probably can be considered a "mini" encyclopedia of everyday living in the United States. It need not be read at one time. When information is needed about a specific subject, the table of contents at the beginning of the book, and the index at the back, will guide the reader to the information required.

Although every effort has been made to use American well-known words and phrases in general use, readers are invited to use a good American dictionary when reading this book. In addition, the reader should ask an American friend for help when there are ideas, phrases, or words that are not understood.

Acknowledgements

The authors wish to thank the following people for their valuable and enormous help and encouragement in making this book possible:

Eric Hayward, director, Department of Pastoral Care, Baptist Medical Center Montclair, Birmingham, Alabama, an immigrant to the United States, who freely gave up many hours to provide ideas, topics, and psychological interpretations and facts for the completion of this book;

Alto L. Garner, Dean Emeritus, School of Education, Samford University, Birmingham, Alabama, who shared his knowledge of the South—providing the bulk of the guidance and encouragement for this book—and spent many hours reading and critiquing this manuscript;

Marie Holley, a Southern lady born in Alabama and brought up in Washington, D. C. who, with vast experience and knowledge of the South, made valuable suggestions and interpretations about Southern culture and corrected errors of perception;

Joan Coombs, a Southerner from Mobile, Alabama, and a musician, proofed the manuscript, corrected misperceptions, and graciously encouraged the authors;

Marilyn Miller Morton, Fellow of the Irish Genealogical Research Society, London, England, founder and retired director, Samford University *British & Irish Institute of*

Genealogical and Historic Research, a native Mississippian who is also a former high school English and history teacher, who willingly helped to proof this manuscript numerous times;

Rosemary Fisk, assistant professor, Department of English, Samford University, Birmingham, Alabama, who critiqued the manuscript, checked facts, and gave invaluable guidance regarding the organization of the manuscript;

Mary Francis Bailey, a free-lance writer and Virginia native, and experienced counselor to international people, who made suggestions and who checked the manuscript for content;

Pat and Jean Massey, native Southerners from Florida and Alabama, with years of experience in the educational and business worlds, who made suggestions and checked the manuscript for content;

Edward Tibbs, Professor, School of Music, Samford University, Birmingham, Alabama, a native of New Orleans, who gave valuable insights into life in the South and the evolution of Southern music;

Richard and Cheryl Lawley, Ralph and Marrianne Coleman, and Anton and Elizabeth Fourie, who shared their insights, experiences, and interpretations of being either newcomers or of being married to newcomers and encouraged their mother;

Jerri Beck, a native of North Carolina, and senior publications editor at the University of Alabama at Birmingham, who organized and edited the manuscript;

Nalini Sathiakumar, an assistant professor of epidemiology, in the School of Public Health, University of Alabama Birmingham, a native of India, who gave the authors invaluable help and suggestions for this book.

Table of Contents

Words To Know

Newcomers, even native speakers of English, are urged to acquire a good dictionary, such as the American Heritage Dictionary of the English Language, for clarification of American English. These phrases and words, frequently encountered, can be easily misunderstood.

Affirmative Action: a phrase referring to measures or programs designed to recruit into educational settings and the workplace members of groups that have been excluded in the past. These measures are considered to be methods for rectifying past discrimination.

Appetizer: a small dish of food served before the entrée (the main dish of a meal).

Auditorium: a large room where a crowd of people can gather for meetings, to hear lectures, or to watch special programs.

Bathroom: 1) a room in a private home, where one can take a bath or shower, use a commode and wash one's hands in a sink. 2) A bathroom in a public building that has only a hand basin and a commode, and is frequently called a "restroom".

Bill: a term for a piece of paper money; a tally indicating the amount owed for services or goods received.

Biscuit: a round, unsweetened cake eaten at breakfast. (British—scone)

"Bless you": a comment made when you sneeze. This is a sympathetic expression with no real meaning.

"Bless your heart": a sympathetic Southern statement made by one person to somebody who is having a difficult, stressful experience. It is sometimes also used in expressing appreciation for a gift or an act of kindness.

Born-Again Christian: a person who has made a conscious decision to become a disciple of Christ.

Bug: 1) to annoy or bother someone; 2) a small insect.

Carry people: to give people rides in one's car from one place to another.

Check: 1) a piece of paper designed for transferring money from one person's account to another person's checking account; 2) the bill a waiter gives you in a restaurant; and 3) (as a verb) to review a document or item to make sure it is correct.

Coke: slang for the illegal drug cocaine; also, short for a popular soft drink, Coca Cola.

Commode: a toilet or lavatory.

Con artist or person (also called a confidence trickster): a person with a wonderful, charming, and friendly personality who tricks one into doing something one does not really want to do. Usually a con man gets money from somebody without the person's knowledge or consent. A con man may also cheat another person or get money from him with his reluctant consent and against his better judgment.

Cookie: a hard and crisp or soft and chewy sweet snack. (British—biscuit)

Cool: 1) pleasant or slightly cold weather. 2) good, nice, enjoyable, attractive, fashionable.

Creek: a small river.

Critter: a little animal.

Den: a room where the family relaxes and, often, watches television.

Diaper: a cloth placed between the legs of a baby which is not yet toilet trained. In many English speaking countries, a diaper is a "nappy" or a "napkin."

Dixie: a term denoting those states that formed the Confederacy during the American Civil War; the Southern states. The term originally referred to New Orleans and derived from dixie, a $10 bill issued by a New Orleans bank. The bill carried the notation dix, from the French word for ten.

Dog days: The time in August when Canis Major and Canis Minor (the dog stars) become most visible in the South. Because this corresponds with some of the highest temperatures of the year, this phrase has come to mean a very hot day when the temperature exceeds 90 degrees Fahrenheit and even dogs have only enough energy to lie down in the shade.

Egg nog: a milky custard drink, usually served at Christmas and Thanksgiving, flavored with almond or cinnamon and decorated with powdered nutmeg. It sometimes, but not always, contains alcohol.

Elevator: electrically powered car that transports people from one floor of a building to another. (British—lift)

Enjoy a person: enjoy the company of somebody; it does not mean Southerners eat people!

Entrée: the main dish of a meal.

Equal opportunity employer: often appears in advertisements for employment to indicate that the company does not discriminate on the basis of sex, age, race, religion, national origin, and other factors having no bearing on one's ability to perform the job.

Every which way: in every direction; also, slang for hasty or sloppy actions.

Fake: unreal, imitation, or to pretend.

Fad: an acronym for "for a day"; means that some item or behavior becomes enormously popular and most people adopt it. After a short time, the popularity fades and the fad is over. Clothing is often faddish.

Favors somebody: looks like somebody.

Fix: to repair something or to prepare something like a meal or one's hair style. Most forms of preparation are sometimes referred to as "fixing."

Fixings: trimmings, special dishes, sauces, or relishes that go with certain foods.

Flashlight: a battery-powered light held in the hand. (British—torch)

Flat: a rubber car tire from which the air has escaped. Flats must be replaced by tires with the proper amount of air in them. The same as "puncture" in British English.

French fries: strips of potatoes that have been deep fried in very hot oil. "Chips" in British English.

Fuck: an obscene word meaning to have sexual intercourse. Although internationals will hear this used in conversation in the United States, they should never use it.

Gasoline: fuel for motor vehicles (British—petrol).

Gas station (or "filling" station): a place where gasoline can be bought.

"Get" somebody: to transport somebody from one place to another; take revenge on somebody.

Good ole boy or girl: see page 31.

Good old boy network: the informal political power group in an organization.

Grits: a well-known Southern breakfast cereal made from corn and eaten with salt and butter with eggs, bacon, and sausage.

Guts: literally, intestines; slang for courage.

Hall: a passage in a home or any building or part of a name given to a specific building, for example, "Russell Hall." Usually if a rich person gives enough money to an institution to build a large building, that building is given the name of the donor and serves as a monument to the donor.

Hallway: an entrance to a house or a passage.

Hamburger: a piece of ground meat that has been fried or grilled and placed between two slices of a bread roll—a standard American meal.

Heartworm: a parasite carried by fleas; heartworms can be fatal to dogs, and preventive medication must be given to dogs in the South every day.

Hello: a greeting which is less formal than "good morning" or "good evening," and which may be used for any time of the day or night. It is usually used when one answers the phone informally.

Hi: informal way of saying "hello."

Holler: 1) to shout or yell. 2) A cove or isolated valley in the country.

Hood: the bonnet of a car, the cover that protects the engine.

Hot dog: sandwich made with a thin pork, beef, or chicken sausage in the middle of a long bread roll. It is not made from dog meat.

How y'all doin'?: How is your life and that of your family? This does not mean you should respond with a list of your health problems. You simply say "just fine, thank you."

Howdy: very informal way of saying "hello."

Hush puppies: a ball of cornmeal about an inch in diameter deep fried in oil and eaten with fried fish.

I'm fine: I do not wish to have something to eat or drink, or I do not need anything now. Also, "I am well," meaning in good health.

Internationals: foreigners to the United States.

Just as soon to: one would rather do something else.

Kidding: joking.

Lavatory: a hand basin or sink; not a toilet as in parts of Europe and Britain.

Lawn mower: a motor driven like a small open car or a machine pushed with both hands and used for cutting the lawn or grass around a building.

Love: like, enjoy, approve, appreciate, or have devotion. This word is used loosely and does not always involve deep feelings.

Money: American coins are the penny, a copper-colored coin less than a half inch in diameter and worth 1 cent; the nickel, a silver-colored coin of about 1/2 inch in diameter and worth 5 cents; the dime, a silver-colored coin about 1/3 inch in diameter and worth 10 cents; the quarter, a silver coin nearly an inch in diameter and worth 25 cents; the half dollar (or 50-cent piece), a silver-colored coin about 1.25 inches in diameter. The most common denominations of paper money are $1, $5, $10, $20, $50, and $100. At one time, a $1 coin and a $2 bill were in circulation, but they proved unpopular and are seldom seen now.

Motor: the car's engine or any equipment that provides power for machinery to operate.

Napkin: a cloth used at the table for protecting one's clothes from spilt food and for wiping one's mouth. This is known in some parts of the world as a "serviette."

Neat: 1) tidy, in order. 2) very good, enjoyable.

Okay (O.K.): yes, everything is just fine.

Panhandler: a beggar on the street who usually asks for money.

Parlor: a living room or formal room where guests are received; rarely seen in the South except in expensive homes.

Pet: a domesticated animal kept for companionship (usually a dog, cat, or bird); also, a person who is someone's favorite.

Phoney: unreal, insincere, pretense.

Pick-pocket: a thief who steals a wallet or any other valuable item from someone's clothing , purse, or bag.

Purdy: pretty.

Raincheck: a voucher given by a store clerk to be used to purchase an advertised sale item that is not in stock and which must be ordered. Also a term used when one cannot accept an invitation or offer at the moment, but would like to be asked again in the future.

Redneck: see page 32.

Restroom: not a place where one lies down; a room with hand basins and commodes (toilets); also known as bathroom. When one is in a public place and needs to use the toilet, ask someone there where the restroom or bathroom is. Restrooms are often found in "filling" stations or "gas" stations.

Rip off: (used as noun) an item or activity priced too high or of inferior quality.

Ripped off: cheated.

Scam: an illegal trick used to cheat someone out of money or other possessions.

See ya: a way of saying "good bye."

Shit: an obscenity that internationals should never use, meaning feces.

Shooting a bird: raising the hand toward someone with all fingers folded down except the middle one. This is a definite insult in the United States, and newcomers should never do this as it could lead to a fight.

S.O.B. (son of a bitch): an insulting and derogatory term that newcomers should never use.

Steal: "a steal" is a bargain; good value for little money.

Teenager: a person from thirteen through nineteen years of age.

Toilet: a room that accommodates a sanitation receptacle called a commode.

Trunk of a car: the separate compartment where the luggage is placed at the rear of the car away from the passenger area. (British—boot)

Uncool: unattractive, ugly, unfashionable; used primarily by young people.

Utilities: services such as electricity, natural gas, and water. Some rental fees include utilities, others do not. Rates vary from place to place.

Weed Eater: electric gardening tool that cuts weeds in the yard close to the ground.

Working on it: trying to achieve something.

Y'all: all of you; a contraction for you all; refers to a group of people.

Y'all come: an invitation to attend a function, or it may simply mean "good bye."

Yer: your.

Yonder: indicates the location of something, usually a long way in the distance, but usually within sight.

You bet: You are right or "I agree."

Zap something: to suddenly hit or grab something.

The United States

As a newcomer, you may find the ways of Americans hard to understand. They encourage individualism while trying to be very much alike; they seem very friendly and open even as violence becomes an increasing problem for society; they want plenty of leisure time even when they spend much of that time working. And these are merely the superficial contrasts one can observe.

As you become more familiar with the United States, you will see many areas where Americans act in ways that are seemingly incompatible. This brief introduction to this country and its way of life gives an overview of some of the philosophies and ideas shared by most Americans.

The American Dream, Freedom, and Individualism

The American Dream

The American dream is the hope that most Americans, if not all, have of one day being successful, of being able to earn enough income to own a home with a little piece of land, and of providing adequately for a family. Usually a car or two is included on this list. American parents also dream that their children will never lack any good thing and will be able to go to college. As the years go by, the American dream seems to grow bigger and bigger, and more items are added to the list.

Americans are able to have such a dream because of the freedoms they enjoy. These freedoms are shared by all citizens, rich and poor. They believe this dream can be a reality for everyone who works hard, is disciplined, uses his or her talents wisely, and saves as much money as possible.

The American dream also includes the desire of people to improve their status in life. Moving up the social ladder from one social class to another does not involve who one's parents are or were, where one grew up, whom one knows, or what race one is. Education and training for highly paid work are the keys to success.

As an individual's salary increases, buying power increases. Many people, after marriage, buy a small house in an inexpensive suburb. When they earn more, they buy a better house in a more expensive suburb with higher social status. This cycle may be repeated several times throughout an individual's lifetime. However, many Americans do not care about social status and are content with an average lifestyle.

Some newcomers think money is the only American yardstick for status. This is not so. Some of the most highly respected professionals in the United States are college and university professors and ministers of religion. Neither of these professions is considered to be well paid, though there are exceptions. Some athletes and entertainers are among the best-paid individuals in the United States. Education and financial success are both status symbols, and sometimes one is gained without the other.

Freedom and Individualism

Every American citizen is equal before the law and is considered to have equal opportunities; thus, no law bars any individual from pursuing a legitimate dream. Americans are not impressed by heritage and inheritance but are impressed by personal achievement and the use of wits, intelligence, and hard work. All individuals are expected to do their best on their own. There is no caste system in the United States, so individuals feel free to pursue their personal goals and dreams—and are encouraged to do so.

Every American has certain inalienable rights, guaranteed by the Constitution and the Bill of Rights. All Americans have the right to choose where they will work, what work they will do, how much they will earn, where they will live, whom they will marry, how many children they will have, whether or not they will be religious, which religion they will follow, what education they will choose, how they will save their money, what they will own, and what they will think, read, and say. Freedoms such as these are guaranteed; however, laws also exist to define where freedom ends and anarchy, crime, and disorder begin.

Political freedom is a cherished possession. Americans have the right to say what they like about any and every political issue, to vote for whomever they wish, to disagree with the government or any politician, to protest action with which they disagree, and to assemble and demonstrate to make their wishes known. Freedom of speech is equally important for journalists in television and the printed word.

These freedoms, Americans believe, have made the United States a leading nation in the world today because they have fostered individualism, independence, and the right of every person to determine his or her own life. These privileges have also enabled Americans to be creative and innovative people.

Americans cherish individualism and the rights of every individual. They enjoy being rewarded for their own individual efforts, not those of the group, the state, or family and friends. This may be one of the reasons why Socialism as a philosophy is only acceptable to the average American in a watered-down fashion and why Communism has no appeal for the majority.

Americans are also aware of the fact that freedom carries much responsibility. Those who violate the rights of others are subject to legal prosecution.

Group Spirit, Individualism, and Privacy

On the one hand, independence and individualism are greatly prized and encouraged in the United States; on the other hand, cooperation in groups is extremely important. Successful Americans must be "team players."

Cooperation is created by encouraging people to be "team" members in nursery schools, kindergartens, schools, sports and cultural activities, and places of employment. Individuals who cannot be good team members need to find employment where they do not interact with many other people—a hard task in the United States. People who are too independent sometimes have difficulty working well with others. In general, eccentricity of behavior is not encouraged in the mainstream of American life.

Americans represent a curious mix of individualism and independence, but they enjoy social interaction with other people, and loneliness is a condition they generally fear.

All over the United States, one notices the lack of fences, hedges, and other boundary lines around homes. This may imply that Americans are not lovers of privacy. While this may be true in other parts of the country, it is not true of the South. Southerners are open about many areas of their lives and, like other Americans, do not object to their neighbors and friends watching them work or play in their yards or homes. They do, however, object to people who are inquisitive, who ask them personal questions, and who do not respect their desire for privacy in their homes and personal lives.

Democracy and the Government

The United States of America is a democratic, constitutional republic, meaning that government officials are elected; there are no kings and queens or any other rulers by inheritance.

Ideally, a democracy means that the government is run by the majority of people through those they elect to represent them in congress. Laws are enacted by congress, which, in its operation and function, is guided by the Constitution of the United States.

Although democracy implies majority rule, minority rights are protected by the **Constitution** and the "**Bill of Rights**". The Constitution is the supreme law of the land. It was written in 1787 and contains the guiding principles upon which the United States government is organized and operates. It also describes the three branches of government: executive, comprised of the president, vice president, and the people the president chooses to assist him; the legislative branch, including the two houses that comprise congress; and the judicial branch, which consists of the Supreme Court and the subordinate courts throughout the land. The members of the Supreme Court and subordinate federal courts are nominated by the executive branch and confirmed and approved by the United States Senate.

The Constitution also states the rules for the operation and function of the three branches and describes their authority. Each branch is designed to be a check on the other two branches.

At the time the Constitution was written, the Bill of Rights (containing ten amendments) was added. The Bill of Rights describes the rights every citizen of the United States inherits. A booklet "A Welcome to U.S.A. Citizenship" may be purchased from the Superintendent of Documents, United States Government Printing Office, Washington, D.C. 20402. In this booklet, one may read the Constitution and its amendments. This document explains some of the American philosophy of life. Without an understanding of the Constitution and the Bill of Rights, much in American life may be confusing to newcomers.

National Government

To achieve a democratic government, the people elect representatives who, ideally, govern the country in accordance with the wishes of the people and the principles of the Constitution. These elections take place in each of the fifty states and, on a national level, for the Congress of the United States.

The United States Congress is the body responsible for making laws, and consists of two houses of lawmakers: the United States **House of Representatives** and the United States **Senate.** Any proposed legislation has to be discussed and agreed upon in both houses separately before it is taken to the president for his signature. Only after the president has signed a bill does it become law.

Each of the fifty states of the United States elects people to the House of Representatives. Each state sends at least one representative to the lower house of congress, with additional representatives based on population size. Thus, a heavily populated state has more representatives in Congress than a sparsely populated one. However, each state sends only two senators, which means that every state is equally represented in the United States Senate.

The President is the leader of the country, and he appoints his chief advisors and major governmental leaders.

Cabinet appointments are subject to congressional approval. While the president establishes national priorities, proposals such as changes in tax law or declarations of war must be voted upon and approved by Congress. Bills that have been passed by both branches of Congress are sent to the president for final approval. If the president so chooses, he can **veto** the bill, stopping it from becoming law. In order for a vetoed bill to become law, it must be passed by Congress again by a two-thirds majority. A president can allow a bill to be vetoed by not acting on it for ten days after its receipt.

The third major branch of the United States government is the **Supreme Court**. This nine-member panel rules on the constitutionality of state and national laws that are challenged by individuals, groups, or agencies. In a sense, this court is considered the highest authority in the land.

State Government

The country is made up of fifty states, each with its own governor and government for overseeing the affairs of that particular state. Each state government has two legislative components (except Nebraska which has only one). Elected officials constitute each component that meet for a specified period of time every year to discuss the affairs of the state and to pass laws, decide how money should be spent, which projects should be pursued, and which new projects should be started. Both the state legislature and the governor must agree before proposed legislation becomes law.

Each state is further divided into districts called counties (except in Louisiana, where they are called parishes). These districts have their own local systems of government, as do the cities and towns within them.

Government in the United States is called "decentralized," which means that local people control as much of the government as possible. It is hoped that this prevents a strong central government, which Americans feel could pose the threat of tyranny.

Two Political Parties—Republicans and Democrats

Currently in the United States, two political parties are represented in congress: the Republican and the Democratic parties. Although there are other parties such as the

Socialist, the Communist, and the Libertarian parties, these are extremely small in proportion to the population. The majority of people vote for either the Republicans or the Democrats.

Newcomers are often confused about the differences in these two parties and sometimes even Americans have a difficult time trying to describe the parties' positions. To an extent, this indicates that the majority of Americans share similar ideas concerning important political, social, and economic issues.

At the risk of generalizing, one could say Republicans tend to support limited government involvement in the affairs of individuals and businesses. They are likely to feel that business should not be hampered by legislation, that the capitalistic system should be encouraged as much as possible, and that individuals should rely as little as possible on the government for assistance when in need.

Democrats also support free enterprise and capitalism, but they tend to feel the government should monitor the economic system and impose certain regulations they consider to be in the public interest. Democrats believe the government should support social programs and help take care of an individual's needs if he or she cannot do so.

Lobbyists, Protests, and Demonstrations

One of the ways Americans make their wishes known about proposed legislation or national issues is by writing to their senators and representatives. "Lobbyist" groups, consisting of people who are paid by special interest groups, try to influence members of congress to vote in accordance with their wishes. Most big industries and organizations have some form of lobbyists working for them at the state and national levels.

People also make their wishes known by staging demonstrations to protest certain actions or to advocate others. Others write to newspapers and magazines to voice their concerns or protests. Demonstrations are legal in the United States because the Constitution guarantees free speech and the right of every individual to voice his or her concern through protest.

The Police Force

In America, the police force is organized at the local level. Thus, towns, cities, and counties recruit, train, employ, and pay the members of the police force. The law enforcement agents (police officers) do not work for the national (federal) government but for the people in the local districts. There is no central police force in the United States; Americans prefer local control over a law enforcement agency in their area. This preference also mitigates against police tyranny.

The **Federal Bureau of Investigation** (FBI) is a federal agency consisting of law enforcement officers responsible for detecting criminals who flee from one state to another and those who commit federal crimes. These officers are stationed all over the United States and keep central computers with information about criminals guilty of offenses deemed to be of national importance and significance.

Federal laws are separate from state laws, although state laws must not violate federal laws. State laws vary from one state to another, particularly regarding requirements for driving licenses, marriage licenses, and other civil concerns. There is less variation in criminal laws.

When an individual, corporation, or group breaks the law, the local police or FBI arrest, charge, and indict that individual, called the defendant. Each defendant is considered innocent until proven guilty and has the right to employ a lawyer to defend his or her rights. When the defendant's case comes to trial, his or her conduct is judged against the law of the land. Each defendant is entitled to a **trial by a jury** of his or her peers. A jury is a group of private citizens, not necessarily trained in law, who do not know any of the people involved in the case. They are required to render an unbiased decision based only on the information presented during the trial. The process from an arrest to completion of the defendant's trial can take months or years.

Capitalism and the Free Enterprise System

The subjects of capitalism and the free enterprise system are described only briefly as there are many resources that discuss them fully.

Capitalism is the economic system that has dominated

Western countries for centuries. In the United States, it is seen as the system giving opportunity to any individual or group of individuals to own and operate a business, factory, or other institution that manufactures goods or provides services to be sold in the marketplace. This business may operate with just one person, the owner, or may employ a few or many people for efficient operation.

The "free enterprise" system refers to the process of one business or institution competing with other businesses or institutions for trade or patronage. Usually the public for whom these services and goods are provided will choose the best price—the lowest price for services and goods of equal value. This competition tends to keep prices down, and it is against the law in the United States for companies to collaborate on prices ("price fixing") to avoid competition. Competition between and among groups, and even individuals, is considered healthy as it is believed to produce the best in everyone.

This system operates on the basic premise of **"supply and demand."** This means that scarce goods are more expensive and plentiful goods are less expensive, and services requiring skillful workers are often more expensive than those requiring less skilled people. In a capitalistic system, everybody is expected to work hard. There are few "free" benefits awarded to people who are able and fit.

The criticism levelled against capitalism and the free enterprise system is that they encourage materialism or the love of possessing goods and money, stress competition, and exploit workers. These criticisms are probably all valid to some degree, but these systems have contributed to the prosperity of the United States and the establishment and maintenance of the enormous middle-class (the largest group) in the United States.

In the United States, trade unions, consumer groups, and other organizations have been formed to protect workers and the public from exploitation by those offering goods and services. Many laws are enacted each year at the state and national levels to protect the rights of people from those who would use business to exploit them. The American public is sophisticated and protects itself; if goods are dangerous, inferior, or inappropriate, they will not be bought.

The materialism of Americans is undisputed, but there is also great idealism. This is apparent in the many volunteer organizations offering help to persons in need. These organizations are run by people who volunteer their time and money to help others without being paid. Most middle-class Americans make monthly contributions to nonprofit organizations that help others, sponsor medical research, or improve society in some way.

Pragmatism

About one hundred years ago, three American scholars and philosophers gave the United States a philosophy that still influences the way Americans think, feel, and behave. They were Charles Sanders Pierce (who named the philosophy pragmatism), William James, and John Dewey. Their philosophy, which has its roots in the Sophist philosophy of the Ancient Greeks, has influenced every part of American life, from education and religion to politics and economics.

In a sense, the philosophy of pragmatism was practiced before these men gave it a system. It was the thinking of the American settlers who, for survival, had to be self-reliant, independent, and innovative because they were so far from help. They learned to defend themselves, to make their own tools, and to handle emergencies and problems. Even today, Americans believe they must do as much for themselves, as individuals, as possible.

Basically, pragmatism teaches that if something works and functions to meet a particular need, then it is good. If it does not work, then it is useless and should be discarded. Another way of saying this is: the degree to which an idea works is the degree to which it is successfully applied. Pragmatism is partly the reason why Americans are practical people concerned with "useful" things.

Pragmatism also teaches that one should seek to improve situations and things whenever possible, even if they are working well. For instance, every year manufacturers promise us that they have improved their products. America, as a nation, is recognized all over the world for its innovative and creative people who are motivated to excel in all they do and to make things "bigger and better" than anyone else.

Pragmatists believe that the only aspect of life that does not change is change itself. Everything is in a state of flux, and change should be accepted as a challenge for humans to adapt to new situations. Change is not to be feared, but should be seen as an opportunity for new adaptations and inventions. Thus, Americans will seek to conquer their environments, whether these be social, political, economic, geographical, or physical.

The developers of pragmatism believed that one should constantly improve the environment, even the social environment in which human beings live, and that people would change through environmental improvements. Hence, Americans have spent many years trying to solve human problems, but many have become skeptical about this belief in recent times and are now looking for other solutions to the growing social problems existing in the United States today.

Many Americans, however, criticize pragmatism. They believe the philosophy tends to motivate people to be more action oriented (which Americans are) and less philosophically oriented. These critics feel that Americans generally tend to be restless, unrelaxed people who are always striving for change, control, and improvement but who miss the contentment of the ordinary situations of their daily lives. Some critics think pragmatism does not stress moral standards adequately and appropriately.

Pragmatism may partially explain the great emphasis on materialism and the desire to accumulate money and things as a way of "changing," mastering, and improving one's environment. At the same time, it has contributed greatly to the development of scientific discovery and the efficiency found in the United States.

This philosophy partly explains the fact that Americans are "future" rather than "past" oriented. Hence, formality, tradition, and glorification of the past tend to be less important than the anticipation of future possibilities, problems, and achievements.

The South and Southerners

The Southerners

Southerners live in the southeastern part of the United States, known as the "South" or "Southern states." The Southern states are Kentucky, Virginia, North and South Carolina, Georgia, Alabama, Mississippi, Louisiana, Arkansas, Texas, Florida, and Tennessee. The area is also sometimes referred to as Dixie. Alabama, Georgia, Louisiana, Mississippi, and South Carolina are considered the "Deep South".

Many people regard Texans as Southerners, and most Texans consider themselves Southerners. Many people born in Florida consider themselves Southerners, but both Texas and Florida have attracted residents from all parts of the country. Neither is considered part of the South anymore.

A number of delightful books are available that discuss the characteristics of stereotypical Southerners. In addition, a brief overview is included at the end of this chapter.

Ancestry of Southerners

The ancestry of Southerners is basically (but not exclusively) Irish, Scots-Irish, Scottish, English, and African. As a region, the South is probably the most Celtic part of the United States. In the seventeenth and eighteenth centuries, English settlers arrived in what is now Virginia and developed farmlands and cotton plantations. From there they moved south and southwest to settle the region now known as the South. They were farmers, cotton plantation owners, and laborers in the fields.

During much of this time, slaves were brought to America from Africa to work in the cotton plantations of the South. Today, many descendents of these Africans live throughout the United States, including the South.

In the latter part of the nineteenth century, Irish settlers arrived to join the work force in the few industries springing up in the South. However, the South was not an industrialized section of the United States, and the great immigration waves of the last century and the early part of this century in the rest of the United States had but limited effect in the South. Consequently, the population in the South did not become as diversified as in the industrialized North.

The Effects of the Civil War on the South

The Civil War (sometimes called the War between the States) took place between 1861 and 1865 and was fought between the Northern and the Southern states. Americans fought against Americans. The war was the result of several factors, among them conflicts over the institution of slavery and the rights of individual state governments as opposed to the power of the federal government.

When the war began, the industrialized North was stronger in military strength, but the South had some brilliant military leaders, which contributed to the duration of the war. The Northern army, however, was much stronger, and eventually the South was defeated.

The war left the South in an enormously impoverished condition. The Southern people had always been used to farming and, therefore, could keep themselves fed after the war, but the road to recovery was extremely difficult. Poverty prevented progress, and the Southern states remained largely unaffected by the growing industrialization of the North. In addition, congress passed laws that prevented the South from quick recovery, for it feared that a rising South would again present problems to the stability of the Union. This situation caused great resentment in the Southern people, many of whom remained rural and poor even as the rest of the country became increasingly urban and industrialized.

The effects of the Civil War have largely disappeared today. However, some of the poverty, poor educational standards, and negative attitudes some Southerners have toward

Northerners are lingering effects of the war. Also, some Northerners have negative attitudes toward the South and Southerners because of the problems mentioned above. These problems and attitudes are not universal in the South, but they continue to affect the lifestyles and attitudes of many older Southerners.

The Southern Personality

Throughout the United States, Southerners are recognized as being polite, gracious people. Courtesy and sensitivity to the feelings of others are two values Southerners teach their children from young ages. Southern charm and courtesy are evident in the supermarkets, the shopping malls, public transportation, sports events, and other places where crowds assemble and do business. People will readily say "excuse me" when they stumble against you. Seldom do people break into a queue, or as they say here, "a line." If you drop something or stumble, generally someone will help you.

Many Southerners are cautious about becoming involved in contentious discussions with anyone other than close friends or family members whom they know will not reject them. Most Southerners strongly dislike conflict and confrontation on a social level; they do not seem to like being asked directly for their opinions in a potentially threatening situation. To avoid conflict, Southerners may seem to agree with you (when in fact they don't) rather than hurt your feelings and risk conflict. Sometimes they will refrain from giving you a direct answer to a question, especially if they think the answer will displease you. Some Southerners are most reluctant about giving you a negative answer, especially if you would like a positive one. The motive is usually to protect your feelings and to prevent your rejection of them. Sometimes Southerners are insincere—not to hurt you but to make you feel good.

Because the necessity for protecting feelings is so important to Southerners, casual social encounters stick rigidly to non-threatening conversations. Safe topics include the weather, natural disasters anywhere in the world, the rising cost of living, the beauty of the seasons of the year, and, of course, sports. However, find out what team your friend supports and do not ever be insulting about that team.

The Southern rule of not offending anybody gives new-comers the feeling that many Southerners, especially Southern women, have no opinions. This is not true. Southerners are strong-willed, independent, and tough people with opinions on every subject, but many are sensitive to others' feelings and don't express these opinions if there is the possibility that they would lead to conflict or give offense.

You may feel unhappy about an aspect of your relation-ship with a friend, colleague, co-worker, supervisor, or associate and may not know what the problem is. Rarely will a Southerner confront you and tell you exactly what the problem is, unless there is some extenuating circumstance. A Southerner in this situation prefers to give indirect indica-tions of displeasure, with the hope that time will solve the problem so that a confrontation will be unnecessary.

For the newcomer, this can be disturbing and cause uncertainty and insecurity. Newcomers who wish to deal with such a situation need to be cautious about using con-frontation. If you should decide to speak to a Southerner about a situation such as described above, do so gently and politely, explaining that you are confused and bothered about the situation. Remember to do so in a manner that allows the other person to save face.

In the area of **politics**, politeness about opinions is disre-garded. Many derogatory statements are made by political opponents at the time of elections. Throughout the United States, it is understood that opinions expressed in the politi-cal area are not intended to hurt the opponent personally but are a part of the political process. Americans everywhere believe that a political candidate should disclose almost everything about himself or herself and should also be pre-pared to take criticism and challenges from opponents. But even at election time, the average Southerner deplores a politician who assaults the character, rather than the record, of his or her opponent. This disapproval, however, does not prevent it from happening, but fortunately violence at elec-tion time is rare in the United States.

You may also notice that Southerners are quickly aroused emotionally. They enjoy loving, laughing, and having fun, but they also feel for the suffering underdog. They have been accused of being too sentimental, too easily reduced to tears by a sad story or situation, and too quickly raucous. Because they are warm, spontaneous, and emotional people, they find it perfectly acceptable to laugh or cry in public or in the presence of other people.

Social Orientation

Southerners are generally people-centered and especially family-centered in their approach to living. Family ties are important, as are family unity and loyalty. They love parties, festivals, sports events, and vacations.

Many people enjoy membership in groups, clubs, associations, churches, and organizations of all descriptions. The group spirit is prevalent and noticeable to newcomers. It is common for people to go to restaurants and other places of entertainment in groups to enjoy friendships.

Southern Compassion

Most Southerners are compassionate and are deeply touched by the suffering of fellow human beings. They are, therefore, generally eager to help victims of unfortunate circumstances and are quick to respond to those in need. However, they are generally reluctant to offer specific help for fear of meddling in your affairs or of appearing bossy. Therefore, if you need help, you must specifically ask for it; do not hint or assume a Southerner will make the initial offer. If Southerners cannot help personally, they will usually refer you to somebody who can. One way to ask for help when you have an urgent problem is to say "I have this problem. Could you suggest a way for me to solve it?" This enables the person to 1) decline to help, 2) help you himself or herself, or 3) put you in touch with someone who can help. However, Southerners dislike what they call a "freeloader," meaning somebody who wants to get something for nothing or somebody who takes advantage of somebody else's labor and good will. Basically, Americans expect individuals to care for themselves, unless this is not possible because of overwhelming circumstances.

While Southerners help others with pleasure, they themselves are generally very independent and tend to be reluctant to ask help from others, except family members and close friends. They are reluctant to accept any form of help that they feel places them under an obligation to somebody else. For this reason, Southerners often prefer to employ people whom they can pay for services when they need help.

Independence of Spirit

Southerners, in common with other Americans, value their independence greatly and do not give others, especially politicians or government agencies, authority over their personal lives. Southerners usually prefer the government, especially the federal government, to have as little authority as possible. This does not mean that they do not adhere to the law of the land or states, but, in matters not legislated, they insist on having total control of every facet of their lives.

To the extent possible, Southerners tend to be democratic in their workplaces, schools, marketplaces, and, ideally, in their homes. They resent being subservient to anyone whom they have not officially elected to a place of authority, and, even then, they prefer to be consulted and included in decision-making.

One term every newcomer needs to understand is "states rights." It refers to the authority vested in the government of each individual state. Some authority is vested in the federal government, but most Americans feel that the authority of the individual states must remain strong.

Story Telling

The South is well known throughout the United States for its good story tellers. The tradition of story telling developed in the early pioneer days before the advent of the automobile, movie theater, and television.

The mountainous, hilly, or wooded and vast Southern terrain made it difficult for people to visit friends and attend organized entertainment. In isolated, sparsely populated communities, Southerners resourcefully learned to entertain themselves by telling stories, and enjoying musical evenings when musicians would entertain groups of people on the fiddle and other instruments.

Newcomers usually enjoy listening to stories the older Southern people tell about places and people. They tell them with vivid descriptions, original perceptions, and quaint language that add to the enjoyment of the tale. The South has produced a number of outstanding storytellers. They include William Faulkner, Truman Capote, Eudora Welty, Thomas Wolfe, Tennessee Williams, Margaret Mitchell, Mark Twain, and Walker Percy.

Hugging

Southerners—spontaneous emotional people—tend to be quick to display this spontaneity in physical gestures. They are apt to hug people, even those they have only known a short time, but rarely do they hug people on meeting them for the first time. Hugging can have many meanings. It can be a display of deep affection between two people of any sex or age, or it can be a superficial expression of pleasure on meeting somebody with no other meaning. Hugging is seen at churches, family and social gatherings, but seldom at business or formal occasions.

Some newcomers, from cultures where physical contact is kept to a minimum, do not enjoy being hugged and are embarrassed by this custom, but other newcomers enjoy being affectionately hugged by their new friends. Regardless of how you feel about this, if you develop friendships and close relationships with Southerners, you will most likely be hugged at some stage. If you feel offended, try to remember that this Southern expression of friendship has no sexual overtones (unless, of course, it takes place in a romantic relationship) nor does it have any meaning except friendship. It does not even connote deep friendship.

If you prefer not to be hugged or if this is against your moral or religious principles, feel free to explain your discomfort to your acquaintance. You may also wish to explain that this is not part of your culture. If you express your preferences, do so in a gentle, kind way, preferably when you are not being hugged. On the other hand, you may wish to be "Southern while in the South" and enjoy this expression of friendliness.

Differences Between the South and the Rest of the United States

In most respects, the South is exactly the same as the rest of the country. The most obvious differences between Southerners and other Americans are the atmosphere of the region, the personality of the people, and their distinctive Southern accent. No accent in the United States, I believe, is as distinctive as the Southern one.

Perhaps the biggest difference between the South and the rest of the United States is the personality of the people. Because Southern people do not have to rush as much as other Americans, they have more time to be courteous on the streets and in the stores. Southerners are more polite than other Americans because they are brought up to value courtesy. Southerners are taught from youth how to converse and make "small talk" in a relaxed gracious way, even with strangers. Rarely is a Southerner uncomfortable with a stranger.

Southern people reputedly are more traditional, and family oriented, with deep family loyalties, than are people in some other parts of the United States. Holidays are celebrated with families, and family members may travel for hundreds or thousands of miles to be with family members over the holidays. Many Southerners do not enjoy moving far away from family members and tend to seek employment near their families. Southern families hold reunions periodically when relatives come from great distances to visit with other family members.

The gentler personality of Southerners tends to make many newcomers feel at ease. Southerners are not as blunt as other Americans and usually do not express negative emotions to people they do not know, so one may feel comfortable about expressing ideas about topics one is unsure about. No one will attack you. Since most Southerners are socially at ease, they are not embarrassed about receiving a compliment. Thus, you may feel free to say nice things about them, knowing these will be graciously received.

Some newcomers, especially those who look foreign and have foreign accents, have complained that Southerners are not always as helpful to them on the streets and in businesses as people in some other parts of the United States. This is out of character for most Southerners, who are usually polite and helpful, regardless of a person's identity. However, some newcomers have been insulted by people, especially when visiting rural areas. This is because it is only recently that foreigners have started coming to the South in sizeable numbers, and some Southerners are not accustomed to newcomers. In addition, some Southerners, especially in the rural areas, feel nervous and threatened by foreigners.

Another difference in the South is that there are fewer cities with populations over one million people. There are few cities like New York, Los Angeles, or Chicago, and the only cities in the South with populations over one and a half million or more are Houston, Texas; Miami, Florida; Dallas, Texas; and Atlanta, Georgia. There are several Southern cities with metropolitan populations of about one million people.

Because the population of Southern cities is smaller, fewer people crowd the sidewalks, streets, and highways. People move more slowly and give the appearance of being less hectic and frantic about their daily affairs. Few people have to rush to catch trains, subways, busses, and other forms of transportation, as they do in many northern cities. Nor are the freeways as congested as in many non-Southern cities. In the South, most people prefer to use their cars, and in many cities there is no comprehensive public transport system. Most Southerners probably spend less time traveling to and from work than do people in the large urban areas of the rest of the United States.

Another big difference between the North and the South is the **climate**. In the South, the summers are much hotter than anywhere else in the nation except the dry Southwest. The South is also very humid, especially in the summer, and air conditioning is almost essential for comfortable survival.

Most of the South has a mild winter, in contrast to the Northern states, and seldom gets snow and ice during the winter. However, most winters bring a few mild snowfalls and ice storms that usually cripple the cities and towns because the local governments do not possess snow- and ice-moving equipment for roads.

The South is still predominantly rural and is considered an agricultural area of the United States. There are small private farmers and large farms operated by corporations, all making a living wage from the soil. The predominant crops are soy beans, cotton, fruits, vegetables, corn, peanuts, sugar, and tobacco. There are many industries related to raising chickens, pigs, cattle, and fish. In addition, much of the land is forest, and the timber industry thrives in the moist, warm climate.

Partly as a result of the Civil War and its consequences, the South is not as industrially developed as most of the Northeastern, Midwestern, and West Coast states even today. The greater industrialization of these regions has resulted in a more wealthy population. Salaries in the South, on average, tend to be considerably lower than in the industrialized areas of the United States, but land and homes are also less expensive.

The South is populated by many socio-economic groups of people. There are rich and poor, middle class, professionals, blue collar workers, unskilled workers, ethnic and racial groups, educated and uneducated people. There is a larger percentage of poor people living in the South than in any other region. However, homes and land are cheaper in the South, and many more people who do not earn large salaries are able to own their homes than is possible in many other parts of the country.

The quality of education is considered to be lower in the South than in other regions of the United States, largely because of the degree of poverty that existed until quite recently. Lately, Southern states have been trying to improve the quality of public education, and scores on the various tests given to children and young people have been rising. Generally, teachers' salaries have not been as high in the South as in some other regions, but this is currently being rectified.

Politically, the South, and especially the Deep South, is considered more conservative than the rest of the United States. This statement is confusing to most newcomers who observe that most of the South votes for Democratic candidates. Although Southern voters voted overwhelmingly for local Democratic representatives during the 1980s, they voted for Republican presidents. Even in 1992, many Southerners voted for Mr. George Bush, in spite of the fact that Mr. Bill Clinton is a Southerner. Generally, Democrats in the South are considered more conservative about government spending and government involvement in business and the affairs of individual states than are Democrats in the rest of the United States.

Southerners are also considered more interested in organized religion than are other Americans. The truth of this assessment is difficult to determine, however. While the many church buildings may make it appear that there is great interest in religion, there may or may not be more affiliated members of an organized religion on a per capita basis than in the rest of the United States. Often the Southern church serves a social function, as well as a religious one, especially in rural areas.

Because of the recent migration of people from other regions of the United States to the South, the influence of television and movies, and the growth of chain stores selling the same merchandise everywhere, the South is becoming more and more like the rest of America. Southerners' homes, eating habits, mode of dress, values, and attitudes are much the same as in the rest of the United States. In time, the regional differences all over the United States will probably disappear completely.

Southern Accent

Some people from the fast-paced and brisk North have criticized Southern speech patterns—the accent and drawl—to the point that many Southerners have a regrettable embarrassment about the way they speak. Southerners find that when they travel to other parts of the United States, they often are good-naturedly ridiculed because of their accents. This has had the effect of making some Southerners feel ill at ease about their accents, especially in the presence of non-Southerners.

Unfortunately, in the past, the rest of the United States has tended to equate the Southern accent with a lack of education, unless the accent is markedly "educated" and only spiked with a Southern influence. In the South, it is a mistake to gauge a person's education, wisdom, or experience by accent or appearance, as many are prone to do in Britain and Europe. Educated Americans have all sorts of accents and appearances.

Regional accents are in the process of vanishing in the United States. However, one still hears the distinctive regional accents of America: the Chicago accent, the Brooklyn accent, the New Orleans accent (strangely different from the rest of the Southern accents) and so on, adding to the interest of this vast, diverse land. Even in the South, there is no one accent that is "typically" Southern. The natives can identify a great variety of accents from different Southern states.

The most common aspects of the accent are the "i" sounds, especially the long sounding "i," sometimes pronounced like "ah," and the ability to make two syllables out of words such as risk (ree-isk), door (doh-orr), bell (bay-ell). Linguists, who can detect the origin of the accent, state that many sounds come from English, Irish, and Scottish accents that have been modified over the centuries. There is possibly also an influence from African languages. Students of English will recognize speech patterns from Shakespeare and other seventeenth century English writers.

Friendliness and Friendship

Southerners are world famous for their insistence on manners and graciousness. This makes it very pleasant to live in the South as, generally, one is courteously treated in public places.

To some newcomers, Southerners appear too friendly. This warmth and friendliness is intended to make the newcomer feel welcome and comfortable, and generally you need not suspect any inherent danger. Southerners do not have ulterior motives when they show you friendliness. This friendliness is sometimes a surprise to newcomers and is often misinterpreted as being an indication that a real friendship is being offered by Southerners. Sometimes this is the beginning of a close friendship, but it should not be assumed so by newcomers.

In many parts of the world, people welcome strangers in a friendly but reserved manner and only after a friendship develops does warmth of emotion follow. The South is different. Southerners express warmth of emotion as part of their initial greeting and often will go to amazing lengths to help newcomers settle into a new home or apartment. The newcomer may (or may not) receive food, the loan of equipment, and other offers of help. As a newcomer in the South, one is generally assumed to be a good person until proved otherwise. However, the newcomer must not suppose that this friendliness and helpfulness indicates a desire to be warm or close friends. Do not be surprised if you never again see your Southern helper once you have settled into your new home. This does not mean, of course, that a friendship will not develop; sometimes close friendships do result from a helping hand, but often they do not.

Distinguish Between Friendship and Friendliness

In the South, newcomers need to distinguish between "friendliness" and "friendship." Friendliness is an obligation Southerners feel they have toward everybody, but friendship is something a newcomer and a Southerner develop only over time. It seems to me that, in spite of their friendly, courteous behavior, which is a learned behavior, Southerners are really reserved people. They usually make acquaintances quickly but make friends slowly, revealing their private selves only after they get to know one well.

The Nature of Friendship

Some newcomers have complained that it is easy to develop casual friendships but difficult to develop close friendships with Southerners and other Americans. Many cultures encourage deep and close relationships with life-long commitments and loyalties to friends. In America this is different, and Americans tend to have many superficial friends and few close friends. Newcomers often ask why this situation exists.

Do not be surprised if Southerners (or other Americans) invite you out to their homes fairly often and appear to be your loyal friends, but, after a few months or years you no longer hear from them. Usually the friendship has ceased because of circumstances, not necessarily because they no longer like you. Americans and Southerners accept this situation as part of everyday life and you should take no offense. If circumstances change, the friendship may be renewed as if it had never been interrupted.

Most people find friends at their places of employment or in clubs. In the South, a great number of people, especially families, find friendships in churches.

Many friends of all ages get together in groups of four, six, or more and go to ballgames, movies, theaters, and restaurants. Conversation is often light and witty, rather than deep and philosophical. Some people feel this recent change in social life was brought about by television—that Americans spend so much time being "talked to" by television that they have little time and opportunity to cultivate the art of conversation.

As Southerners get older and busier and assume more responsibilities, friendships tend to play a smaller part in their lives. It cannot be denied that many Americans are lonely and wish they had better quality friendships. The reasons they don't are complicated and varied, and a number of factors contribute to this situation.

The hectic lifestyle that has developed since World War II has undoubtedly affected the quality of friendships most Americans experience. Modern life for many people is too hectic and busy with work and family obligations for deep friendships.

Many people move from town to town frequently, particularly once they leave their parents' homes and become employed. As a result, some do not remain in one place long enough to develop lasting friendships. For others, the knowledge that they will possibly be moving in the future leads them to avoid deep friendships and the resulting pain of separation.

Since close friendships require more time and attention than most people can give, people settle for casual friendships that focus on having fun. Conversation consists of telling humorous anecdotes, jokes, or discussions about sports, personal incidents, and events. Intense intellectual and emotional interaction is usually avoided.

Maybe Americans do not need friendships to enrich their lives as much as people in some societies do, because the country has so many resources, choices, and opportunities for activities and diversion. Also, individuals have the financial and other resources to fill their lives with many interesting experiences and activities that are time consuming.

Because the spirit of independence and individualism is encouraged and middle-class people have financial resources, people rely on other people as little as possible. Consequently, Americans do not expect their friends to take responsibility for them. Friends will help friends when necessary, but rarely beyond a certain point. For example, rarely do friends become financially committed to each other. This is understood by both parties. Most Americans in financial trouble turn to welfare organizations and institutions for help when family members cannot help them.

Marriage as Friendship

American marriage is not just an arrangement whereby two people live together in economic harmony and loyalty, raising children together; it is also expected to be a friendship. Consequently, most husbands and wives expect spouses to be their closest friends, as well as loyal and faithful sexual partners.

This type of marriage is fulfilling and enriching and sustains individuals in the struggle for survival. It is also time consuming. Many Americans place more emphasis on developing and maintaining this type of marriage than on developing close friendships with many other people. In a sense, a good, close marriage lessens an individual's need for many close friendships.

Southern Hospitality

Traditionally, Southerners are hospitable. In bygone days, newcomers were lavishly welcomed into the Southern community. But lately, changes in the South mean that the lavish welcomes are not as prevalent.

You may be fortunate enough to start a new job or join a church or club where people really care and rally around you and give you a conspicuous welcome by inviting you to their homes, restaurants, etc. However, if you do not receive this attention, do not be discouraged. This does not mean that you are not welcome. It only means that life in the South, as in the rest of America, has become too busy for many social meetings.

One word of caution. You may settle in a part of the South where the natives are not used to having newcomers. You will usually find the natives polite, friendly, and courteous. However, you may feel that you are being kept at arms' length, and you are probably right. There are many parts of the South where newcomers have only recently started moving in. Sometimes these newcomers have been outspokenly critical of the South. For this reason, some Southerners want to observe the newcomer among them before extending a hand of friendship.

Southern people tend to be warm and open hearted, provided they feel you do not criticize them and accept them as they are, not as you wish them to be. It is profitable for newcomers to make an effort to read Southern history, learn to understand the events that shaped this part of the country, and to learn to understand why the people are as they are.

Offers and Promises

Newcomers also need to understand the difference between offers and promises. Because Southern hospitality demands courtesy, newcomers can easily misunderstand the meaning behind polite statements made by Southerners.

An offer is like a suggestion and is usually made on the spur of the moment as an emotional response to a particular situation. For instance, you will often hear "come see us." This is not an invitation; it is merely one way of ending a conversation, or it is a suggestion, not a promise of an invitation. Other ways of ending a conversation are: "take care," "see you later," "talk to you later," "see you again," "let's get together," "we must go out sometime," and "phone me sometime." These are usually perfunctory statements, although they could lead to friendships later. Sometimes, however, you can receive an invitation in this way, so it is best to ask your acquaintance what he or she means if you are in doubt.

Often suggestions have been made to newcomers that have been interpreted as promises. This has led to disappointment because promises have not been fulfilled. A suggestion might be something like this: "Maybe I could come round sometime next week and help you." This statement has no firm day or time and one should not expect a visit. People do not often make definite suggestions about how to help you; they wait for you to tell them what you need—a humiliating thing for some newcomers to do.

A promise is a definite, firm offer or commitment that is usually followed with specific details. For instance, someone may say "I will come and help you next week on Thursday at 7:00 p.m.," or " I will speak to my boss tomorrow about a job for you. Phone me tomorrow evening to hear what he says."

Another statement you need to interpret correctly is: "If you are ever in our town, come visit us." This is not an invitation to spend a vacation, short or long, in the home of your acquaintance. It may only be an invitation to phone them when you are in their town so that arrangements can be made to have a meal together. On the other hand, it may be an invitation to spend some time in their homes. The point is, don't take such statements at face value; always check with the speaker about what is intended.

You may receive a real invitation to spend "a few days" in the home of a Southerner. If so, find out how many days your host has in mind. Usually a day or two, or sometimes three, is all that is involved in the invitation. If you don't do this, you may find yourself disappointed and disillusioned with your Southern (or other American) acquaintance or friend.

Invitations

Invitations are discussed more fully in a later chapter. However, a brief note seems appropriate here. Throughout the U.S.A., there is a tendency for friends to gather at a restaurant instead of in someone's home. When friends meet in restaurants, everybody goes "Dutch," meaning each pays for his or her own meal.

When Southerners feel comfortable with you, they may invite you into their homes for meals, sometimes formal, sometimes very informal. You might be invited with other people; sometimes you and your family will be the only guests. However, if this is not your experience, remember that people across America are too busy these days for such entertaining, and most people can cope only with the essential demands of their lives.

Younger people seem to have more invitations extended to them by young Southerners than older people and families. This is possibly because young people have fewer demands than older people, are naturally more curious about people from other countries, and have a more casual and relaxed attitude to entertaining, which means they don't feel they have to prepare as extensively for guests.

Some Stereotypical Southerners

Southerners, like other Americans, differ greatly among themselves. Some are more casual than others, some are better educated than others, and lifestyles run a range from subsistence to luxurious. This makes it difficult to give an accurate picture of the people of the South. The following are some common stereotypes. As with all generalizations, these are not to be taken too literally, nor will all Southerners fit easily into one of these categories.

Southern Men

There are different kinds and stereotypes of Southern men, but almost all are characterized by their polite and gentle manner of dealing with other people. Many are strong, independent, and determined men who love the land and region they claim as their home.

Like all people from the South, Southern men usually speak slowly and have the distinctive Southern accent, even after they leave the South. They love a good story, and many of them have a facility for recounting an event in a fresh, interesting, and often witty way.

One well-known stereotype of the South is the **Southern**

gentleman, portrayed in the movie "Gone with the Wind," a popular movie about the "Old South."

Typically, a Southern gentleman is concerned about education, even if he is not highly educated himself. He reads widely and encourages his children to be educated. He is courteous and kind, always in control of his emotions, especially his anger, works hard, and provides for his wife and family. He is solicitous of the opposite sex, which includes holding a door open for a lady and giving up his seat for her, taking a lady by the arm should she need help up and down steps or while walking on a rough surface. As a son he is dutiful and sensitive and is helpful to the elderly, the poor, and children.

In addition, he does not use profanity in public, nor in private if women are in his company. His word is his bond, so he balances his courtesy with honesty.

A **good ole boy** is another Southern male stereotype of considerable interest. The term refers to a specific type of Southern man, although they are found in many areas all over the United States.

The good ole boy is a sensible, simple, hard-working man who usually grew up in a rural area and prefers to live there. Even if he moves to a city, he still feels he is a "country boy" and has no emotional attachment for city life and values. He loves hunting and fishing, drives a truck (often with a gun in the cab), and often enjoys chewing tobacco. He also enjoys country and western music and football.

He has had enough education to prepare him for a reasonably good job and lifestyle, but he rarely aspires to a professional career. He usually has a lot of what he calls "walking around sense"—common sense.

He adheres to traditional roles in the home, and expects his wife to do the housecleaning and cooking and to take care of the children. He assists with the discipline of the children, which usually means corporal punishment. Sometimes he encourages his children to go to college and earn degrees and/or other technical qualifications. He is extremely proud of his children who do graduate with qualifications and skills.

Some good ole boys, though not all, believe in settling

arguments with a fight. In certain circumstances, they may feel their honor is at stake if they don't fight an opponent.

Good ole boys are interesting people. They are usually friendly and happy to converse with newcomers if they are sure that the newcomer is not critical or superior toward them, but they can be mean and prejudiced against all who do not belong to their group.

Redneck is a term given to a special kind of Southern man, although this type of man can be seen in other parts of the United States and, certainly, in other parts of the world. And while people in the South tend to laugh about its redneck reputation, a newcomer should never call anyone a redneck.

The redneck Southern man usually has a disdain for education for himself and his children, for cultural activities, formal clothing, and fancy homes. Often rednecks have deep racial prejudices and will be threatening, at times, to people of another race. However, many rednecks have friends of other races, so one is hesitant about generalizing.

Rednecks prefer to live in rural areas, although they are sometimes found in city suburbs. Some rednecks are unreliable and irresponsible and do not always take their jobs seriously. Often they do menial work which does not pay well nor demand much of them. Many are forced to accept welfare support.

In fairness to rednecks, remember that this is a stereotype, not a real person. Some fine people who call themselves rednecks are not at all like the stereotype.

Men as Husbands and Fathers

Many Southern men, like other American men, are caught in the transition of the American woman from traditional woman to the new, independent, self-assertive woman who no longer stays at home to rear children and keep house. With the call for equality, Southern women have rejected the traditional Southern roles for men and women with which most men grew up. Because so many wives work, many Southern men are expected to help with chores in the home. However, because their fathers played out traditional roles, many Southern men are still uneasy about helping in the house. Some men feel housework is "woman's work" and should be done by a woman, and this issue presents problems in many American marriages.

On the whole, Southern men love their children and are willing to work hard and make sacrifices for them. Most middle-class Southern men are ambitious for their children and want them to go to college, even if they themselves did not go to college. Many men want their sons to be first-class athletes and encourage them to participate in sports from an early age. They want their sons to be tough and manly, and they encourage pursuits perceived as manly, often at the expense of artistic or academic pursuits.

Daughters are special to Southern fathers, especially if they are pretty and feminine. Middle-class fathers want their children (of both sexes) to go to college, and both male and female children are equally valued by American parents.

Although most Southern men are loving husbands and fathers, some are physically or emotionally abusive to their wives and/or children. There is growing concern all over the United States regarding the growing number of reported cases of wife abuse and family violence, and authorities are investigating causes and cures for this social ill. Although wife and child abuse occurs, it is still considered scandalous for a man to beat or verbally abuse his wife and children.

Southern Men and Careers

The stereotype of the relaxed, leisure-loving Southern man has given way to the middle-class Southern man who is concerned about advancing his career, making and investing money, and earning esteem in his community. Like other American men, many Southern men enjoy having their own businesses and enjoy the independence this gives them.

Until World War II, Southern men left the South in significant numbers after earning their college degrees, seeking better opportunities for employment and advancement in other regions of America. This is now changing as business and employment opportunities increase in the South.

Southern Men and Leisure

Undoubtedly, one of the favorite pastimes of Southern men, regardless of age, is watching football, either at a stadium or on television. Friday nights in the fall are football nights for high schools, and Saturday afternoons are the time for college football games. Professional football games are played on Sunday afternoons. Other sports, such as basketball, baseball, and golf, are also popular in the South.

Many Southern men enjoy hunting and fishing, and many own hunting guns that are displayed in their dens or other rooms in their homes. All over the south, there are areas where one may hunt during specified months of the year, but only with a hunting license.

Southern men hunt everything from squirrel and opossums to deer and bear. They hunt in groups and alone. There are hunting lodges in numerous places, and men will take a few days off from work, leave their families, and go hunting in the woods. They may go for a weekend or for only a day. Those who can afford it go as far as Alaska, Canada, and even Africa to go hunting.

Fishing is another popular sport. The South is blessed with many lakes, streams, rivers, and creeks, and the Gulf Coast has rich fishing grounds. Unless the weather is really cold, men can be seen fishing at any time of the year in the South. A fishing license is required for this activity.

Homosexual Men

Some people estimate that the homosexual population in the United States makes up about 5 to 10 percent of the population. This figure is probably the same in the South as well. Although every city in the South has its homosexual population, Southerners have conservative views about homosexuality in general and feel that homosexuals should adjust to their sexual orientation without openly co-habiting and forming relationships with other men. Generally, homosexuals in the United States do not feel fully accepted. Newcomers will soon observe quite a lot of media coverage about homosexuals, especially as they campaign for full recognition.

Southern Women

Southern women are like other American women in most

respects. The few Southern characteristics that make Southern women different from other American women are that Southern society has traditionally expected women to be "ladies" and always to be feminine in appearance and behavior. Southern women generally seem to pay more attention to their appearance than women in other parts of the United States do. Beauty contests are very popular in the South, not only for teenage girls and young women, but also for little girls from about four years of age.

You should remember, however, that the people of the United States are becoming more alike each decade, and the term "Southern lady" will, no doubt, soon disappear. Other differences, too, will likely diminish over time. Contemporary Southern career women do not always wish to be called a "lady".

The middle-class Southern **lady** is trained by parents to be gracious, polite, patient, and kind and to suppress her anger. She is aware of other people's feelings and is polite in all circumstances. She does not raise her voice in public, nor have an argument in public, even if she is provoked. She does not use abusive or blasphemous language, nor does she get drunk.

Appearances can be misleading, however. Although the Southern lady appears gentle and gracious, she is often a strong, determined, and motivated woman with goals for herself and her family, which she pursues with courage and resolution. Southern women are known for being strong women.

An older Southern stereotype is the **Southern belle**, a vivacious, pretty, very feminine, and coquettish woman with good manners. She is sweet and coy. Generally, the stereotype is a good one, though many modern Southern women feel it connotes a pretty woman without much intelligence who is too concerned about pleasing men. Modern young Southern women prefer to be considered tougher and more career oriented.

Like the "Southern gentleman," Southern "ladies" are kind and generous and willing and ready to help everybody needing assistance, especially newcomers. They do not mind being directly approached for help and, usually, they will do whatever is possible to assist all who ask. Southern women also feel a responsibility to contribute their time, talents, and money to improve their communities, especially through charitable works.

Today's Women

Today women are recognized as having rights equal to those enjoyed by men, and their employment opportunities are protected by law. American women are some of the best educated women in the world and are represented in all professions, vocations, and workplaces at all levels of employment. American, and therefore, Southern women, enjoy one of the highest standards of living and professional status in the world.

Many newcomers perceive some American women as being strong and aggressive and lacking the traditional, outward signs of femininity. They are not intimidated by men and do not have to treat men as superiors; neither do they have to obey men who are not their work supervisors. Because they are as well educated as men and are their legal equals, they are able to question and challenge men's authority and abilities.

The feminist movement has encouraged women to be equal with men in practice and in their perception of themselves. Women's traditional role, therefore, is different in the United States than in the male-dominated societies of much of the developing world. However, beneath this less traditional feminine behavior and appearance, the majority of American women are still caring, concerned, and nurturing individuals.

Women and Education

Middle-class Southern parents encourage their daughters to be financially self-sufficient, and education is considered the key to this independence. Several universities now have more female students than male students, and women pursue college degrees in virtually all academic fields.

Many women work because they have professional training, not because their husbands earn inadequate salaries.

Women and Marriage

Most American (and Southern) women favor an "egalitarian" marriage. In this marriage—predicted to be the standard marriage format of the future—neither the husband nor wife is head of the household. In an egalitarian marriage, the husband and wife become a team, sharing in household chores and cooperating in managing family affairs. Though this arrangement may not be fully acceptable to many Southern men yet, it is rapidly becoming more and more accepted as greater numbers of women work outside the home.

If you are a newcomer and plan to marry an American Southern man or woman, before you become too deeply involved, be sure to discuss attitudes and expectations of marriage, especially with regard to the division of labor in the home. This is particularly important if you and your potential mate are young, since younger women tend to be more deeply committed to the egalitarian approach to marriage.

Women and Sex

Most women in this country believe that they should be active sexual participants, for their own benefit, as well as for their partners. They also believe they are not sexual objects just for the pleasure of men, and they expect their partners to be knowledgeable about sexual behavior and sensitive to fulfilling their sexual needs. They also understand and accept their sexual obligations.

It is impossible to generalize about American women's attitudes about pre-marital sex, but probably a third (or more) of unmarried women are involved in pre-marital sexual intercourse. A similar number of married women are involved in adulterous liaisons. From magazines, books, movies and television, newcomers may get the impression that all women are promiscuous. This is not the case. Recent studies suggest that Americans are becoming more conservative in sexual habits and practices. Women who are practicing Christians do not approve of premarital sex or adultery.

Idealistically, most American women insist on monogamy in marriage. Few women condone their husbands' sexual infidelity. They do not tolerate their husbands' developing emotional and romantic relationships with other females, even without sexual relations. The American wife wants her husband to help in the home, be an economic partner, help rear the children, be a satisfying sexual partner, and also be her closest and best friend.

Women as Mothers and Homemakers

American women are currently going through a period of emotional conflict. They want to be educated, have careers, be married, have children, and be good wives—all at the same time. The majority of American mothers work outside the home, and many suffer from guilt about leaving their babies in day care centers. Many women have to work as sometimes two salaries are needed to support the high standard of living of Americans.

Mothers are expected to play an active part in their children's education. They are expected to attend meetings at the school and to help with special school activities, such as fund raising, sports events, field trips for the children, and making costumes for school plays. In addition, parents should help children with their homework, arrange and provide transportation for the extracurricular activities of the children.

American parents can consult many books (available at libraries and bookstores) on child rearing practices. In addition, special lectures and workshops are held in the community from time to time. The local mental health agency provides information about support groups and resource material to assist parents in rearing their children.

Older Women

Aging women have problems in the youth-centered American culture. (See "Old Age and Retirement Centers" for additional information about old age in America.) Most middle-class, middle-aged and older women try to look as young as possible, sometimes devoting great amounts of money and energy to this effort. Consequently, many Southern grandmothers look very young to newcomers. During the 1950s and 1960s, many Southern women married young and had children early, but their youthful appearance is often the result of diet, exercise, good health care, grooming, cosmetics, and an active life style.

Southern grandmothers tend to be very proud of their grandchildren, and many carry "brag" books filled with photographs of their grandchildren. Some grandmothers help their families by taking care of grandchildren while the parents work or go out for recreation. However, many grandparents live great distances from their children and grandchildren and see them only during visits.

A number of older women work at service institutions and charity organizations for no pay at all. They are called "volunteers" and are a valuable part of American society.

Women in Business and Professions

Women are employed at every level in the workplace, including managerial positions; many are supervisors. There are women teachers at every level of the educational system, and students from other parts of the world will almost certainly have women teachers and professors. In many places of business, you may find a woman dealing with your business in any commercial, industrial, or governmental establishment.

When a position for a job is being filled, it is illegal for an employer to discriminate against any person on the basis of race, ethnic origin, sex, religion, or age (over forty). Women, therefore, have a right to bring a lawsuit against a potential employer if they feel they have the qualifications for a particular position and were not given the job specifically because of their gender or age.

Newcomers, unaccustomed to seeing women in prominent positions, may feel uncomfortable when confronted with the equal status of women. But newcomers should be careful to understand this aspect of society without feeling threatened or insulted. Women have the positions they fill because of their knowledge, efficiency, skills, and abilities.

Newcomers appointed to managerial positions need to understand the thinking of American women. Some newcomers from male-dominated societies have encountered much resentment from American women coworkers because they have brought with them to the United States the attitudes

toward women from their cultures. To gain the full cooperation of American colleagues, newcomers must adopt the
American cultural patterns of male-female relationships in
the workplace. See the section titled "Newcomer
Supervisors" on page 187.

Women as Lesbians

Lesbianism (also called homosexuality) is the name given
to women who prefer their sexual partners and their emotional, romantic relationships to be with other women.
Many newcomers are surprised and, sometimes, shocked to
find this subject openly discussed and acknowledged.

Some lesbian women form permanent attachments and
live together, developing a family unit. Some even adopt children, though this is not a common occurrence. Although
American society has accepted lesbianism to a certain extent,
this lifestyle is not acceptable to most Americans, especially
in the more conservative South.

Southern Families

As is the case with many American families, Southern
families are in transition. As more and more women enter
the workplace, traditions concerning housekeeping and child
rearing are giving way to new, highly individualized, family
roles. This is due, in part, to the Women's Movement, which
stresses equality, and, in part, to the growing tendency for
both married partners to work. Southerners will continue to
struggle with the individual changes resulting from these
social changes.

The Women's Movement is a term applied to efforts on
the part of many women across the United States to obtain
rights and opportunities equal to those enjoyed by men. As
with the Civil Rights Movement, the Women's Movement is
bringing both legal and personal changes to the attitudes and
lifestyles of many Americans.

Unlike many societies, the United States has no specific
pattern of child discipline, and this goes for the South as well.
In the traditional Southern family, the father disciplined the
children, and the mother supported the father in this role.

But today's social changes have brought shifts in the pattern of child rearing and discipline. Young parents often try to share this role, while older parents tend to mix the traditional role with current ideas.

Divorce

An issue that frequently perplexes newcomers, especially those from Asia and the Middle East, is that of divorce. This is a complex problem, but some reasons for the high divorce rate, which currently is about one in three marriages, are discussed.

The expectations of marriage in American society are very high. Spouses are expected to be best friends, loyal partners, companions, entertainers, co-partners in child rearing, economic partners, and emotional nurturers. Yet the American lifestyle is busy, hectic, and demanding; the choices for careers and entertainment are great; and the pressure to succeed requires great attention to one's profession. With so many demands on one's time, spouses and families are highly stressed, and spouses' expectations are often neglected.

Another reason for divorce is the fact that people change over the years, and the changes do not always suit the spouse. When a more suitable person is found, one spouse may sue for divorce. Men and women work together, and each spouse may meet and "fall in love" with a person who seems more suitable. Even if this is not the case, individuals have the opportunity to know many members of the opposite sex, and they may compare their spouses with others. When they feel the spouse does not measure up, they may decide on a divorce. In addition, men and women may freely mix socially, in private and in public, so alternative, potential spouses can easily be found.

In the past, women were forced to accept the disappointments and problems in a marriage for economic reasons. Today, more than 50 percent of middle-class American women work outside the home and are able to divorce because they can support themselves, and often their children, on their salaries and the financial support the ex-husband has to pay by law.

Except in some religious organizations, there is almost no

taboo against divorce in American society anymore, so people are free to end a marriage without the fear of being socially ostracized or severely criticized. Christian Americans consider divorce a tragedy and do not promote divorce. Many churches have counselors and programs to help couples strengthen their marriages to prevent divorce.

Teenagers and Young Adults

Newcomers will find that Southern young people are much like most other young Americans. Young people constitute a subculture with its own attitudes, values, behavior patterns, and activities.

Southern young people spend many hours each day in front of the television set and view the same shows, advertisements, movies, talk shows, and other programs as other Americans. Thus, it is not surprising that there is a similarity in appearance and behavior.

American young people are some of the most privileged young people in the world. Nevertheless, they are subject to stresses because American culture, and, therefore, Southern culture, is highly competitive, with emphasis on achievement and success. Middle-class young people are expected to do as well or better than their parents did. In general, American young people are expected to be sociable, good looking, and academically or vocationally successful. In addition, they are also expected, whenever possible, to be successful at sports, as well as in academic areas.

American society is faced with the problem that each individual family has to develop its own ways of organizing itself and rearing the children. As children compare their families with those of their friends, unhappiness can result when some parents appear more lenient than others.

Contributing to the problems of discipline is the ease with which American young people become mobile. Young people can get vehicle driver's licenses at age sixteen in most states. Once they have earned their licenses, they tend to feel they are adults, able to go where they please. Many work after school to earn money for gasoline or cars, enhancing the sense of independence.

In the United States, middle-class parents aim at rearing

their children to be independent, self-sufficient, and self-reliant from an early age. Ideally, by eighteen years of age, the young adult should be emotionally mature enough to leave the parents' home, choose employment after graduating from high school, or attend college in preparation for a career. Most parents expect their college-age children to contribute financially to their college expenses. This does not mean that the parents abandon their children; they are usually willing to help, advise, and support them. Parents generally expect their children to become emotionally mature enough to make their own decisions and to live a responsible and independent life taking financial responsibility for themselves as much as possible.

Southern young people are reputed to be more conservative than other young American adults in many ways: politically, religiously, in their attitudes to society, and in their dress. It is true that many young people in the 1980s and 1990s have materialistic goals and pursue careers they hope will help them become wealthy. However, once young Southerners are confronted with the problems and suffering of others, they usually respond with a highly idealistic, generous, and compassionate side of their personalities. The many young people who join the Peace Corps, mission teams of all religious denominations, and other volunteer organizations all over the world, often for no pay, are such young people. Most young people are not addicted to alcohol or other drugs, and the majority care about their parents, families, and living a productive life.

African-American Southerners

Black Americans prefer to be called African-Americans. They are descendents of the slaves who were brought to North America during the seventeenth and eighteenth centuries from the West Coast of Africa. After the slaves were freed, many moved to the more industrialized Northern states, a trend that continued into the twentieth century because the South offered few good employment opportunities for them.

During the early 1960s, the Civil Rights Movement,

under the leadership of Dr. Martin Luther King, Jr., won equal legal rights for African-American people and resulted in their becoming politically aware of their power. The federal government was forced to pass civil rights legislation to ensure that African- Americans would receive equal opportunities in such areas as education, employment, housing, and welfare services.

African-American people have suffered a great deal from the segregationist policies of the past and from discrimination in general; today there are several organizations that monitor and protect the quality of life, investigate cases of discrimination, and study legislation at every level to guard the interests of the African-American community. Among them are the Southern Christian Leadership Conference (SCLC) and the National Association for the Advancement of Colored People (NAACP). The government also has established an agency that monitors the way all employees, but especially those from minorities, are treated by employers. The agency (Equal Employment Opportunity Commission— EEOC) also investigates complaints of employees of unfair labor practices.

Greater numbers of African-American people are entering politics, and several Southern cities currently have, or have had, African-American mayors who have earned the respect of all population groups. Today there are many African-Americans in congress and in top administrative positions in the federal government.

As is true for other Americans, most African-Americans nationwide are middle class, although this may be less so in the South, and the number in positions of leadership is increasing. Colleges are encouraging African-American students to enroll, often by offering scholarships and other incentives. However, the number of students who drop out of high school and who do not go on to college remains a concern for society as a whole.

Another great concern of the African-American community leaders in the nineties is the erosion of the African-American family and the resultant problems. In recent years, African-American leaders have expressed concern about the number of single-parent families and the numbers of teenage girls who have babies out of wedlock. (This is also a concern in the white community.) Some African-American leaders feel that government policies of giving aid to single mothers have discouraged mothers from marrying because once married, the aid is terminated. The absence of the father in many families has created problems in rearing children and has eroded the traditional family structure, which has long been a strength in African-American communities.

African-American teenaged males are currently the group with the greatest unemployment rate in the United States, compounding other societal and personal problems. Some of them are involved in youth gangs and illegal drug activities. For these and other reasons, African-American parents face grave and difficult problems.

Generally African-American Southerners are patriotic, and many have careers in the armed forces. Certain sports also have outstanding African-American participants in numbers disproportionate to their presence in the general population. Some have become highly visible, top-ranked athletes and entertainers, and this may leave the impression that African-American Americans have special skills and talents in these areas. However, as is the case with white Americans, the majority never achieve these positions of extreme respect or adulation.

Usually African-Americans are friendly, warm-hearted, and generous people who are people oriented in their approach to life. They are excellent at understanding people and can quickly assess a person's intention and sincerity.

Many African-American Southerners are very religious and belong to well-organized and dynamic churches. Historically, African-American churches have been an enormous help to their members, offering comfort and strength, as well as organizational and political structure. A number of civil rights activities were originated by church leaders, particularly in the 1960s.

Race Relations in the South

Racial problems in the South, especially the Deep South,

have attracted attention all over the world. Prior to the 1960s, many institutions and facilities were designated as "white" or "colored." ("Colored" was the polite term by which black Southerners were known at that time.) This policy was known as "segregation," and it kept black and white Southerners living apart, although they frequently worked and shopped together in the market places.

During the 1950s, the Civil Rights Movement unofficially began when Rosa Parks in Montgomery, Alabama, refused to give up her seat in the section of a bus designated for white people. African-American Southerners also drew attention to their separate and unequal educational institutions and demanded entry to white schools and universities. Under the leadership of Dr. Martin Luther King, Jr., a Baptist minister, who had studied the Indian leader Gandhi's philosophies of nonviolent means of protest, the movement gained momentum. African-Americans all over the United States, not just in the Southern states, demanded the civil, legal, social, medical, and educational rights and opportunities that white people enjoyed.

In 1964, African-Americans won their civil rights and congress (then composed primarily of white Americans) enacted the law known as the Civil Rights Act. This act opened all public schools, colleges, universities, residential areas, and public facilities to all Americans (and newcomers), regardless of race, religion, or ethnic origin. Subsequent legislation has expanded the coverage of this act to other groups—such as those older than forty and the handicapped.

In understanding race relations in the United States, one has to understand the terms "discrimination" and "discriminate." In their negative meaning, these words refer to behavior or attitudes based on another person's race, religion, age, sex, ethnic origin, or age. Such discrimination may take the form of not hiring a person, denying a person admission to a certain school or club, or treating a person in a negative and different way. (Today, most Americans believe that all people must have equal rights and opportunities before the law, regardless of race, color, religion, or ethnic origin.)

There are many laws in the United States today designed to prevent discrimination and to insure that people are treated fairly and equally before the law. Many Americans feel this ideal has not been fully achieved, and they continue to campaign for greater equality.

Southern Love of Music

Southern people, like many other Americans, love music. Newcomers can expect music to be played in stores, shopping malls, restaurants, sometimes even in airports and on parking lots. Sometimes music is too loud for some newcomers, but one does become accustomed to it.

Country Music

The South is well known for its country music, which often tells stories of life situations, particularly sad ones. While the words may be quite sad or sentimental, they are frequently set to catchy tunes. Though always popular in the South, country music and gospel music are enjoying new interest and popularity in the rest of the United States. Country music is promoted by the "Grand Ole Opry," an institution in Nashville, Tennessee, and newcomers interested in country music would enjoy a visit to this concert hall. A travel agent can advise you about a trip there and can make reservations for seats. The hall is usually heavily booked, so reservations are advised.

Another way one can enjoy country music is to attend local concerts by different groups in towns and cities. An interesting experience is to visit a country music festival where different bands, soloists, groups, and individuals perform, usually for a whole day. Often dancers will demonstrate clogging and square dancing, also activities enjoyed by many Southerners. These festivals are joyful, happy events, offer plenty of food for sale, and provide the newcomer with a pleasant opportunity for observing the culture of the rural South.

Jazz

New Orleans, a city in the South, is the home of jazz now considered a classical art form. Jazz is a uniquely American music developed by mostly African-Americans and somewhat influenced by African musical rhythms in the early part of the 1900's. Tourists visit New Orleans to hear this distinctive blend of musical cultures. Some of the original jazz musicians, now fairly aged, still play there. Those who do still perform are a delight to listen to and observe, as is the new generation of jazz musicians. A visit to Preservation Hall, the original home of jazz, is strongly recommended.

Church Music

Newcomers are often amazed at the standard of church music performed in the bigger churches of all denominations throughout the South. Even in rural areas, large churches often have trained and paid choir masters or ministers of music who train choirs. The type of music performed in churches depends on the selection of the minister and the minister of music and usually takes the preference of the congregation into account. One can expect everything from classical music to contemporary gospel music in rural or urban churches in the South. Some larger churches have small orchestras or ensembles comprised of church members.

Many churches have choir programs for young people. The standard of music is good and often these choirs go on concert tours in the United States. Exceptional choirs will raise money and go on tour overseas as well as in the United States.

Classical Music

There is a symphony orchestra in some large Southern cities and some of these are considered very good. The symphony season is usually during the winter and spring months. Usually, music lovers can purchase season tickets at a reduced price, but unfortunately tickets for musical performances are a bit higher in the United States than in some countries. In some Southern cities, music clubs bring outstanding musicians and performers to the cities. In addition, famous American and international performers often include the larger Southern cities in their itineraries.

The New York City Opera tours the United States, including parts of the South, and brings excellent opera to many who cannot afford to travel to the music centers of the United States, which include New York, Chicago, San Francisco, Los Angeles, Cincinnati, and Atlanta.

Colleges and High Schools

In many public and private schools throughout the South, music, especially choral and band music, is taught. If the school your child attends does not teach music, there are usually music teachers in the community who teach privately.

Most junior colleges, colleges, and universities have choral programs for which students usually have to audition. During the spring and summer vacations, it is common for the best of these choirs to tour the United States, and some even go overseas. Larger colleges and universities offer music degrees and most have orchestras, ensembles, and marching band programs in which students may participate.

Sometimes the universities and colleges present concerts for the public free or at a nominal price. Some universities and colleges present famous musicians on special occasions to which the public is invited, again for a reasonable fee.

Other Music

Throughout the South, concerts feature music that is very much a part of American culture. One can frequently attend concerts and hear over the radio various types of rock and roll, popular, reggae, and, rap music. Recordings of this music are sold in music stores all over the South.

Popular singers tour the United States and include the South in their tours. Their concerts are usually fairly expensive, but popular. Rock and roll concerts are described as "soft rock" or "hard rock" music. Many parents are concerned when their teenagers go to rock concerts as there is sometimes, but not always, a group of people who take drugs or smoke marijuana at concerts. Sometimes the words of the songs are considered sexually suggestive, obscene, violent, or otherwise offensive. Usually the police are present at these concerts to supervise the crowds, but many parents try to prevent young teenagers from attending rock concerts featuring singers who are known to attract a rowdy, drug-taking crowd of people. Newcomers attending these types of concerts need to be aware of these potential problems.

Humor

Using, abusing, or misunderstanding humor can probably get one into more trouble than any other single social interaction in the United States. Since humor is culturally defined, this should not surprise anybody. What is funny to one person is boring or insulting to another. You will even find that what is funny in one part of the United States is not funny in another part.

You may find that the lack of your own national brand of humor is one of the aspects of being a newcomer that you will miss most. If you have fellow ex-patriots in your city, get together to laugh.

If you do not want to offend Southerners, a few observations are relevant. First, unless you are sure a story, incident, or joke will be acceptable, do not tell it. Reserve it for your fellow expatriates or family members who will understand; you could place yourself in a poor light and could create tension between yourself and a Southerner.

Second, humor with sarcastic or hurtful overtones is not socially acceptable. The most important rule about humor in the South is that you never laugh at the expense of somebody else, and you never joke or tease in a manner that might hurt someone's feelings. Racial or ethnic jokes are considered in bad taste and should be avoided at all times.

It is not acceptable for a newcomer to correct anybody's grammar, speech, or pronunciation, even if it is done humorously. Current, local usage tends to determine the use of grammar, and this is regionally defined, so a particular rule you learned about English may not be observed here.

Southerners often joke about themselves, their drawls, their accents, or slow speech. You may find yourself being kidded about your accent, but this is usually done in a good-natured way; rarely, if ever, is it meant to be a correction. Southerners make a distinction between humorous kidding and correcting; one is acceptable, the other not.

Be careful about joking or teasing someone about politics, religion, and football. These are subjects dear to the hearts of many Southerners, and you can easily upset them by inappropriate joking about these subjects.

Americans from other parts of the United States sometimes make mistakes by making detrimental comments in a
jocular manner about Southerners and education,
Southerners and culture, Southerners and poverty,
Southerners and farming. These type of comments, however
humorous, usually are not acceptable to Southern people
because they imply a hint of criticism and a stereotype that is
untrue and which Southerners have tried hard to overcome.

Southern Homes and Gardens

Generally, Southern middle-class homes are spacious and
comfortable and are in no way inferior to homes in any other
part of the United States. In fact, you can buy a great deal
more land and house in the South for your money than anywhere else in the nation.

Many people improve their homes by adding rooms or by
refurnishing and remodeling. Often visitors will be invited to
view the new acquisitions. You need not feel embarrassed
about seeing the home if your host or hostess invites you to
view it, but do not walk through a home without permission.
You may also feel free to make complimentary comments
about the home, the furnishings, or the furniture. These
comments will be regarded as compliments and will not be
interpreted as hints for a gift of the admired item, as is the
case in some cultures. Southerners, generally, are happy to
know that you like their choices.

A typical middle-class Southern home consists of three or
four bedrooms, one or two bathrooms, a living room, a dining
room, a kitchen, and a "den" in which the television is placed.
The living room, furnished in a somewhat formal style, is
used when people have "company" (visitors) or for formal
entertaining. The "den" or "family room" is used by the family for relaxing, usually in front of the television, and is
furnished in a casual, informal way. Often the family eats in
the kitchen, and the dining room is used when visitors are
being entertained. Many homes do not have separate living
rooms and dens, but have just one "great room".

Most occupants of a house like to have their own bed-
room, but often children have to share a room. Many families

also have a "guest" room in which visiting friends can be accommodated.

Most middle-class Southern homes have an area with a washing machine and a clothes dryer where the laundry can be done, usually in a separate room or in the kitchen or garage. Homes usually have a garage or an open area with a roof called a carport in which one or two cars can be parked.

Some Southerners employ interior designers to help them decorate their homes because an attractively decorated home is important to them. Many middle-class home furnishings and decorations somewhat resemble those of the old ante-bellum homes on a much smaller scale, of course. (Ante-bellum is the name given to homes built before the Civil War of 1861.) Some people furnish their home with antiques, which are very expensive.

Most Southerners own a variety of appliances that make house cleaning and meal preparations simple, such as vacuum cleaners, rug shampooers, electric brooms, washing machines and clothes dryers, electric cake mixers, electric carving knives, toasters, microwave ovens that cook and defrost food in minutes, electric coffee makers, stoves, refrigerators, freezers, and many other household items. These appliances enable the husband and wife to spend as little time as possible preparing food and cleaning the home.

Throughout the South, homes are built of a mixture of brick and wood, or wood alone. Sometimes a home is predominantly wood with a veneer of brick on the outside. There are also wooden homes with vinyl siding, a veneer attached to the outside of the house that never needs painting.

Wooden homes (or aluminum, as in trailers) that are built on concrete blocks (not concrete foundations) are able to be moved. Sometimes on a highway, one can see a home being moved on a special vehicle that is preceded and followed by a warning vehicle with flashing lights. Many people in the South live in mobile or trailer homes, which can be purchased or rented and constitute a relatively inexpensive way of owning a home. These homes can be luxurious or basic and are surprisingly comfortable with all the usual amenities of a regular American home. They can be moved to a site equipped with electricity and sewage outlets and rented to mobile home dwellers. The parks in which these homes are placed can range from luxurious to those with only the bare essentials. One can also frequently observe a solitary mobile home under some trees out in the country.

Not all Southerners live in these circumstances. Those with low incomes often live in slum areas of cities or in "housing projects" that are owned or subsidized by the government. These are rented at low rates to poor people. Often these projects are run down and look dismal and shabby and often are the sites of crime and drug dealing. Other poor people rent privately owned apartments or small homes, while others buy small, inexpensive houses or buy or rent mobile homes.

Yards and Gardens

A yard is the area of ground surrounding the home on which one grows grass, shrubs, and flowers, and a garden is the piece of ground on which one grows vegetables.Vegetable gardens are most often behind one's home, and flower gardens may be either in front or behind the home.

The South has rich soil and high rainfall, which accounts for the green grass and forests. But the humidity poses problems for an inexperienced gardener. Plants that grow successfully in your homeland will not necessarily grow well in the South. A plant nursery, where you buy your plants, will tell you which plants will grow in your yard. Sometimes you may have problems with your soil, in which case you will need to have it tested and evaluated. Most Southern states have an "agricultural extension agent" in each county who can answer your questions about the soil in your area. The number for this office will be listed in the blue pages of the telephone book.

Many pests plague the Southern yard. Shrubs and trees need spraying periodically and a plant nursery or hardware store with a garden shop can advise you about the use of pesticides.

Southerners, in middle-class city suburbs especially, pride themselves on their lawns and shrubs and disapprove of neighbors who do not keep their yards tidy and clean. They also keep the exteriors of their homes in good repair and expect their neighbors to do the same since shoddy-looking homes and yards tend to lower the value of properties in a neighborhood. Poorly maintained yards also encourage snakes, rats, and other critters. Newcomers should make every effort to maintain their yards like their neighbors do, especially in the fall when fallen, dead leaves are raked from the lawns.

Yards in the spring in the South are a wonderful sight. The flowering tree with white and, sometimes, pink, four-petalled flowers is called the dogwood tree. In many yards, azaleas bloom, adding touches of color. In many Southern cities, one can get a map of the routes to tour during the spring to see the flowering trees and shrubs. Many beautiful homes and gardens can be viewed on these routes, and sometimes historical homes will be open to the public, for a fee.

Are Southerners (and Other Americans) Parochial?

Newcomers often complain that Southerners know very little about the rest of the world. This is not a problem confined to the South; many other Americans also know very little about the world outside the United States.

There are probably many reasons for the poor knowledge of world geography, history, and current affairs. Education in the United States has, as one of its goals, the training of an individual for living in a democracy. The school subjects relevant to this goal tend to focus mainly on the United States.

Another factor leading to ignorance of other cultures and countries is the lack of emphasis on teaching foreign languages in elementary and secondary schools. Usually only college and university students have to take a few years of a foreign language. In addition, many Americans feel little need to learn a foreign language because English has become a world language. Furthermore, in the 1970s, computer languages replaced the teaching of foreign languages in many colleges.

In contrast to many other countries, where information about government affairs and political events is censored, limited, or not given much prominence, the goal of the American news media is to inform Americans of the political events of their country, county, and neighborhood. This is an enormous task in a vast geographical area with a population of at least 250 million. Many Americans feel overwhelmed by the amount of information their media give them each day about their own country and feel they already suffer from "information overload" without trying to keep up with events in the rest of the world. Some psychologists suggest that having too much information to process creates an emotional problem for many people.

For many years, the United States has led the world in most fields of human endeavor. Leaders of many different fields from countries around the world study developments in the United States to benefit their own countries. For this reason, some Americans feel they do not need to study other countries for ideas on improving their way of life. This has had the effect of encouraging Americans to look to themselves for improvement and answers, instead of to others.

This is changing at the moment, and knowledge about other countries is increasing in many different ways. For instance, some universities are encouraging students to study in other parts of the world through exchange programs. Research in foreign universities and visits by students to foreign universities during the academic year or summer vacation are also encouraged.

As trade expands between the United States and the rest of the world, information about other countries is also being gained by the many Americans who travel or live abroad for their companies. A developing network of scientific research projects among different nations also promotes knowledge. Global problems, such as the threat to the environment and the AIDS epidemic, are having the effect of making Americans more aware of other countries and peoples. In addition, the amazing development of Japan has resulted in the Japanese "business culture" being studied and imitated.

The collapse of communism as a political ideology and economic system has caught the attention of many Americans who have not had any special interest in the rest of the world. Possibly there will be more interest in the international scene in the 1990s than at any time since World War II.

The advent of an emerging united Europe and the

progress of so many developing countries will probably force Americans to become better acquainted with other countries, their cultures, and perceptions. Americans wishing to maintain their international trade links will have to pay more attention to the larger world, and parochialism will naturally diminish.

Religion

Religion is important all over America. At the time of this writing, probably 80 percent of the population believes in God and about 40 percent attend a church, synagogue, or mosque regularly. In the South, people are particularly serious about religion. Probably half the Southern population goes to church regularly and supports a place of worship by attending its religious activities and by making regular financial contributions.

Religious Freedom

The Constitution of the United States guarantees its citizens religious freedom and the separation of church and state. This means that the government never interferes in the affairs of any church or denomination, however large or small.

All citizens (and visitors) have the right to follow any religion in the manner of their choice. No individual or government may persecute any person for any religious practice unless it violates a law. The principle, "separation of church and state," is the reason that public schools may not have public prayers for students, and no religious organization may hold meetings on school or government property. There is, therefore, no official church recognized by the state, and no religion or religious agency receives money from the government for its operation. Religious organizations, however, are not required to pay taxes.

The belief in the separation of church and state does not imply that clergymen may not preach about political, social, moral, or ethical issues related to government. However, because freedom of speech is also a dearly held belief, the government may not dictate how a minister preaches.

Diversity of Religion

Every major religion in the world has its adherents in the United States and in the South. There are over 200 organized church denominations, some large, some small. But the Jewish-Christian religious heritage and tradition is by far the predominant one and has influenced religious thinking in the United States most strongly.

Besides the major Christian and Jewish denominations, there are religions such as Buddhism, Hinduism, Islam, native American religions (American Indian), and also some vestiges of African religions. These do not have great numbers of adherents. In some parts of the South, especially Florida, a form of voodooism is practiced, although its adherents are very few. There are also a few isolated churches that promote Satan worship.

The Christian religion is the predominant religion in America and, therefore, the South and consists of two main groups: Protestantism and Roman Catholicism. Protestantism is the predominant group in the South.

The Roman Catholic Church is the largest single denomination in the United States, although all the Protestant denominations grouped together claim greater numbers in membership. The Protestant denominations are Baptist (nationwide, the largest group divided into many sub-groups), Presbyterian, Methodist, Congregational, Episcopalian (Anglican), the Christian Church, the Assemblies of God, Disciples of Christ, Church of God, Full Gospel, Lutherans, Quakers (Society of Friends), Seventh Day Adventists, the Church of the Nazarene, to name some denominations that are considered "main stream." Smaller in membership but active in many parts of the United States are the Orthodox denominations: Russian Orthodox and Greek Orthodox.

There are other, smaller groups with religious beliefs that are somewhat different from mainstream denominations. These include Jehovah's Witnesses, Mormons, and Unitarians.

Many newcomers ask why there are so many religious denominations. The answer is simply because diversity is not feared in the United States, choices are encouraged, and individuals have the freedom to live their lives as they please.

Although the mainstream denominations basically believe the same Christian doctrine, they have different ways of conducting their organizations and worship services. People tend to belong to organizations that suit them best.

Churches of all denominations are to be found all over the South, although some denominations are more strongly represented in certain areas. The two predominant Protestant denominations in the South are the Southern Baptist Convention and the United Methodist Church, followed by the two Presbyterian denominations. The Roman Catholic Church is also represented in the South, as is, to a smaller extent, the Jewish Faith.

The churches can fulfill many functions: spiritual, social, sociological, cultural, recreational and educational. Church life consists of not only attending a worship service on a Sunday, but also attending recreational functions such as sports meetings like ball games, arts and crafts meetings, music and art festivals, fitness classes, cooking classes, daycare facilities for young children, etc.

In most Southern towns and cities the residents have a selection of churches within the same denomination. Hence one can sometimes find a church more formal in its worship and a less formal type one down the road. Americans tend to visit many churches within the same denomination in a particular city before they decide which church they will join.

What Christians Believe

This section discusses the beliefs of most major Christian denominations, especially in the South. One of the most important beliefs is "salvation by faith, not of works," by which Christians mean that they enjoy harmonious relationships with God while on earth and receive the gift of living in His presence in Heaven after they die. Salvation cannot be bought or won by good deeds; it must be accepted as a free gift and, on earth, the individual must request it from God. After salvation is received, the Christian should live to please God.

God is one God existing as three persons—the Father, Son, and Holy Spirit—each with a different function. The

Father plans salvation, the Son makes it possible through his death and resurrection, and through the Holy Spirit, the believer experiences the reality of a loving relationship with God.

When God created the first human beings, Adam and Eve, he enjoyed a perfect relationship with them. Later in their lives Adam and Eve disobeyed God and so sin and a spirit of evil entered the world. This broke the perfect relationship of harmony with God. God, however, loved his people so much that he sent his only son, Jesus, to the earth to heal the relationship.

Jesus Christ lived on the earth 2,000 years ago in the part of the world we call the Middle East today. He went about teaching and performing miracles. His teaching emphasized turning away from evil to love and obey God, and to love fellow human beings.

Because one of the purposes of Jesus's life was to heal the relationship between God and man, he allowed himself to die as a sacrifice for the punishment of human sin and evil. He died after his enemies nailed him onto a wooden cross, which is the symbol of Christianity. After being dead for three days, Jesus Christ came back to life and showed that he had conquered evil and death. This return to life is called the resurrection. After spending forty days with his earthy family, friends and followers, Christ returned to live forever with his father, God, in heaven.

Though the death of Jesus Christ makes possible a reconciliation with God, each individual person has the responsibility of making a conscious choice to have a relationship with him, by accepting this "salvation." This is usually after an individual realizes that his or her life does not please God because of evil and a broken relationship with him. At this time of realization and enlightenment, the person then sincerely admits evil and asks God to forgive him or her. This is known as confession and repentance and is the first step to becoming a Christian. At this time God then grants to that individual salvation. Sincere confession is followed by a decision to obey and follow Christ and his teaching as his follower, or devotee. Followers are known as "Christians."

On earth a Christian enjoys a harmonious, joyful relationship with Christ who gives the help and strength to live a spiritual life. Help is necessary because a Christian is constantly being tempted to do evil by Satan. Spiritual help also comes through reading the holy scriptures (called the Bible), prayer and meditation, and by attending religious services.

Many people who belong to churches do not practice Christianity. A practicing Christian is one who has salvation and lives according to Christ's teachings. These teachings include the ten principles called the "Ten Commandments." These state that the disciple: should love and serve only God, should have no idols, should not abuse God's name, should keep one day holy each week (usually Sunday for Christians), should honor parents, should not kill, commit adultery, steal, lie, and desire other people's possessions. Jesus emphasized that one should love God and one's neighbor as one loves oneself, and should live a moral, good life. This life is characterized by kindness, love and helpfulness to those with any need. The Christian should treat everybody with equality and justice and should be especially concerned about the poor, sick and imprisoned. Christians should not engage in sexual relations outside of marriage, should not become intoxicated with alcohol and drugs, and should not be corrupted by riches, nor exploit or defraud others.

Christ taught that his disciples should develop loving, and helpful relationships with other Christians. This is one reason why Christians meet in groups to worship God once a week on Sundays. During the worship times, called "worship services" often two important "ordinances", sometimes called "sacraments" are observed. One is baptism, the other is communion, also called "The Lord's Supper" or the "Eucharist".

After Christians become followers of Christ they are "baptized" as an outward sign of their resolve to live as Christians. Some churches baptize a baby by sprinkling water on the forehead of the baby, and the parents promise to bring the child up as a Christian. When the child is grown he or she will "confirm" the decision the parents made. Other churches only baptize people after they make a decision to become a disciple. These churches completely immerse the disciple in a container of water in front of a group of worshippers.

When Christians observe communion they gather together in a group to remember, with thankfulness, Christ's death. They participate in a ceremony in which the minister shares bread and wine (or grape juice) with them. These are symbols of Christ's body, which was broken on the cross (the bread), and his blood (the wine), which flowed from his body when he died.

Followers of Christ do not have to live in seclusion from the world and everyday life. The Bible teaches that disciples may live in the material, secular world and enjoy its benefits, provided this enjoyment does not clash with the teachings of Jesus, and lead them into evil deeds (called sin). Christians are expected to earn their living through employment because work is considered pleasing to God. They should also give financially to support their church and the work of those who go throughout the world (missionaries) to teach all people about the "gospel" which is the good news of what Christ has done for everyone. They should also give of their earnings to those in need.

In the Roman Catholic church some disciples choose to live in monasteries, and priests in this denomination do not marry. In all the other denominations, the ministers (priests) marry, have children and live as other Christians in the secular world.

See the section "Holidays" for the Christian festivals and celebrations of Christmas (Christ's birth) and Easter (Christ's death and resurrection.)

Culture Shock

One problem all newcomers face is culture shock. Culture shock is the combination of the emotions of unhappiness, confusion, homesickness, insecurity, and loneliness felt when one realizes that so many aspects of life in the new society are unfamiliar, uncomfortable, and different from past experiences. People here think, speak, eat, sometimes dress, and behave differently. They have different customs, traditions, values, child-rearing practices, and attitudes about everything from recreation to religion, and it is normal for newcomers to feel uncomfortable and unhappy while getting used to these differences.

Making the Adjustment
(Getting used to the new country)

Every newcomer or immigrant family goes through its own unique phases of adjustment. Usually the last weeks spent in the homeland are sad and fearful, but also exciting. In addition to packing, discarding, farewells, etc. there are dozens of details about the trip and the arrival in the new country that need attention. This time can be tiring and frightening. In addition, there is a deep, painful and natural grief about leaving so much that is loved: family, friends, sometimes pets, and usually, possessions. For some newcomers (especially refugees), there may also be relief at being able to escape danger and threat.

However, once the newcomer family arrives in America, the emotions of upheaval are lessened temporarily because exciting, interesting, different, and new sights and situations are constantly confronting everyone. The pain of departure is further dulled by the activity of settling in: finding a home, purchasing equipment and furniture, finding stores, selecting new foods, meeting people, and getting settled in your new home. After some of this has been completed, most members of the family feel full of hope about adjustment in the new country.

Generally newcomers find the first three months in a country just wonderful; for the next three months, the country is no longer new, it is less wonderful, and the newcomer feels homesick and begins to be critical of the new country, especially if dreams or expectations do not materialize. Sometimes this criticism becomes hostility, and nothing seems good in the new country. After about six months, the newcomer feels everything at home is better than in the new country and wishes to go home. Between twelve and eighteen months after arriving, the newcomer begins to feel more comfortable, and at ease. Of course, not everyone goes through these feelings exactly in the same way.

It takes most people one to two years to feel emotionally settled. During these two years, one is alternately happy and sad, glad and mad, appreciative and critical, sometimes all at the same time!

After one gets used to American food, one begins to long for native food; after the novelty of the mall and department stores wears off, one longs to shop in a quaint native store in the homeland; after one gets used to Southern English and American T.V., one longs for one's own language and pictures of home. The list goes on and on, and one spends two years see-sawing back and forth between excitement and homesickness.

Depression

At first, you may be intrigued by the differences. Occasionally you may be irritated, and often you will find the differences confusing. For newcomer adults, the feeling of being "different" can sometimes, though not always, have the effect of making them feel isolated from other people, and this, in turn, can lead to feelings of loneliness and depression.

Depression is part of the immigrant and newcomer experience. However, if one's feelings of isolation and depression cause fatigue, loss of energy, sleeplessness or desire for too much sleep, changes in appetite, feelings of hopelessness, much weeping, and inability to enjoy normal experiences, then it is necessary to consult a doctor. This condition can be treated, and one need not feel embarrassed about discussing problems of depression with a doctor in the United States. Most doctors are sympathetic and will understand the newcomer's depression.

Sometimes the stress of adjustment results in husbands and wives quarreling, arguing, accusing, and blaming each other. Spouses sometimes find it difficult to give much emotional support and help to each other when there is a great deal of emotional stress.

If you and your spouse no longer can live together peaceably and happily and you cannot solve your problems, do what Americans do and see a marriage counselor. These counselors help people handle crises and difficulties and are helpful, especially when there are no relatives in the new country to help one with stress and problems. Counselors' names and phone numbers should be obtained from a reputable clinic, hospital, or the Mental Health Society in your area.

Feeling Different

Most adults will probably never fully understand the culture of a society other than his or her own. You should understand that feeling different is no disgrace; it is a normal part of the immigrant and newcomer experience. You will probably always feel a little different from the natives because your earliest emotional and cultural experiences took place in a different country or state. Generally, however, your being different makes no difference to Americans. What will matter to most Americans is that you do your work properly and obey the law. If you are pleasant, polite, noncritical, and cooperative in your workplace and neighborhood, you will be accepted.

Try not to let feelings of being different isolate you from others. Most Southerners like foreigners and people who are different, provided they are polite and do not criticize the South or Southerners. If you try to understand and like them, they will respond with acceptance and warmth to you. People who are not accepted socially in the South are those who insult Southerners and the South and those who constantly talk about the superiority of the place from which they come.

You can probably reduce feelings of isolation by trying to understand the host culture and its problems. While understanding does not always ease the pain of adjustment, it does enable one to adjust more easily and relate to the people in a warmer, friendlier manner. Also, newcomers should identify and focus on the many positive, happy aspects of the new culture and try to enjoy them.

To understand the South and the United States, read history books and something of the cultural patterns of your region. You might want to read about the philosophy of pragmatism; something about John Dewey, B. F. Skinner, the Puritan philosophy of the work ethic, the philosophy of Christianity, American attitudes toward human sexuality, and the influence of religion on the United States. It is important to understand the philosophy of capitalism and the free enterprise system, the philosophy of democracy and its political and legal systems. You may also want to read about the Democratic and Republican political parties for politics is an important part of life in the United States.

Helping Children and Young Adults Adjust

The adjustment for **young adults** and **teenagers** may be very difficult after the initial stage of settling in. They may feel insecure about the unfamiliarity of their surroundings, their inability to speak the language, their lack of friends, and their lack of understanding about the culture of their schoolmates. They may feel they look different. Sometimes newcomer children do not understand their teachers' instructions or the speech of their peers. In addition, newcomer children are sometimes shy and do not know how to make new friends. Many children and most teenagers will still feel a degree of grief about the loss of many relationships in the homeland. These and other problems can lead to depression in both children and teenagers. Parents need to observe young people and children closely. If symptoms of depression are observed by parents, medical help from a pediatrician should be obtained.

Children and young people need assurance of the understanding, interest, concern, friendship, and love of their parents through the adjustment stage. One way parents can reassure their children is to communicate effectively with them. This does not involve merely telling them what they should do and feel. Parents need to encourage children and young people to share their feelings, problems, and thoughts with them and should avoid scolding the children. Teenagers and children need to feel that they can express their negative thoughts about their problems and that their parents are able to understand the uncomfortable feelings they have about the new environment. Being able to express these feelings without being criticized will help children feel better. They need their parents to be their friends, not their judges, in the adjustment period.

Of course, this kind of sharing and communication between parents and children must fit your cultural background. If family discussions are not part of your culture, have talks with your children in a way that fits in with your culture. In most cases, talking about your feelings and allowing the children to talk about theirs will be helpful in making the adjustment to your new life.

It is important that a parent who is going through a phase of homesickness not be too negative about the new country and community in front of young children and teenagers. A child can become fearful and insecure if its parents appear unhappy and unable to adjust. Attitudes usually form the basis of adjustment, and a desire on the part of the parent to adjust and enjoy the new home will help the child's and teenager's process of adjustment. Parents should not pretend to be happier than they are because this will be evident to older children. Parents should be reassuring and say something like "I am sad and homesick, but I will adjust in time."

School teachers and counselors can also be a great help to parents who are helping children and teenagers to adjust. In the South, you can get help from several mental health societies, schools, and churches. Many services are offered free of charge.

One way parents can help their children and teenagers through the adjustment phase is to plan family activities that accentuate family love and "togetherness." These can include picnics, visits to the amazing shopping centers all over the South, and visits to zoos, parks, and such places. The important point is that parents need to provide love, understanding, and activities that reassure their children and teenagers that the family is still a loving and united one, in spite of the many changes it has undergone.

Many churches throughout the South have programs for children and teenagers where newcomers are welcomed. Other helpful groups are sports clubs, Boy and Girl Scouts, and cultural clubs. Find out about the various activities for young people and children in your area as these may contribute towards the positive adjustment of your children and teenagers.

Aids in the Adjustment of the Older Newcomer

Probably young newcomers adjust to a new culture more rapidly than older people do. Couples in their twenties with young children find the adjustment of living in a new country or community easier than older parents with teenage or young adult children. There are several reasons for this: older immigrants have lifetimes of loving memories and loyalties in their homelands and friendships forged over many years, they have developed more analytical and critical abilities, and their own cultures are embedded in their personalities.

Older and teenage newcomers may find the social group in which they wish to mix a much more reserved and cautious group about admitting foreigners than the group into which a young child will merge. Not only Southerners, but most people over forty years of age, tend to have their friendship patterns already established. They have enough friends already and no longer have time or energy to create new friendships. The section on friendship (page 24) discusses some of the reasons older newcomers may find it difficult to make new friends. Under these circumstances, perhaps you should make friends with other "newcomers." These could be Americans from other areas in the United States or foreigners from other parts of the world.

It is relatively easy to make friends with other newcomers—they are also looking for new friendships and have some of the same problems you do, even if they come from a different country. These friendships can be rewarding because you can share the challenges of adjusting to new circumstances, and you can help and encourage each other.

It is rewarding to pursue friendships with Southern people because they are generous, warm, and kind. They are prepared to explain the Southern way of life and help newcomers with problems of adjustment and will sometimes share special holidays and celebrations with you. Provided newcomers are not critical of the South or Southerners and do not make them feel inferior or uncomfortable, Southerners will be warm and gracious friends.

Homesickness

It is normal for newcomers to feel homesick, to have times of deep sadness, and to miss family members and friends, especially parents. These feelings are to be expected. As time goes by and you adjust to living in the United States, this situation usually improves, although most newcomers always miss their parents and relatives.

Newcomers suffer from homesickness in different ways. Few people never feel homesick, and older people are likely to suffer more bouts of homesickness than younger people. You will miss the familiar people, places, sights, smells, and sounds. And of course, the food! Newcomers staying in the United States for a specified period of time are less prone to homesickness than are immigrants.

Feelings do settle down, and it is important to know that most people go through these same experiences. After about six to nine months—when the acute phase of shock has passed—new friends are found, and life returns to some normalcy again. This has been the experience of millions of other newcomers for three hundred years in the United States of America—the land of immigrants.

If you or one of your family members have real difficulty adjusting, seek help from the mental health society in your area—the number is in the telephone directory, or you may ask the telephone operator to find the number for you. Many employers provide counselors you may consult. Americans frequently see counselors in times of crisis and difficulty, so your search for help will be considered normal.

Reducing Homesickness

While homesickness is a normal aspect of adjusting to life in a new country, there are ways to reduce this feeling. Different ones of these suggestions may be more beneficial for some families (and some family members) than others.

Trips

When the excitement of settling into a new environment begins to wear off, taking a trip may ease some feelings of homesickness. The South is full of inexpensive and interesting places to visit for a day, a weekend, or longer as there are many lakes, mountain resorts, state parks, beaches, historical sites, etc. Seek advice from your local automobile association or from the Chamber of Commerce in the area you wish to visit (telephone numbers are available from the telephone operator). A change of scenery can do wonders for the whole family in the process of adjustment. When going on a trip, it is helpful to concentrate on enjoying the trip and to make a conscious effort to put aside the problems of adjustment for the duration of the trip.

Free Entertainment

Because many newcomers and immigrants have limited funds during the adjustment period, they can take advantage of the free or inexpensive entertainment offered in the South. The local newspaper will give details of a variety of events. For instance, through the spring and summer, the South is well known for its many festivals—many with free admission. Of course, there is always something to buy at a festival, but it is not necessary to spend anything. Festivals are usually held out of doors. Some have sports or exhibition events, dog shows, craft shows (Southern people love making all sorts of items, useful or otherwise), and food stalls. Many festivals are related to agriculture or industry in a particular area, and some feature beauty contests.

Sometimes there are free concerts in shopping malls, free craft shows, and a variety of free exhibitions. In some

Southern cities and towns, free symphony concerts and dramatic productions are sometimes held outdoors.

There is always the American recreation of shopping. A walk around a mall in the evenings is usually interesting, even without making a purchase. This is called "window shopping." In winter, the mall is cosy and warm; in summer, cool and refreshing. Malls for Americans seem to be the equivalent of the European park or the open air cafe, the South American market, or the Oriental or African bazaar.

Remember that America has an excellent public television system (PBS -the educational channel) that often broadcasts famous concerts and fine plays. Check the local newspaper for the schedule for PBS.

Continuing Education Courses

Local junior and senior colleges sometimes offer courses for enrichment. These can be taken without having to work toward a college degree. Usually they are inexpensive and provide a venue for meeting people and stimulating your ideas. Some Southern cities and towns also have community centers that offer courses of general interest like painting, ceramics, cooking, etc., for a fee.

Churches

Almost without exception, churches welcome newcomers. Churches are becoming more accustomed to foreigners, and many have programs designed especially for international people. You may have to spend time finding a church of your choice, but in most large Southern towns, you should be able to find a church that will suit your needs. Some churches offer free classes in conversational English and American culture for newcomers, as well as the opportunity to mix with other internationals and Americans.

Friends from the Old Country

One way to deal with homesickness is to meet with other people from your homeland. If you live near a university or an organization that employs internationals, you may be able to get information about such people. To get together for a familiar meal and to talk about "home" is usually helpful and provides an opportunity to discuss common problems, difficulties, and complaints.

Writing

Letter writing is good therapy for newcomers dealing with the pain of adjustment, particularly if one can write to a sympathetic friend about feelings, impressions, and experiences in the new country. Some newcomers do not feel they can write about their feelings to others. For them, writing a daily journal in which feelings and thoughts are recorded has proven to be a great help and is considered a therapeutic activity.

Going Home

Some immigrants and resident aliens are fortunate in being able to visit their homelands frequently and do not lose touch with their relatives, friends, and the atmosphere of their countries of origin. These visits keep them aware of the changes, difficulties, successes, and developments in their homelands.

Other immigrants seldom, if ever, go back home. Some refugees are not permitted to return; others cannot afford the fare. These people are prone to have nostalgic feelings about the places where they grew up and to idealize their friends and family. They tend to remember the pleasant times, and the bad times fade in their memories, unless, of course, they were traumatized refugees.

Sometimes newcomers become disillusioned with the United States when dreams do not come true and expectations are not met. When this happens, feelings of homesickness return with much intensity, even after living in the United States for years. Some people get so discouraged that they decide to sell everything they own and go back home. Before one makes a decision like this, a preliminary visit for as long as possible can reveal if the homeland is the same in reality as it is in memory.

One's homeland changes in one's absence. Family and friends have changed, though they may love one just as much as one remembers. Places have changed, buildings have been altered and redecorated, and some have deteriorated or been torn down. Economic conditions and attitudes have changed, for better or worse. You may even notice that your native language has undergone changes, and you may not be familiar with the latest expressions and idioms. You may feel foolish because you have to ask people to explain what they mean when they use the latest slang.

Though you may be aware of the changes you will find, you may not be prepared for the emotional shock these changes will bring. It is like having culture shock in reverse. It is wise to consider all aspects of life in your new country and in your homeland before selling out and ending your life in the United States.

If you do decide to go back home, do not be surprised if it takes you at least six months to a year or more to settle down there. You should also be prepared for the fact that some people in your homeland envy those who have had the opportunity of living, studying, and working in the United States.

The most important aspect about returning home— whether permanently or for a visit—is to maintain or re-establish warm relationships with family and friends by paying attention to their conversations, being sensitive to their feelings, and understanding their dilemmas. You will have lost touch with the everyday events in your homeland, and you should avoid criticizing the country and its people or comparing it to the United States.

Daily Living

This section covers some of the general aspects of moving to and living in the South. Specifics will change from city to city and state to state; however, certain considerations will be true in virtually all areas. Ask your contacts in the city to which you are moving if special laws or codes apply to such things as pet ownership, garbage pick-up, or parking.

The Weather

In the South, one can expect hot, humid summers and mild, rainy winters. From early fall in October until Christmas, the temperatures are cool but rarely go below 40 degrees during the daytime. In many sections of the South, days will frequently be warmer than 40 degrees. After Christmas, the weather gets cooler, with temperatures in the 30s and 40s for days on end. Nighttime temperatures are even colder, often dropping to freezing or below. From Christmas until March, the South may have occasional snow or ice storms or periods of frigid weather when the temperatures fall below 20 degrees. However, these cold snaps and storms are rare and are usually short lived.

During **snow and ice storms**, most businesses, schools, and colleges in the South are closed because the roads become icy and dangerous. Some roads are deemed impassable and are closed by highway or law authorities. Because such weather is rare in the South, most cities and towns do not find it necessary to own expensive snow-removal equipment. As a result, only essential services are maintained, and other functions are suspended.

When extreme or dangerous weather is anticipated, radio

and television stations announce what to expect, and newcomers should pay attention to the weather report each day. When bad weather is expected, one should purchase emergency supplies before becoming ice or snow bound. Electricity and telephone services are likely to be stopped by the storm, so everyone tries to be prepared do do without these services during the storm—and sometimes for several days thereafter.

Supplies to be obtained before the storm arrives include food that does not require refrigeration or cooking. This includes canned food, fruit, bread, and beverages. Families also need flashlights, batteries, and candles for light. Many Southerners buy portable gas appliances that can be used to heat canned food and make instant coffee, and some of these appliances can also be used for heating and lighting. However, they operate on a potentially dangerous gas and have to be used very carefully. A battery-operated radio or television is also essential for staying informed about weather conditions.

During the fall, people living near the Gulf Coast of the South are constantly alert for **hurricanes.** These storms can be extremely dangerous and destructive and should always be taken seriously. Hurricanes consist of very high winds, ranging from 75 to nearly 200 miles per hour. Newcomers living in hurricane areas should follow instructions given on the radio or television when a hurricane is predicted. Neighbors can also help with information about how to prepare for the storm. If possible, one should leave the area. If this is not possible, one should go to a sturdy shelter recommended by the weather forecasters and civil defense authorities.

A hurricane brings windy and wet weather for miles around the place where it strikes land. Power lines are often damaged, leaving the area without electricity, and heavy rains bring flooding. This means the same emergency supplies described for snow storms should be purchased.

Tornadoes also threaten parts of the South, as they do many other sections of the United States. These wind storms are dangerous and destructive, and newcomers should heed the warnings about them on radio and television. Some towns have sirens that sound an alarm when a tornado has been sighted, and one should determine if such a warning system exists in one's area.

If a tornado is sighted in your area, you should go to the basement of your home. If you do not have a basement, follow the instructions given on the radio or television. Usually a hallway, closet, or beneath a stairway will be the safest place inside a dwelling. Stay away from windows, and leave a few windows on all sides of the residence slightly open to help accommodate the intense pressure a tornado can cause.

All over the United States, radio and television stations broadcast information about the weather throughout the day. When an announcement is made concerning bad weather, follow the instructions carefully. Your primary concerns should be seeking shelter in a safe location, having sufficient and appropriate supplies, and avoiding activities and locations that could prove dangerous.

How to Rent a House or an Apartment

When looking for an apartment or house to rent or purchase, you have to consider several aspects before making a decision.

Transportation

If you do not own a car, you probably need to be within walking distance of your work or college as many Southern cities and towns have inadequate public transportation systems. If you plan to walk everywhere, check with local police and neighbors in the area to determine if the area is safe for walking. Even if you have transportation, you need to find out how much crime there is in your neighborhood. Never assume the streets are safe, particularly after dark.

You also need to find out how crowded the highways are between your home and your work or college. If you will be using a popular route, the travel time to and from work may be much greater than the distance would indicate.

Schools

If you have children, find out about the schools in the

neighborhood you are considering. Check on the quality of their academic programs, whether or not each school has problems with gangs, alcohol and other drugs, and what type of school discipline is practiced. Some schools have problems with students who are poorly disciplined, and some schools are in areas where crime is quite common.

The Area

Find out if the tenants in an apartment building or neighborhood are noisy, particularly if the area is known for "partying" and drug transactions. These can be areas where one has to take care when walking around at night. Some people do not mind being next door to noisy neighbors, but remember that construction materials in American buildings are not soundproof.

Rental Charges

When discussing the rental charge, find out what the charge includes. Sometimes, though not often, the price for your electricity, gas, and water (called "utilities") is included in your rental. Some rental charges include one of these utilities, but you are required to pay the monthly fees for the others.

You will usually be expected to pay an amount of money—a deposit—before you move in. This covers any damage you may inflict on the house or apartment. If you leave the place in good repair, your deposit will be refunded. (In some cases, a portion of the deposit may be used to repair damage and the balance will be returned.) Often you have to pay the rent for a month in advance.

The Lease

Before you agree to take a home, be sure you understand the terms of the lease. This is a legal contract, and you should read it carefully before signing it. Usually a lease includes rules about how you should pay each month, how much notice you have to give when you wish to vacate, and how you should behave in the place. Some leases allow for the rent to be increased if additional people move into the house or apartment, and some allow for rental increases after a stated period of time.

If there is any requirement in the lease that you do not understand, ask the person from whom you are renting to explain it. Some landlords are willing to delete some requirements from a lease, but that is not common. (If both you and the landlord agree that a specific clause will be deleted, the landlord and you should both sign the deletion of that clause and place your initials beside it.)

One usually has to take a lease for a year. This means that you cannot move out of the apartment or house in less than a year without paying all the rent for the remaining portion of the year. Sometimes landlords may work with you to arrange for somebody else to take over your place, but this is not always the case.

Renting (Leasing) Furniture and Furnished Apartments

If you plan to be in the United States only a short time, you may wish to rent a furnished apartment. These apartments come with standard items of furniture and kitchen appliances. Such apartments are usually advertised in the "classified" section of the local newspaper. As with all legal documents, the lease should be carefully read and understood before it is signed.

Furniture may also be rented from rental stores. Usually one pays rental for each month, although some items can be rented on a weekly basis. You can find the names of companies that rent furniture (and other household and garden equipment) in the yellow pages of the local telephone directory under the heading "Rental."

Behavior in Rented Apartments and Homes

Noise

Most people living in houses in suburbs and in apartments do not tolerate noisy neighbors. The landlord, or local police, receive complaints about disturbances regularly. People living in apartment complexes are expected to be quiet after ten o'clock at night. If you have visitors, ask them to speak softly after ten and to be quiet in the parking lot when they leave. Also, when going in and out of your apartment, try not to make any noise late at night. One should also refrain from banging doors, playing a radio, tape player, or the television too loudly, as this also could disturb neighbors at any hour of the day or night.

Odors

In many kitchens there are vents above the stoves for pulling cooking odors and oily vapors out of the apartment. If you have an apartment with a vent, always use it. This will prevent your cooking odors from spreading to your immediate neighbors and will help to prevent your apartment from getting an oily film on flat surfaces. Try to vacuum carpets regularly to keep odors from becoming permanent in carpets, especially if you cook highly spiced foods. Open windows regularly to dissipate food odors with fresh air.

Unpleasant Neighbors

If you find yourself next door to unpleasant neighbors, what should you do? You may discuss your problem with your landlord during daytime hours. If you suspect that criminal activity is being conducted in a neighbor's apartment, or if a party seems out of control, you may call your nearest police. You may sometimes refrain from giving your name to the police. If they insist on your name and address, request that your name remain confidential. Unfortunately, neighbors may take revenge on you if they know you have called the police.

If you feel your life is in danger, by all means see your landlord and ask to be moved to a safer part of the apartment complex. If this fails, you may wish to get legal advice, but do not go to a neighbor's door and complain in person. You do not know what reception you will get or if you will be attacked, verbally or physically.

Pets

Often landlords do not allow pets in apartments, but most renters of houses allow tenants to own pets. Before leasing a house or an apartment, come to a clear understanding about whether or not you may have a pet on the property.

The two most popular varieties of pets in the United States and the South are dogs and cats, although there are many other types of pets. They are kept for a variety of reasons, including companionship, but are never eaten.

There are laws about the type of pets people may own. Certain animals, considered health hazards or too dangerous, are outlawed all over the United States, and some animals are not allowed as pets inside city limits. Certain exotic animals are illegal as pets because of their status as endangered species. Newcomers who want an exotic pet should check with local government authorities before acquiring it.

Dogs, cats, and other pets are required to have annual rabies injections in most areas of the South. If a pet bites a person and proof of a rabies injection cannot be produced, the animal is placed in quarantine, and the animal's victim has to undergo painful treatment to prevent rabies. In addition, the owner of the pet can be sued by the victim.

Most Southerners are unusually kind to animals, but there are those who abuse them. It is against the law to be cruel to any animal, and people are indicted, charged, and sentenced for cruelty to animals. Persons who mistreat animals may be reported to the police by their neighbors, who can remain anonymous if they so choose. Special animal doctors, called veterinarians, treat sick animals and give preventive injections to healthy ones. Fees for these services can be fairly expensive.

How to Purchase a Home

Before choosing a home, consider the factors discussed under the heading "How to Rent a House or Apartment." Think carefully about what type of house you need and where it should be located. Do not allow anyone to persuade you to buy something you do not want or which is too expensive for your budget.

In the daily local newspapers and home-buying guides that are often found in the front of grocery and book stores, restaurants, and other public places, there are listings of houses for sale (or lease.) Or you may phone a real estate company and make arrangements for a realtor to help you find a house.

It is a good idea to use a real estate agent because buying

a home is extremely complicated. Before choosing an agent, check that he or she represents a firm that is a member of the Board of Realtors, whose telephone number is found in the telephone directory. Or you may wish to ask a reliable and trusted colleague or friend to give you the name of an agent.

You should also obtain the services of a lawyer who specializes in real estate law and who can take care of your interests when you have decided to purchase a house. Your lawyer should examine the contract you will need to sign to purchase the house, to make sure that you are being protected from fraud or unusual requirements.

Usually people need some money for a "down payment"; however, you will not need the entire amount of money required to buy the home. Most home buyers take a bank loan, called a **"mortgage,"** on which one pays interest. This interest is added to the payments you make each month to pay off the loan. The rate of interest depends on the type of loan and the type of bank. One can get a "fixed mortgage" with an interest rate that remains the same for the length of the loan. Another type of mortgage is the "adjustable-rate mortgage" with interest that varies according to changing interest rates nationally. A real estate agent or your lawyer can explain this in detail to you, but be sure you understand these concepts before you purchase a house.

A mortgage can be taken for ten, fifteen, twenty, or thirty years. The shorter the period, the more you will have to pay each month on your mortgage. If one does not have enough money for a down payment, one can sometimes arrange to have a "second mortgage" that is issued for a shorter time at a higher interest rate than the first mortgage. This is a complicated process, and one needs to get the advice of a lawyer.

Once you have bought a home, remember to purchase home owners insurance to protect your home against fire and other dangers, as well as coverage for accidents to others occurring on your property. You should also get "title insurance" at the time you purchase your home to prevent somebody else from claiming ownership of your property.

After you have bought a house, you will need to arrange with your local utility company to have electricity, water, maybe natural gas, and sewerage services connected. Usually you are required to pay a cash deposit before these services are provided. A telephone is essential in the United States as so much of your business is done over the telephone. Arrange to have a telephone installed as soon as possible after you move into your home. Your real estate agent or lawyer can advise you on how to get these services.

Insurance

Every newcomer should understand the importance of insurance in the United States as a protection against some financial catastrophe. Except in rare circumstances, the government does not take care of private citizens, because each individual is expected to be prepared for problems. The best way to be sure about insurance coverage is to ask a trusted friend or employer to introduce you to a reliable and honest insurance agent from whom you can get advice.

When you purchase insurance, you will pay a relatively small amount of money (called a premium) to an insurance company on a regular schedule. Depending on the type of insurance you have (known as the coverage), the insurance company will pay certain bills or reimburse you for certain expenses in the event of a specified accident or situation. One buys insurance according to one's needs, and the cost is determined by what is bought.

Insurance is necessary for financial hardship caused by death, health care costs, home disasters, vehicle accidents, physical disability, and litigation. Private homes should be insured against fire and storm damage, theft by burglars, and injury to someone visiting in your home or on the property.

Fire Insurance

Usually the owner of a building buys fire insurance just for the building. If you are renting a house or an apartment, consult an insurance agent regarding insurance to cover your household belongings.

If you buy a house on credit, you are required to have "homeowner's insurance" that covers fire and other hazards. Make sure that the home and your belongings are adequately covered because fire is always a hazard in an American home.

(Should you have a fire, your coverage may be limited, based on the cause of the fire, so be familiar with the policy and with ways to prevent home fires—see page 125.) If a home damaged by fire is mortgaged, the portion of the insurance covering the building will normally be paid to the person or institution to whom the mortgage is owed.

Health

Caution: There is no comprehensive free health care in the United States. All newcomers must get medical insurance immediately upon arrival in the United States because medical services, medicines, and hospital costs are the highest in the world, and free medical care is not offered.

Large employers usually contribute toward health insurance for employees. If you have such insurance, be sure you understand what it covers. For instance, some health insurance policies do not pay maternity benefits until you have been in the employ of the company at least nine months. You should also know what amount of the medical bill your insurance policy does not pay, how much of the bill you have to pay, if your spouse and children are covered, and if hospital expenses are covered. Also find out how medical bills are paid. Sometimes a doctor's office will file the insurance claim directly. In some cases, you will be required to pay the doctor and then file for reimbursement from your insurance company.

If you work for a company that does not offer insurance, you need to take out your own insurance with a reliable and well-established company. This is usually expensive; however, health care costs in the United States can be very high, and, in many areas, it may be difficult to obtain the care you need if you cannot show proof of insurance.

You can find the names and telephone numbers of insurance agents in the yellow pages section of your local telephone directory. An agent can guide you in the selection of an insurance policy. Be sure to check an agent's reputation with your friends.

At the present time legislation regarding medical insurance is being discussed. Great changes are anticipated in the next few years. The information in this section may change depending on the new proposals presented to Congress.

Liability Insurance

Certain professions require liability insurance to protect practitioners against the cost of a lawsuit should a client believe the services or goods provided were improper, harmful, or otherwise unacceptable. Find out from colleagues about any insurance you need to carry for professional reasons.

Travel Insurance

If you make a reservation on an airline, you can get life insurance at no cost to you if you pay for the ticket with a credit card from a company that offers this service. If you travel for your company, find out what travel insurance the company has on your life. This insurance will pay a certain amount to your family if you are killed in a transportation accident involving that flight.

Before traveling around the United States and/or going to foreign countries, find out how much medical coverage you have should you get sick away from home. You may find you need additional medical insurance. (Be sure to carry proof of insurance with you when traveling.)

If relatives from your homeland visit you, be sure they obtain traveler's medical insurance before coming to the United States. Free medical care is not provided for them in the United States

Life Insurance

You also need to have adequate insurance so that your family's needs will be provided for in the event of your death. This type of insurance is particularly valuable if you plan to send your children to college. If you have insurance in your land of origin, it might not be adequate when it has been changed into dollars.

Often your company provides some life insurance for you, but it might be inadequate for your specific needs. Discuss this with acquaintances you trust, and talk to several insurance agents about what your insurance needs are and how they are likely to change with time.

Disability

Some employers provide disability insurance as a fringe benefit. Should you become disabled and unable to work while you have this insurance, you will be paid a reduced monthly income while you are disabled. Both husband and wife should have this insurance if the household depends on the salaries of both.

Automobile Insurance

In most parts of the South you are required by law to take out "liability" automobile insurance so that your insurance will pay the medical expenses and the automobile repair expenses of somebody with whom you are involved in an accident. Never operate a car without adequate liability insurance as it is a serious offense to drive without it, and should you have an accident without liability insurance, you could be in serious trouble.

You can also take out additional insurance for your own car and medical expenses in the event of an accident. Of course, if another person causes you to be injured in an accident, that person's insurance should take care of your expenses. However, many times people ignore the law and drive without insurance. This means you could be left with the entire bill yourself.

A car can also be insured against theft. If you take out a loan to purchase a car, you will probably be required to have theft insurance. See the section on buying a car for additional information.

Termites and Other Nuisances

All over the South, homes are plagued by **termites** that bore into the woodwork of a building. Termites are tiny insects that eat into a piece of wood and destroy its interior. Thus, a piece of wood may look perfect but in reality be just a shell. In this way, a building can be seriously damaged without the owner realizing what has happened. Termites can also enter through cement or brick steps and destroy the wood in and around the foundation of a house.

Property owners employ specially trained technicians to

inspect and chemically treat their properties regularly to prevent termite damage. There is a fee for this service but it is essential to have this done if you own property in the South. This service should be repeated once a year or more for constant protection against termites. Ask colleagues or friends to recommend a properly bonded firm to perform this service for you.

The humidity and heat of the South tends to attract other insects that also invade houses and apartments. Among these are large and small **cockroaches, crickets, spiders, and moths**. Cockroaches love kitchens, and they carry germs. Because moths destroy certain types of fabric, especially wool, woolen clothes must be stored in a way that protects them. Drycleaning establishments can moth-proof your clothing, and chemicals are available to be placed in your closets. Be careful how you use these chemicals as they are very poisonous.

Fleas are another source of annoyance, especially in the summer. These insects live in the soil but attach themselves to pets and humans. In this way, they can invade a house.

There are products available at hardware and grocery stores for killing and controlling all these pests, but these products should be used and stored only according to the instructions. They usually contain hazardous chemicals that are a danger to small children. Sometimes household pests become so annoying that professional exterminators are necessary to get rid of them. Neighbors and friends are usually able to give advice when you have problems with insects (called "bugs" in the South).

Additional information about insects common to the South (but more likely to be found outside) is contained later in this chapter on page 121.

Air Conditioning

Like cars, air conditioning is almost a necessity in the South. The hot humid summers with temperatures often in the 90s can be extremely uncomfortable without air conditioning or fans to cool the interiors of buildings.

Often the air conditioning unit is also the heating device used in the winter. A neighbor can show you how to switch the unit from a cooling to a heating function.

Many newcomers to the South are not accustomed to air conditioning, so be aware of the fact that it is expensive and that the cost is included in your power bill. The cooler you keep your house or apartment, the higher your bill will be. One should understand how to operate the thermostat that controls the internal temperature of a building. As with all appliances, be sure you know how to operate the air conditioning unit before turning it on.

Air conditioning is a mechanical device that cools air, pumps it through a building, sucks it back through a filter that cleans the air, cools it again, and sends it back through the building. This process is repeated only when the unit is in operation. One must remove the dirty filter at regular intervals and replace it with a new one as a dirty filter can damage the air conditioner's motor. An exceptionally dirty filter can also cause the air conditioner to leak water into the rooms surrounding it.

Air conditioning units should be inspected by a certified mechanic at least once a year—at the beginning of summer. A faulty air conditioner can be dangerous and could start a fire.

If you live in an apartment, ask your landlord whose responsibility it is to maintain air conditioners, including the replacement of dirty filters.

Telephone

The telephone system in the United States is the best in the world. Most of the time, even public telephones (called "pay phones" in the South) work efficiently. Public telephones are found almost everywhere in the South, from restaurants to street corners, and few are ever out of order.

You do not have to be a specially privileged or wealthy person to have a telephone installed in your home in the United States. Many ordinary Southerners have more than one instrument in their homes.

If you desire and can afford a telephone, simply phone one of the telephone companies (phone numbers are in the yellow pages) and find out the cost of having a telephone installed and what the monthly charges will be. You will have to pay for the installation and a monthly fee plus all charges for long distance calls (calls made to places outside the city where you live and overseas.) You should pay your monthly telephone bill promptly; otherwise, your service may be discontinued.

When the telephone rings, you should try to answer it as soon as possible, preferably after the first ring. In the South, people do not let their telephones ring too many times. When you answer, you should be as polite as possible and first ask "How are you?" after you have said "hello." Should a Southern friend ask what you are doing, he or she is not being inquisitive, but is merely showing interest. It is quite all right to respond by telling your friend what you were doing when the phone rang—or you can say "nothing much, what are you doing?"

The termination of a telephone call is also expected to be courteous. The initiator of the telephone call should be the person who terminates the conversation. You can say something like "I won't keep you from what you are doing." If, as the receiver of the call, you have to terminate, be careful to be tactful by saying something like "Don't let me keep you. ... I appreciate your calling." Because many people go to bed early, one should not phone people after 9:30 p.m., unless you are certain the person you are calling will not be asleep, or if you have an emergency.

When you speak over the telephone, remember that to your hearers, you have an accent. Therefore, speak deliberately, clearly, slowly, and maybe a little louder than usual if you have a naturally soft voice. If you don't do this, you may be misunderstood.

In this country, you may obtain a credit card for making telephone calls. This is useful when you are away from home; however, it can be used by others if it gets lost, and the card holder will be billed for the amount of the call. If you lose your card, let the telephone company know immediately so you will not be liable for calls after you have notified them.

Do not let anyone overhear you giving your credit card number over the telephone when making a call because a dishonest person could use your number to make calls on your bill.

Yellow, White, and Blue Pages

Once you have a telephone, the telephone company will give you one or more directories listing the telephone numbers for individuals and businesses in your area. Directories are divided into white pages (for private, residential phone numbers with a separate section for business numbers), blue pages (for governmental numbers), yellow pages (for business companies and service organizations). White and blue pages are in alphabetical order. Yellow pages have an alphabetical listing by type of service or business. However, not all businesses are listed in the yellow pages—only those that pay to be included.

If you cannot find the number of a person or company in your telephone directory, call the operator (often at 411) if the number is in your area. If the number you seek is outside your local calling area, dial 1, then the area code for the region you want, then 555-1212. You should remember, however, that calling the operator for a telephone number carries a charge in many areas, and you will need to know the exact name of the person or company you want to reach.

Long Distance Calls

The front pages of the directory will supply information about long distance and overseas calls. The charge of long distance calls varies according to the time of day, the day of the week, the type of call you make, and the company with which you have your service. Some companies offer special overseas rates. Sometimes one is billed for a long distance telephone call if the telephone rings more than five times, even if nobody answered the phone. Check to see if this is the policy with the company you choose.

Person-to-Person Calls

A person-to-person call, where one tells the operator the name of the person to whom one wishes to speak, is more expensive than just calling a number and speaking with any person who answers the phone, but it means you pay for the call only if the person you are calling answers. It is a good idea to phone the operator and find out the cheapest time and method of making long distance and overseas phone calls.

At the time of this writing, one needs a quarter to use a **pay phone**. These phones usually have clear instructions written on the instrument, but if you have difficulties, place a coin in the slot and dial the operator (usually "O") and explain your problem. Operators are usually courteous and helpful. Most pay phones accept only coins, so one should have several quarters handy when making a call from a pay phone. Some pay phones also accept credit cards, and those that do indicate this on the instrument.

Free Numbers

You may call numbers in your local vicinity without paying an individual charge for each call. In addition, there is a system of "800" numbers used by mail-companies, national businesses, airlines, special interest groups, and other businesses and organizations that serve the entire country. Charges for calls to 800 numbers are paid by the companies, not by the individuals making the calls.

To use these numbers, dial 1, then 800, then the number provided by the company or organization. Public libraries usually have directories for 800 numbers where you can look up numbers for companies or organizations in which you are interested.

Caution: Some companies use 900 numbers. These are not free and may cost as much as $50 a minute or more. Many of these numbers are advertised on television and radio in ways that appeal to children, so be sure your children understand they should never call a 900 number without your permission. In some areas, you can ask the telephone company to install a device on your telephone line that makes it impossible for anyone to use that line to dial a 900 number.

Emergency Numbers

A telephone is a great help in any emergency requiring medical help or police assistance. In most towns and cities in the South an emergency number will obtain all types of help. Often this number is 911, but find out what that number is in your area.

Telephone Solicitors

Sometimes people may try to sell you items and services over the phone. Unless you really know that the seller of the product or service is reputable, it is best to refuse all offers over the phone. This is important for a newcomer as these people may be dishonest, and you may commit yourself to a purchase that never arrives or is inferior. Never give your credit card number to anybody over the phone unless you are positive that the company asking for this information is reliable, like an airline with which you make an airplane reservation.

Food

Generally Southern food is tasty, so most newcomers acquire a taste for Southern food quickly. Since much of the food is fried and sugar or pork fat are often added for flavoring, it is easy to gain weight in the South. Also, many vegetable preparations are called "casserole" dishes, which means that the vegetables are baked in a sauce, often with cream as an ingredient. They are usually delicious!

Southerners have three meals a day. For breakfast, served anytime between six o'clock till about ten o'clock in the morning, many Southerners nowadays have cereal and milk, toast and coffee. But the traditional Southern breakfast consists of eggs, scrambled or fried; bacon; ham or sausage; grits and toast or biscuits with jelly or jam. Coffee is usually served with this meal.

At lunch time, served from about 11:30 a.m. until about 2:00 p.m., many people will have a sandwich (consisting of two pieces of bread with a filling of meat). Salads, meat, and vegetables served with iced tea are also lunchtime favorites. At night, supper is served from 5 p.m. until about 7 p.m., although some people without children may eat later. Dinner consists of two or three vegetables with meat, either cornbread or a bread roll, and sometimes a dessert. Iced water and iced tea are usually served with the meal. Often coffee is served at the end of a meal. Fruit is sometimes eaten instead of dessert, especially when people are trying to limit calories for weight loss.

Well-known Southern Foods

Fried chicken: A whole chicken is cut up into pieces, dipped in a corn meal or flour batter and then fried in a deep pot of oil until the meat is thoroughly cooked and the batter is crispy and brown. Many fast food stores serve fried chicken.

Fish: Many varieties of fish, from the ocean, rivers, lakes, ponds, and creeks are eaten in the South. A popular Southern fish is cat fish, which is found in rivers and creeks but is also raised in ponds on fish farms. Though fish may be broiled, steamed or fried, fried fish is the favorite method of cooking fish in the South.

Grits: One of the best-known of all Southern foods, this is a porridge made with ground corn. It is seasoned with salt and butter and eaten at breakfast with bacon, egg, and sausage, or alone. The term "grits" is used regardless of the size of the serving.

Hush puppies: These bread-like balls are not made from dog meat, but are deep fried cornmeal and onion balls about one and a half inches in diameter. They are usually eaten with fish.

Baked ham: Ham in this form is often glazed with a sweet sauce and baked thoroughly. It can be eaten hot or cold.

Beef steak: This is a favorite meat in the South, and steak houses are found in almost every town and city. If you order a steak, you will be expected to tell the waiter or waitress how well or rare you would like your steak cooked. Thus one orders it: well done, medium, medium well done, medium rare, and rare (which will hardly look cooked at all).

Lamb: This is not a favorite Southern meat, but it can be purchased at grocery stores sometimes. Some restaurants, usually those serving Middle Eastern fare, also serve lamb.

Vegetables

Southerners are known for their love of vegetables, especially well-cooked ones. A great variety of vegetables are grown in the South and can be purchased in grocery stores and at farmers' markets during the summer months.

Legumes (seeds contained in a pod) are usually flavored with pork fat, called hog white meat. These include butter beans, navy beans, black eyed peas, and lima beans. They are highly nutritious and an excellent source of fibre.

"Greens" is the generic name given to vegetables that are really leaves. These can be spinach, collard tops, turnip tops, mustard, or kale. They are often steamed with hog white meat (called fat back) and are eaten with corn bread.

There are many other Southern vegetables available in cafeterias and some restaurants, and these include okra (a green elongated vegetable either fried in a batter or steamed), sweet potatoes (orange root vegetables with a sweet flavor), squash, beans, potatoes, and an all-American favorite, corn, an indigenous vegetable.

Salads are also favorite dishes in the South. These are usually made from vegetables or fruit and are eaten raw with a sauce, called "salad dressing" for flavoring.

Iced and Hot Tea

Iced tea is one of the South's favorite beverages. This is usually made from orange pekoe and pekoe cut black tea with boiling water and then cooled, after which ice is added. It is usually served in a tall glass. The tea is not taken with milk or cream, but is sometimes flavored with lemon juice and sugar, or a sugar substitute. If one asks for tea in the South, one will be served iced tea.

If you would like hot tea, you will need to specify that you would like it hot. Usually you will be given a cup of hot water with a tea bag in the saucer. You are expected to place the tea bag in the hot water yourself and infuse it till you have the required strength of tea. Sometimes you will be given lemon for your hot tea. If you prefer milk for hot tea, feel free to ask for it.

Drinking Water

Water that comes out of a tap (faucet) and a drinking fountain, anywhere in the United States, is usually water that has been purified of bacteria and is safe for drinking. Water in many cities is treated with chemicals to assure that it is safe for human use, and many cities add fluoride to water in order to prevent dental caries. Water from streams, rivers, and lakes should only be drunk if the local people drink it. Some mountain streams, especially in the West, have bacteria and should not be drunk.

Desserts

The favorite desserts in the South are cakes, pies, and ice cream. There are an amazing variety of these. Many are available in the freezer sections of the grocery store for reasonable prices.

Southern pecan pie, a favorite dessert, is a pastry shell filled with a sweet jelly-like substance with a layer of pecan nuts on top. Apple pie is an all-American favorite dessert. These can both be eaten with cream or ice cream. Pumpkin and sweet potato pies are favorite desserts, especially at Thanksgiving and Christmas time.

New Orleans or Cajun Cuisine

New Orleans food is world famous and is a cuisine of its own, even though it is part of the South. Characteristically, this cuisine has a gravy or sauce base, called a "roux" and various foods are cooked in this sauce. Another distinctive feature of this cuisine is the combination of exotic spices, some of them very hot, added to food. There is a great deal of literature and information about this style of cooking because it is currently popular all over the United States.

Restaurants

There are many types of restaurants; from fast food restaurants, where food is prepared in a few minutes and costs very little, to expensive restaurants, where one can spend many dollars. Restaurants can be self-service or those where one is served by a waiter. Some restaurants specialize in one or two different dishes and serve nothing else, like the fast food stores, while others offer a confusingly large variety of choices.

In most places, restaurants are regularly inspected for cleanliness by health inspectors from the government. In some areas of the South, the restaurant inspection rating is displayed near the entrance. If restaurants fail the inspection, they are closed until the sanitation standards improve.

Cafeterias

These inexpensive restaurants are popular in the South. They serve home-cooked style vegetables, salads, desserts, and meat dishes. The food is displayed on long selection counters, each item is individually priced, and one places one's choice on a tray that is provided at the beginning of the counter. Usually one pays at the end of the selection counter or when one leaves the restaurant.

Fast Food Restaurants

If you are in a hurry, go to a "fast food restaurant" where hamburgers, sandwiches, fried chicken, Mexican food, or Italian food (such as pizza) are sold. These are usually inexpensive meals and are served quickly while one waits. While standing in line waiting to be served, look at the menu displayed prominently, usually above the heads of the assistants, and make a selection. While you pay the cashier, another worker gets your order ready. Many fast food restaurants also have "drive through" lanes so that drivers can pull up to an outside speaker, place their orders, then drive around the restaurant to the other side and receive, through a window, their orders already prepared. This can be done without even getting out of the car.

Steak Houses

Steak houses are also popular in the South, and some serve steak similar to that pictured on a menu above the counter where orders are taken. In some steak houses, one can choose salads and sometimes cooked vegetables from a salad and vegetable bar. Manners dictate that you do not fill your plate too full, but that small portions of a number or all of the foods displayed are taken. In some restaurants, you may return to the salad bar for as many times as you wish, provided you use a clean plate each time. This is called an "all-you-can-eat" food bar.

Seafood Restaurants

Seafood is becoming increasingly popular. The American Heart Association recommends that a person eat at least two fish meals a week for a healthy heart, and this probably contributes to the popularity of fish. A seafood restaurant specializes in a variety of fish, cooked in different ways. One may usually request the type of cooking one prefers at these restaurants, i.e., grilled, fried, or broiled.

Expensive Restaurants

An expensive restaurant can vary in price from moderately expensive to enormously expensive, depending on the location, the type of atmosphere, and the food served. Currently, less expensive restaurants range in price from about $12.00 to about $25.00 per person and expensive restaurants range from $30 to $50 and more per person. Of course, it is possible to spend even more than this at fine restaurants in large cities or if alcohol is ordered with the meal.

These restaurants usually are decorated in a stylish, tasteful manner and play soft music to create a relaxed and luxurious atmosphere. One can be served appetizers, salads, entrées (the main course) which usually consists of a meat or fish with a baked potato or rice and sometimes a choice of vegetables. Often the food is served with fancy sauces and is flavored with secret ingredients. One usually pays for each individual item, including the beverages, separately. This is called paying "a la carte." Sometimes these restaurants offer a "special" that includes several items for one price.

If children are taken to these restaurants, they should be well disciplined and should be quiet to avoid disturbing other patrons.

Family Restaurants

Family restaurants usually serve plain food that all the members of a family can enjoy, such as salads, sandwiches, hamburgers, meat, vegetables, fish, and, sometimes, salad bars. The prices are low to moderate, which in the early 1990s range from about $7.00 to $10.00 per person. All members of the family are welcome here, and some family restaurants offer special meals and prices for children.

Restaurant Manners

In most restaurants, one is expected to be appropriately attired. Often a sign outside a restaurant signifies that shirts and shoes are required. Of course, other clothes are also required! Sometimes expensive restaurants require men to wear ties and jackets.

If one goes to a restaurant with others, good manners dictate that all members of the group wait until everyone is served before beginning the meal. People should speak in low voices so that others will not be disturbed, unlike in some cultures where loud conversations ensure privacy. Children should be strictly controlled and should not be allowed to be noisy or to visit the tables of other patrons.

Alcoholic beverages are served at some restaurants (not all), and one is expected not to drink much alcohol at a restaurant. Drunkenness is frowned upon, and drunken behavior is sometimes a reason for a manager to ask a diner to leave.

In the South, one eats with a knife and fork. With the knife in the right hand, one cuts food, one piece at a time into small pieces, and then places the knife across the side of the plate. The fork is then used in the right hand to take small portions of food from the plate to one's mouth. The fork is placed on the plate while one is chewing, and the process is repeated until all the food is eaten. The left hand is placed on one's lap while one eats with the fork.

Unless one is eating fried chicken, tacos, hamburgers, hot dogs, or similar foods, one never eats with one's fingers. In fast food restaurants, one may eat french fries and other foods with the fingers.

A napkin is always provided to be placed on one's lap to catch food dropped from the fork by mistake. The napkin may also be used for wiping one's mouth during and after the meal. It is not to be used as a handkerchief. One should not place one's arms or elbows on the table, and one should not raise the plate to one's mouth, nor should one stretch one's arms in front of other diners to reach items on the table.

From the menu, one selects a choice and, if there are items that are unfamiliar, it is acceptable to ask the waiter or waitress to explain what foods they are. One is expected to be polite to the waiter and to give clear instructions about selections and how meat is to be cooked. At the end of the meal, the waiter gives you a "check" (the bill for the meal). It is customary to leave an extra amount of at least 15 percent of the total bill in cash, on the table, as a tip for the waiter or waitress. This is <u>not</u> subtracted from the amount you pay. If payment is made with a credit card, the tip can be added to the total on the invoice.

Fresh Foods

Numerous foods are frozen, but fresh foods are also available in the grocery stores, both in and out of season. However, food which has not travelled great distances, nor been refrigerated, can be purchased at the farmer's markets, where many local farmers display and sell their produce. Sometimes farmers will sell food at the side of a highway, particularly during the summer.

Food and Drug Administration (FDA)

This is a government agency that supervises the testing for safety of medicines before they are sold in stores or made available to doctors for prescribing to patients. All drugs and medical treatments have to undergo extensive testing before they are available to the public.

This agency also supervises the control of food processing, farming, and distribution of all food eaten in the United States to make sure that foods are safe and are of a high quality. The standards of food control and production in the United States are high, and one may safely consume what is offered in food stores. However, look for an expiration date printed on all items and do not buy foods after the expiration date.

Financial Affairs

Credit Cards

Credit cards, or "plastic money" as they are sometimes called, are little plastic cards with a person's name and an assigned number on them. These are issued by banks and credit companies, upon approval of an application submitted by you. The credit card indicates that a company will allow you to buy on credit with the card so that you do not need cash at the time of the purchasing transaction. With a credit card, you may buy goods only from a merchant who does business with your credit card company. When an item is purchased, the store will stamp a sales slip with your card, obtain your signature and then give you a carbon copy of the transaction. At the end of the month, the merchant sends an account of the amount of purchases you have made to the company that issued your card. This company will pay for the item on your behalf, and you will be billed for it. You will then be expected to pay the whole amount or a portion thereof, depending on the type of card you have, when you receive the monthly bill. One should consider how the repayment is to be made before making any purchases, especially if they involve large amounts of money.

The credit company will charge interest on the amount of purchases, depending on the conditions of the card. Some cards do not charge interest if you pay within a specified time. **But** often the interest is very high, so understand the conditions of your credit card. Adding the interest a credit card company charges you raises the cost of your purchase.

Usually a credit company will allow you to buy goods up to the value of a certain amount. You should not exceed that amount. The company will inform you of how much you have to repay each month. It is important to pay this amount as the repayment of your debts is computerized on a central computer, and the promptness with which you pay each month contributes towards what is called a "credit rating." One should always aim to keep an excellent "credit rating" as this provides an open door to many different types of business transactions. A credit rating is like a character reference: it infers reliability or unreliability to a creditor. Without a good credit rating it is difficult to buy anything without cash.

There are different kinds of credit cards: major cards, individual store cards, gas cards, etc. Major cards like Visa, Mastercard, American Express are cards that can be used all over the United States and some other parts of the world. Most merchants or traders will take major cards. Individual stores also issue cards, but these can be used only for purchases at one of the branches of that particular chain of stores. Gas cards, which are issued to you on application to a major gasoline company, can be used to purchase only that company's brand of gasoline at a service station selling that brand.

Many people have many credit cards, a practice that can be dangerous. It is easy to buy too much and to find one's whole salary almost totally committed to repaying credit card accounts. One should consider the following questions before applying for a card: what is the maximum I can charge; what is the interest every month; is the interest simple or compound; how much will I be required to repay each month; by what date must I repay each month and what are the penalties for failure to pay on time?

The advantage of having a credit card is that one does not need to carry much cash, which can be lost to a pick-pocket or robber. Another advantage is that one can charge items in an emergency, as when one's car breaks down and repairs are necessary, or when medication is needed for which one does not have enough cash. A credit card is also valuable for emergencies when going on a trip.

Always sign your credit cards and keep a record of your credit card numbers. (It is best to have a list of account numbers hidden at home.) If you ever lose a credit card or have one stolen, you should notify the company or bank issuing the card immediately and give the card number; the company or bank will issue orders to merchants not to accept that card. When reporting a lost or stolen card, you can also obtain information about having a new card issued for your use. If you do not report that your card has been lost or stolen, you might be responsible for charges made by another person.

How to Get a Credit Card

For newcomers, getting a credit card may be complicated. Credit and credit cards are given to individuals who meet several requirements, including a previous reputation for paying bills on time. Most newcomers will not have a credit rating in the United States and will not have worked here for two years—usual requirements for qualifying for a credit card. Do not be surprised or embarrassed if you are not granted a credit card until you have established a good credit rating.

One way to establish a good credit rating is to negotiate

with a business to purchase an article large enough in price to warrant your paying for it in "installments." This means you pay only part of the purchase price at the time of purchase and continue to pay a portion of the remaining balance each month until the item is paid for. The amount you pay each month is established by the merchant, and this agreement also includes additional charges for the privilege of making monthly payments. For instance, a major household appliance or a car may be purchased in this way. To establish a good credit rating, these monthly payments must be made on time each month.

Payment of your utility bills (electricity, natural gas, and water) and your telephone account will also help you establish a good credit rating. Again, you must pay the required amount promptly to build a good credit rating.

Sometimes employers are able to give newcomers a recommendation to banks that are considering credit card applications. Ask your employer if such a service is available to you.

The four major credit cards are Mastercard, Visa, American Express, and Discover. The first two cards are issued by individual banks, and the last two can be applied for directly. The international representative at a bank can help you apply for a card. Telephone numbers for credit companies are obtainable from Directory Information. Most credit card companies have "1-800" numbers.

When applying for a credit card, be sure you understand:

1) the maximum amount you can charge to the card—your "line of credit,"

2) the date each month by which your payment is due,

3) finance charges you have to pay if you do not pay in full or on time,

4) the annual fee for having a credit card,

5) the interest on your purchases that the company charges.

Checking Accounts and Banking

Because it is dangerous to carry large sums of cash, it is advisable to get a checking account from a major bank.

Briefly described, with a checking account you place your pay check or other money in a bank for safe storage. The bank in which your money is stored issues you a book containing little paper coupons, called checks, that can be used instead of money for paying accounts or making purchases. The amount for which you write the check will be deducted from the money you have placed in the bank. Writing a check for money which is not in one's bank account is an offense for which the bank will impose a fine. The check is said "to have bounced," and it is called a "bad check." The merchants from whom purchases are made may also fine one for a "bad check." If this mistake is made often, one's credit rating is jeopardized. In some cases it is a crime to write checks for money which is not in a bank account, and this could lead to arrest and prosecution.

Each time one wishes to pay for something with a check, the name of the person to receive the money is written on a designated line; the amount of the purchase is written on another line; and on another line the date is written. Your signature is written on the last line. Often you will be asked for identification when you write a check. A driver's license or your passport will be acceptable.

One needs to keep an accurate record of the names and the amounts for which checks have been written. At the end of the month, the bank will send a "statement" that indicates what checks have been cashed and in what amounts. It also shows the amount of money remaining in the account. These statements need to be kept for your records.

A check can be mailed through the post office to creditors or to stores in another city in the United States. Special checks can be purchased at a bank for mailing to other parts of the world.

Some stores, particularly grocery stores, will not take credit cards, and since it is not advisable to carry too much cash, a check is valuable at such a store. Another advantage of having a checking account is that a record can be kept of people one has paid and can constitute proof of payment should one be accused of failing to pay a creditor.

Not all stores and restaurants accept checks. Some businesses accept only local checks, meaning that the bank with which you have your account must be in the same area as the store. Because these decisions are left to the individual businesses, you will not be able to use a check at every business place.

Another advantage to having a checking account is that you can apply for a "bank card" that allows you to withdraw money from your account when the bank is closed. Some shopping centers also have machines in them where you can use your bank card to withdraw cash from your account. These **"automated teller"** machines require you to have the card issued by your bank, and you will need to know your identification number, which the bank supplies at the time your card is issued. Usually instructions are flashed on a computer screen, and you answer requests for your identification number and tell the machine the amount of money you wish to withdraw. Be careful never to let anyone else learn your identification number or that person may be able to remove money from your account. Some of these automated teller machines are accessible and operational 24 hours a day. However, due to a growing crime problem in the vicinity of some outdoor automated teller machines, some are open only during daylight hours. Regardless of the location of the automated teller machine you use, be careful and alert for robbers when withdrawing or depositing money at the machine.

Report stolen or lost check books to your bank immediately and arrange to have payment stopped on checks that might be used against your account.

When selecting a bank, ask a trusted colleague or American friend for information and advice. Be careful to use an established, reputable bank. After you have chosen a bank, see the international representative (or someone else experienced in dealing with foreign nationals) and ask questions until you understand the system and the agreement with the bank. Never sign anything you do not understand.

Saving Accounts

Savings accounts are designed to help you save money, and you usually cannot write checks to get money from your saving account. However, there are many different kinds of saving accounts, and you should find out about the various options offered by banks in your area. The money in a savings account earns interest, but interest rates vary based on the type of account and the amount of money, so look for the best saving account for your situation.

In opening a saving account, be sure you understand what is involved in making a withdrawal. Some bank cards (see above) will include your savings account number so that you can make a withdrawal from your saving account by using the automated teller machine. Some saving plans charge a fee if money is removed before a certain amount of time has passed, and the length of time varies from plan to plan. Again, shop around for the best interest rates and conditions of banking.

Shopping

One of the most impressive aspects first observed by most newcomers to the United States is the superb marketing and display of goods in the stores. Everywhere one goes, one is greeted by the most tempting displays of merchandise.

Most newcomers are delighted with American stores and find they spend too much money on items they really do not need and did not intend buying, especially when they first arrive in the United States Credit cards make this temptation especially difficult.

In most places in the South, Monday through Saturday, general stores open at 10 o'clock in the morning and stay open until 9 o'clock at night. Some stores in bigger cities, like convenience stores and some grocery stores and pharmacies, stay open twenty-four hours a day. On Sundays, some stores are open all day, some are closed all day, while others open at lunch time and close at six o'clock in the evening. On some public holidays, like Thanksgiving and Christmas, many stores are closed all day.

Types of Stores

There are many different types of stores in the United States. **Grocery stores** (sometimes called supermarkets) sell food: meat, fish, poultry, pork, sometimes lamb, vegetables, bread, dairy products, canned or tinned goods, household cleaning products, items for babies, cosmetics, paper goods, and pet requirements. Sometimes they also sell photographic equipment, flowers, hardware, automobile supplies, and small appliances. In these stores, one gets a cart or "buggy" to hold the grocery items, and one pushes it up and down the aisles while making selections. When the selection is complete, the buggy is taken to the cashier at the cash register who totals the prices of the individual groceries and takes one's money. The groceries are then put in paper or plastic bags and taken home by the purchaser.

If one buys frozen foods in a grocery store, they must be placed in a freezer or the freezer section of a refrigerator immediately when one gets home. Frozen food should not thaw and then be refrozen because bacteria can then develop in the food and could make one sick.

Usually only at **filling stations** can one purchase gasoline. These are usually located close to an interstate or freeway and on main suburban roads near shopping centers.

Pharmacies or drug stores sell medicine, both prescription and "over the counter drugs," (medicines one can purchase without a doctor's prescription). Newcomers who are not familiar with American medicines may ask the pharmacist for advice about which medicine to buy and how to use it. Pharmacists are trained to help one select a medicine for illnesses that do not require the help of a medical doctor. One should also ask them if more than one medication can be taken together as it is sometimes dangerous to mix medicines. In addition, you may find a variety of other items: greeting cards, toys, clothes, candy, hose, and garden equipment. Pharmacies often accept photographic film for developing and printing.

Hardware stores sell supplies required for repair and maintenance of the home. These include paint, nails, wood, fencing, bathtubs, commodes, sinks, glue, electrical wiring, outlets, etc. Some stores also sell plants, seeds, animal feed, and garden equipment.

Department stores usually sell sports, semi-formal, formal and dressy clothing, cosmetics, costume and fine jewelry, bed sheets, pillow slips, towels, table cloths, shoes, plates, dishes, knives, forks and spoons, glass and silver goods, and general items for use in the home. Some department stores sell appliances and furniture. Department stores employ clerks who are happy to assist the customer find suitable purchases.

Prices for **appliances** vary from store to store, so it is worth shopping around before making a final choice. Appliances usually can be bought at major department stores or at an appliance store that only sells small and large appliances. Some discount stores also sell appliances. When buying appliances, be sure you understand the guarantee, the service contract (if any), and how to have the appliance repaired should it break down. Always keep the sales check (receipt) so that you can have a faulty appliance repaired or replaced by the appropriate supplier. Complete and return the warranty information card. Avoid buying any appliance that cannot be adequately serviced and repaired in your town.

A **"dime" store** is usually the store you select when you do not know where else to go. Here you can find a variety of miscellaneous items, including toiletries, costume jewelry, some non-prescription medicines, clothing, sheets and table cloths, pillows, blankets, candy, household items, appliances, plastic goods, and sometimes, small pets. Prices are usually low at these stores, but these stores are disappearing as stores like Wal-Mart and K-mart replace them.

Convenience stores are often located at or near service stations and keep only items one would need in an emergency, such as butter, milk, bread, drinks, some processed foods, candy, etc. They are usually open twenty-four hours a day. Often they will not take personal checks but sometimes do take major credit cards, and, of course, they take cash.

Discount stores sell almost everything, sometimes at a discounted price. Some operate drugstores and some have small eating areas where light refreshments are sold. Usually there are a minimum number of clerks available, so the shopper often has to hunt for purchases without much assistance.

If one needs money desperately and cannot get a loan, a

pawn shop will offer money for a valuable item, on the understanding that within a certain time, the same item will be bought back by the same customer at a slightly higher cost. If the customer fails to buy the item back on time, it will be sold (usually at a higher price) by the pawn broker to cover the loan.

At a **"deli" (delicatessen)**, one can purchase several varieties of cooked food and sometimes salads and vegetables to eat at the store or to take home. Some delis specialize in a particular type of food, especially ethnic food.

Throughout the South **"yard or garage sales"** are popular. Private persons may sell items they no longer need or want. Sometimes neighbors get together and have a large yard sale. These items can include adults' and children's clothing, furniture, appliances, household goods, toys, books and various bric-a-brac. Usually goods are inexpensive, and often good quality items may be purchased. These sales are advertised in the newspaper, or signs may be posted on posts or trees near the home where the sale is to take place.

One is expected to pay the price an item is marked at a yard sale, although sometimes one is invited by the organizer to make an offer. Usually one is expected to pay in cash, although occasionally some people do accept personal checks. These are good sales where newcomers can often find bargains.

Flea markets consist of small stalls operated by one or more persons selling every type of used and new items. Usually (though not always) prices are lower than in regular stores. However, one should be discriminating as it is possible to find items of poor quality for too high a price.

Thrift stores are generally operated for the benefit of needy people and sell used (and sometimes new) items donated to the charity at a low price. Often one can buy good, used household goods, including furniture, for reasonable prices.

Mail order buying is popular in the United States. From a variety of catalogues, one may purchase all kinds of merchandise. These can range from expensive, luxury goods to inexpensive items. One can either send money and an order form to the company or can phone an order using a credit card. Either way, one must keep a detailed list of prices and descriptions of items ordered. Merchandise takes from a few days to six weeks to be delivered through the mail. This method of purchasing saves time, energy and money spent traveling to shops. The disadvantage is that one cannot inspect the merchandise and one has to make decisions based on a picture in the catalogue. In addition, the goods take time to arrive. If the goods are not what the customer ordered, most companies will take the goods back and refund one's money. However, before you order, make sure that you can return goods you do not like.

Factory outlets are becoming increasingly popular. These are stores where specific manufacturers sell their products at a discount. Usually the items do not pass the manufacturer's quality control standards. When considering a purchase at a factory outlet, check the item carefully, as sales are usually final, and you will not be able to return defective merchandise.

Sales

Throughout the United States, sales are popular. At specific times, stores offer most, and sometimes, all their merchandise at reduced prices. Sometimes items are marked down fifty percent, sometimes even more. Big sales, called "white sales," are held in January (after Christmas), and this is a good time to buy sheets, table cloths, towels and other household items and clothing. Other significant sales are held near July Fourth, Veterans' Day, Memorial Day, Labor Day, Thanksgiving, and any other special occasion. These are good times to buy new, expensive items.

Returning Unsatisfactory Merchandise

Most stores allow one to return purchased goods if they are found to be unsatisfactory and if they are returned within a reasonable amount of time after the date of purchase. Sometimes merchandise is the wrong size, color, or in some other way is not what one wanted. Or merchandise can be found defective and therefore unable to be used. In these cases, one may return these goods to the store where they were purchased if the store has a policy about returning goods. When purchasing an item, find out if it may be returned before you leave the store.   Most stores have a return policy but some do not.   Often "sale" goods are not returnable.   If you wish to exchange or return goods, you must keep your sales receipt.   No store is obligated to accept returned merchandise without a receipt.   Also, merchandise that is not defective but is not what you want must be in perfect condition when you return it.

Warranties

Some merchandise carries a warranty against defects for a limited time.   Usually one has to complete a card that comes with the merchandise and mail this, sometimes with a sales receipt, to the manufacturer so that goods that do not perform satisfactorily can be returned for replacement or repair.   Make a copy of your warranty card and your receipt before sending them to the manufacturer.

Pay the Price

In the United States, one pays the price at which an article is marked.   It is not the custom in this country to bargain with the shop assistant for a lower price.   Occasionally, customers are invited to make an offer on an article, especially if it is slightly damaged, and then the assistant will either reject or accept it.   At some car dealerships, one may negotiate the price of a car, and sometimes an offer will be accepted which is less than the amount the car is priced.   When one purchases several expensive items such as appliances or expensive household goods and clothing, a store manager may offer one a discount or may be willing to reduce the overall price.

Sizing of Clothing

Clothing, shoe, and hat sizes in the United States differ from those in some other countries.   Usually the more expensive brand names start the sizing of their garments with smaller numbers, or size designations, so do not be surprised if you find a brand name article fitting you perfectly in a much smaller size than the size you usually wear. Clothing and shoe sizes are not standardized.   Always try on clothing and shoes in the store before purchasing garments to make sure that they fit properly.   Shoe store assistants prefer one to wear hose or socks when trying on shoes. Merchants all over the United States expect customers to try on clothing and shoes.

Be Cautious

Scams

From time to time, you may receive phone calls or mail from people trying to sell you unbelievable bargains on goods, travel opportunities and such, or offers for you to invest in some scheme claiming you can make a lot of money very quickly. Do not discuss your finances with these people. Do not allow them to mail you any of their merchandise and do not promise to send them any money. End the conversation as quickly as possible. You are never obligated to spend time discussing financial matters with anyone, particularly someone you do not know. And you should not make purchases over the phone unless you have initiated the call to a reputable company.

You may receive "checks" from companies with which you have not agreed to do business. Often these "checks" are good only on merchandise purchased from that company or their use obligates you to make purchases from that company. Do not cash these "checks." Read the fine print (tiny type) on all material you receive. Sometimes this is difficult to read or to understand. If it is, discard the material or seek the counsel of a trusted American friend.

Better Business Bureau

Consumers who cannot solve problems they have with businesses like stores, hospitals or companies can report these organizations to this bureau, which exists in most cities. The bureau will investigate the problem and try to resolve the problem for you. The Better Business Bureau can also be contacted any time a consumer would like information about the business reputation of a company. The telephone number is found in the business section of the telephone directory, or you can call 411 and ask for the number.

The Media

The word media is the generic term for all printed publications such as newspapers, journals, magazines, and also television, and radio. Most newspapers in the United States are printed each day, although some communities have newspapers that are printed once a week. **Daily newspapers** usually contain brief reports of international news and concentrate on national and local news of more direct concern to the communities they serve. Each contains a section of "classified" advertisements in which items for sale and lease, job vacancies, and other special announcements are included. Newcomers can learn a lot about the United States by reading the daily "Ann Landers" or "Dear Abby" columns.

Most daily newspapers also include sections on home decorating, arts and entertainment, and items of general interest. The Sunday edition, especially the New York Times, usually features greater coverage of international news (very useful to newcomers), travel and air fares, book reviews, reviews of plays, movies, and music, as well as tips on making money, buying or selling a home, recipes, and other topics.

News magazines like *Newsweek, Time,* and *U.S. News and World Report* are published each week or each month and report on news of the past week or month in greater detail than newspapers. Many include essays of general interest about the business world, international events, people, trends, and such events as sports, entertainments, and cultural activities.

General magazines are published to suit virtually every taste and interest. Subjects range from sports and entertainment to financial matters, politics, and automobiles. These are generally inexpensive and are often offered at discounted subscription rates to college students, new subscribers, and through special promotions.

Journals are magazines published within specific academic or professional disciplines. Journals present discussions and research findings in a particular field and are usually of little or no interest to the general public. Because the audience is small and specialized, the subscription price for a journal is usually relatively high.

Tabloids look like small newspapers and are generally sold at supermarket checkout lines and in convenience stores.

Articles in tabloids are intended to be read for entertainment and often have only limited and dubious news value. Much of the information is not intended to be taken seriously.

Newspapers and magazines can be purchased at news-stands, in supermarkets and other shopping areas, or from newspaper machines. If you want to receive publications regularly, you may "subscribe." This means you pay for a year, and the publication is mailed to your address. (Usually, the total cost for a year is less if you subscribe than if you purchase each copy at a newsstand.) You can have your local newspaper delivered to your home by phoning the newspaper and requesting this service. You will be billed for the period you request.

Why so Many?

Americans believe in the constitutional right known as the "freedom of speech" and the "freedom of the press." These freedoms guarantee the right of all individuals to say and print their opinions about any subject, provided the statements are not false (an individual may be sued for making an untrue statement about another person). Therefore, you may be very surprised to find a host of opinions in the media.

The government does not own, control, or financially support any branch of the media to guarantee that the media are entirely free and independent of the government. The media are supposed to be the "watch dogs" on behalf of the people, checking on government officials and politicians constantly to make sure that these people are not deceiving the people. Therefore, journalists are expected to investigate any (and preferably all) incidents of public concern and interest such as scandals, dishonesty, dangers, threats, mistakes and all forms of crime. After the investigation, reporters are expected to provide the public with the facts so that appropriate action can be taken by those concerned.

Reporters are supposed to be fair and accurate and to present both sides of an event or situation. But being human, they often are not. Often reporters for the media are unable to give both sides of a story because of the limited space and time available in their media, or because they often do not know both sides, and because they have personal political preferences. Reporting is therefore necessarily biased by the available information and the perceptions and inclinations of the reporters. Reporters in the United States as a group (not individually) are reputedly more liberal than the general population.

Of course members of the media also report international news and general interest items, such as weather, crime, financial, ad educational news. Each type of medium varies in its coverage and opinions of events, depending on its goals, ownership, and staff members. Often reporting focuses on sensationalism because this sells well.

International business professionals will find the following publications interesting and helpful as they discuss financial, as well as news, items:

The New York Times (newspaper)

The Wall Street Journal (newspaper)

The Washington Post (newspaper)

Financial World (magazine)

Kiplinger Magazine (magazine)

Money (magazine)

Forbes (magazine)

Subscriptions to these publications are sometimes expensive, but the local library will usually subscribe, and you may read them there at no charge.

The Library

Even small towns in the United States have free or inexpensive libraries. You may go to the library to look up information or to read, or you may apply for a library membership card and use it to check books out to take home.

Requirements vary from one place to another; however, to qualify for a library card, you will usually need to show proof of a permanent address in the area where you have lived for a certain amount of time. Once you are issued a library card, you will be asked to present it each time you borrow books from the library.

Library cards issued by a specific library system are valid only at libraries within that system, and you cannot use one city's library card in another city's library. You should also remember that each book you check out is due back to the library on a specific date, which will be stamped on a piece of paper inserted in the book. If you fail to return the book by that date, you will be charged a fee. If you do not return the book, you will be required to pay for it.

Movies

Movie theaters operate in all Southern cities and towns. Many are open every day of the week and have several shows each day. These are advertised in the local newspaper giving the locale, the times of the show, and sometimes the prices. Sometimes it is possible to get discount coupons from stores, colleges, and places of employment.

Movies are rated according to codes to guide parents in selections for children and to protect young people and children from material deemed inappropriate for them. These ratings change from time to time, so check the rating of any movie before allowing your child to see it. Any movie other than those rated with the code "PG" may contain explicit language, scenes of sexual behavior, violence, nudity, or other scenes inappropriate for children. Because the codes are subject to change, consult the codes in effect at the time you consider a movie.

Television

Television in the United States is free, and you will not be able to avoid becoming familiar with television. From television one can learn a great deal about life in the United States, but one will also see many programs that have no basis in reality and which are presented only for their entertainment value.

The major networks are the American Broadcasting Company (ABC), Columbia Broadcasting System(CBS), National Broadcasting Company (NBC), and Public Broadcasting Service (PBS). Through cable hook-ups, television viewers can receive a wide variety of specialty channels—such as those featuring educational and nature programming, comedy programs, movies, sports, business, and twenty-four-hour news channels.

On cable television, you can get Cable News Network (CNN) and many other interesting channels, including Home

Box Office (HBO), Cinemax, Showtime, and the Disney Channel, which show movies. In order to receive cable, you must subscribe through a local company, pay an installation fee, and pay a monthly fee that is based on the equipment and channels you receive. (The movie channels and certain other channels require payment of an additional monthly fee.)

The many talk shows on television invite viewers to phone in questions and comments. Before you call one of these shows, you should consider that the expense of the long-distance call is paid by the viewer/caller if it is a 1-900 number, and can be quite expensive.

Many daily and Sunday newspapers list the television programs for each 24-hour period, and most daily papers include a listing for the entire week in the Friday edition of the paper. In addition, a weekly publication, TV Guide, gives a comprehensive listing for the weekly programs. It is available at supermarkets or by subscription.

The major networks practice a form of self-censorship and do not air material deemed unsuitable for family viewing during certain times. However, newcomers should be aware that standards for "suitable family viewing" have changed during the past two decades, and some newcomers (like many Americans) may consider some programs to be unacceptable for children. Therefore, parents are urged to monitor what their children watch. In many areas, public television offers good entertainment for children most afternoons, and these programs will probably meet with your approval.

Radio

There are hundreds of radio stations in the South, and the major networks (ABC, CBS, and NBC) also broadcast over the radio. Most stations feature a certain type of programming, and music stations usually play only a specific type of music (country/western, classical, rock, jazz, etc.). "Talk programs" involve listeners, who call in during the broadcast to voice opinions and ask questions of the individuals on the radio program. Many of these programs help newcomers understand some of the concerns of Americans.

Sometimes newcomers are not interested in many of the

topics discussed on radio programs and consider the news programs to contain inadequate international news. Newcomers may wish to purchase short-wave radios that have the capacity to pick up broadcasts originating in other parts of the United States, as well as many overseas countries.

Mailing and Sending Items

Letters

The United States Postal Service is run by the government, and the clerks are federal workers. If one has questions about how to mail letters or other articles, the clerks should be consulted. From the post office, one can purchase an "aerogramme," a thin piece of blank paper that can be used as a letter. One writes a letter on one side and the address on the other. It has to be folded in three sections and secured with glued flaps that are part of the aerogramme. It contains a stamp, and it is an inexpensive way of sending a letter overseas as it contains the paper, envelope, and stamp all on one sheet. This is the best way of assuring that a letter to an overseas person goes by air as it is easily identified as an airmail letter.

If you have a bank account, it is quite safe to send a personal check in an envelope through the mail anywhere in the United States. Be sure to write the name of the person to whom you are sending the money in the appropriate space. This will ensure that only the person for whom the money is intended will be able to cash the check. That person will have to put it through a bank account to receive the money or have a friend put it through his or her account. Never send cash through the mail.

If you do not have a bank account, you may purchase a money order (which is like a personal check) from a post office or a store that sells them. Many convenience stores (see page 107) sell money orders. You will have to pay a small fee for the money order, but it is a safe way of sending money. You may also purchase a special check, called a cashier's check, at a bank, which you may also safely mail at the post office.

You may send a check, money order, or cashier's check through registered mail at a post office for a fee. You may also pay a small fee for a receipt to be sent to you when the person receives your envelope with the money. To register and request a return receipt is a good way of mailing any important item in the United States as you will have proof that the person to whom you have mailed the item has received it.

To send money overseas, you purchase an overseas "draft" (similar to a cashier's check) from a bank that deals in international financial matters. This draft will be in the currency of the country to which you are mailing the money. Check that the bank clerk clearly and correctly types on the draft the name of the person receiving the money on the draft. Unfortunately, there is no way to register or insure mail sent overseas, but this may change at any time, so if you ever decide to mail money or a valuable package, ask a clerk in the post office to advise you on the safest way to mail money overseas.

You may send urgent mail through the post office for an extra fee, and it will be delivered the next day. (Note, however, that it may be delivered only to the postal station of the individual to whom it is addressed. If you are sending urgent mail to someone at a large company or a university, the delivery may be considered complete once that company or university receives the mail.) Federal Express, DHL Worldwide, and United Parcel Service will also deliver urgent mail (for a fairly high fee). Some of these companies will pick the mail or package up at your home or place of business for special delivery elsewhere. The telephone numbers for these businesses can be found under "mailing services" in the Yellow Pages of your telephone directory.

Sending Valuable Items

There are several ways one can send packages and letters containing valuable items: through the United States Postal Service or through a delivery service such as United Parcel Service. Both these agencies have branches in most Southern towns and cities.

If you send a valuable item through the mail, ask the clerk in the post office to send it "registered" and "insured" and request a return receipt that will be mailed back to you once the goods have been delivered. The clerk will explain the procedure and the advantages of this to you. If you insure the package and it gets lost, the post office will pay you the declared cost of the article.

Before mailing or sending a valuable item, find out from the delivery or postal agency how to pack it. In the United States, one should have all material in a strong, reinforced envelope or box securely taped with strong plastic tape. Usually string or rope is not permitted as a substitute for tape.

Emergencies

In many towns and cities in the south, there is a telephone number one can call in the event of any emergency. It is usually, but not always, 911, and the operator who answers this number will direct a call to medical, police, or fire fighting personnel. It is a good idea to place this and all other emergency numbers in your area next to your telephone.

Medical Concerns

Doctors

One of the first tasks of a newcomer is to find a doctor. Friends, acquaintances, and colleagues can assist in this search but if you have nobody to advise you, the hospital nearest to your home can give you the telephone numbers of doctors. Doctors appreciate a telephone call or a visit from new patients before they need medical attention in order to get acquainted, but this procedure is not essential. Usually, the first visit to a doctor is more expensive than subsequent visits.

Most Southern cities have excellent medical centers, especially the cities with medical schools. Some rural areas have few doctors, especially in the area of gynecology and obstetrics, but nowhere in the South are doctors and hospitals inaccessible. Some medical centers in the South are linked to rural areas by emergency helicopters.

The Public Health Department in all cities offers information about immunizations, epidemics, innoculations for travelers, AIDS, and other diseases. The number can be found in the "county" section of the blue pages in your telephone directory.

Paramedics

In many Southern towns and cities, emergency medical personnel (paramedics) are on call twenty-four hours each day to give immediate emergency assistance in the home of patients suffering from serious, unexpected medical problems when a patient cannot be moved or there is not time to get to a hospital. These paramedics can be reached by telephone and respond immediately. Usually they give life-saving treatment and aim to keep the patient alive while en route to the hospital. They are especially trained to give treatment for heart attacks, strokes, choking, and similar acute emergency situations.

Keep the number of your nearest paramedic station at your telephone in the event of an emergency. You can usually summon the paramedics by dialing the emergency number for your area—which is usually (but not always) 911.

Emergency Rooms

The majority of hospitals in the South have "emergency rooms" that operate twenty-four hours a day. If you or a member of your family becomes extremely ill or injured during the day or night and requires immediate attention and there is no time to contact your own doctor, you may take the patient to one of these emergency rooms. But make sure you do this in accordance with the procedures of your insurance company. One does not need to make an appointment before going to an emergency room.

Poison Control Centers

In many towns and cities there is a poison control center that can be reached by telephone, sometimes twenty-four hours a day. Should any person, especially a child, accidentally take poison, one can phone this center and receive advice immediately from specially trained personnel. If you have children, it is advisable to phone the poison control center when you first settle in the South and find out what medications you should keep on hand in case a child swallows a poison or dangerous substance.

You will notice that all medicines in the United States have warning labels advising that medicines should be placed out of the reach of children. One can also buy medicine with child-proof lids, and pharmacists can be requested to put all medicine in containers with child-proof lids. These help to keep children from swallowing medicine accidentally.

Common Dangers

Snakes

Snakes are found all over the United States. Many snakes are harmless and are essential for the ecology, while others are poisonous. Some poisonous snakes in the South include coral, rattler, water moccasin, and copperhead. If you live near trees, shrubs, and grassy areas, you need to be aware of snakes, especially in hot, humid weather for they love these conditions. Some poisonous and nonpoisonous varieties swim in creeks, streams, and rivers, and children should be warned about swimming in these places. Local people can advise newcomers about the areas to be avoided. Libraries have material that will help you identify both harmless and poisonous snakes in your area.

If you are ever bitten by a snake you should get to a hospital emergency room immediately. It is also advisable to be familiar with the appearance of poisonous snakes, so that you can describe its appearance to the doctor in the emergency room. The medical staff will be able to treat you more quickly and with greater certainty if you or a family member are able to kill the snake that bit you and can take it with you to the emergency room.

Spiders

Spiders are another hazard in the South. The black widow spider and the brown recluse spider are both poisonous and extremely dangerous. The victim of a spider bite should get to an emergency room immediately after being bitten. Libraries can provide you with information about recognizing these spiders. If you live in a wooded area, it is a good idea to shake your shoes and socks every morning to dislodge any hidden spider.

Cute Little Animals and Rabies

Much of the South is wooded and overgrown with bushes, shrubs and grass, and there are many attractive little animals living in this terrain. Most of the squirrels, chipmunks, and rabbits are too fast for children to catch, but sometimes children are able to trap them. However, these animals are wild and should not be handled or petted. Children should be taught never to touch them as they can, and do, bite. Also, they are potentially dangerous as their bite can carry rabies, a serious disease for humans. If bitten by any wild animal, a victim should receive immediate medical attention.

Poisonous Plants

In the South, there are several varieties of poisonous trees, vines, shrubs, creepers, and other plants. Children should be warned about them and told never to eat any berries or plants. Newcomers are advised to become familiar with these if they go camping, back-packing, hiking, or just strolling through the woods. The general rule is: never eat or handle any vegetation with which you are not familiar and wear protective clothing when you are walking through thick undergrowth.

At Christmas, many homes are decorated with attractive green branches of the holly tree. The bright red berries are poisonous and are a temptation for children. The poinsettia plant, another traditional Christmas decoration, also should not be handled by children.

Poison ivy and poison oak are hazards when one walks or works in the yard or woods. These plants grow on a vine and are hard for newcomers to recognize. Ask a neighbor to teach you to identify these and avoid all contact with them. In allergic individuals, these plants will cause skin lesions that are alternately painful and itchy and which require medical attention.

Mushrooms

Mushrooms abound in the heat and humidity of the South, but these should NEVER be eaten and should not even be touched as many are extremely poisonous and can cause death. Poisonous mushrooms are difficult to differentiate from the edible variety, so eat only mushrooms bought from a food store.

Insects

Many insects in the South are not poisonous but their sting or bite can cause serious and, if neglected, fatal allergic reactions in some individuals. These include yellow jackets, hornets, wasps, and bees, among others. The sting of these insects is usually extremely painful and often requires immediate medical attention. If a victim of an insect bite begins swelling or having trouble breathing, emergency medical help should be obtained immediately as this condition could lead to death. If you live in an area where there are bees, you should find out from your doctor how to determine if you are allergic to them and then take the necessary precautions.

After a short time in the South, newcomers notice the viciousness of the mosquitos' bite, and some people who are allergic to mosquito bites have particular difficulty. There are several products on the market for such bites, and your pharmacist can help you select the best medication for this condition and explain how to use it correctly. Many Southerners (and other Americans, for this is a problem in many parts of the United States) apply insect repellents to all exposed areas of their bodies. Ask your pharmacist or physician to advise you about such products and use them with care if you are going outdoors, especially in the summer months.

You should also be cautious when walking through the woods or in long grass because of the danger of ticks. Ticks are tiny insects that imbed their heads under the skin of animals or people in order to suck blood from their victims. Ticks carry several diseases, the most serious of which are Lyme's disease and Rocky Mountain spotted fever. After being in the woods or tall grass, inspect yourself and your children for ticks— being especially careful to check the scalp. Consult your doctor if you are bitten by a tick as the diseases they carry must be treated immediately.

Tampering

Although such criminal acts are rare, there have been instances of poison being placed in medication and in food, especially fruit. To protect yourself and your family, check the packages of any product that will be eaten. Medication bought off the store shelf should have a protective and sealed covering under or around the lid or some other safeguard. The packaging of food, whether it be a packet, box, or bag should be intact. If it is not intact or if the seal looks broken or if the container looks as though it has tiny holes, do not use it, even if you have already bought it. Beverages usually have lids that are sealed and, if tampered with, are recognizable as such. Newcomers should be alert to this form of poisoning whenever purchases are made anywhere in the United States. If an article looks suspicious, take it to the manager of the store.

Household Cleaning Products

All products have labels that carry warnings about their use and storage. These should be read carefully and observed; improper use and storage could harm your health. Some cleaning chemicals should never be used together, and warnings about this are included on the containers. These products should be placed where children cannot get them as most are potentially dangerous, even fatal, for children, especially if they get them in their mouths and eyes. Many children die each year from eating or drinking household cleaners.

Police

There is no national police force in the United States. Each city and town is responsible for recruiting, training, and maintaining its own force, which can consist of both male or female officers who are on call twenty-four hours a day. If you suspect that somebody is on your property, trying to break into your house, is already in your home, or if you witness a disturbance in your neighborhood such as a fight, drunkenness, or any threatening situation, you may call your local police station for help, and officers will come to your assistance.

Fire Emergencies

This section is written especially for newcomers who are not accustomed to living in wooden homes with American appliances.

In towns and cities, fire stations can be reached by telephone and in the event of a fire, one can expect firemen to arrive quite promptly after receiving a request for help. However, people living in rural areas are sometimes miles from the nearest fire station, and their homes may burn to the ground before a fire engine has time to reach them.

If you are buying or renting a home or apartment, make sure you live in an area that has fire protection by a crew from a fire station. In some areas, you will be required to contract and pay each month for this protection. In other areas, this will be a regular service provided by the city or county to which you pay taxes. Keep the telephone number for the fire department near your telephone.

Some Precautions Against Fires

Since there is so much wood in the construction of the average American home, fire is always a hazard. However, by being careful in your home, you can do much to avoid the horror of a home fire.

Do not leave any appliance—like your washing machine, television set, dishwashing machine, drying machine, stove, kettle, iron—operating when you go out of your home. Do not leave anything cooking when you leave your home.

If you see a fire starting anywhere in your home, get everyone out of the building and stay to put out the fire only if it seems small enough for you to handle by yourself. However, always call the fire department; you may not be able to extinguish it yourself.

Keep a home fire extinguisher (available at a hardware store) in your kitchen and in your garage, near the doors of entry, and learn to use it. This will enable you to fight a fire while someone else in the family calls the fire department. Be sure the person who calls the fire department speaks clearly, slowly, and loudly when giving the address to the fire department, especially if your home language is not English.

In addition, you may purchase a smoke detector from any hardware store. This is easily installed and is run on batteries. Be sure to replace the batteries regularly. Smoke detectors will warn you of a fire, especially important when you are sleeping. If you live in a house with a second floor, you may consider buying special ladders that can be hung from the windows to enable people to escape from upstairs.

Many fires in American homes start with grease burning in a pan on the top of the stove. For this hazard, keep a box of bicarbonate of soda (baking soda) near the stove so that you can sprinkle this powder on a small stove fire to prevent it from spreading all over the kitchen. If the fire is too big for soda, use your fire extinguisher.

You may find many products on the American market with which you are unfamiliar, but which may be highly flammable. Cleaning chemicals, aerosol cans, paints, hair sprays, and deodorants are all fire hazards. Read the labels for warnings about flammable ingredients on all packages you buy and check for special instructions in the use and storage of these items. Keep the flammable items far from stoves and other hot surfaces to prevent a fire from starting. Also, do not use matches or smoke near flammable items, including hairspray and perfume when using them.

You may enjoy the Southern cook-out where meat is grilled on a gas grill or on an open fire. If you use one of the many fire starters, be sure you understand the instructions for using it. If the English sounds unfamiliar to you, ask a neighbor to explain the instructions to you.

If you use a space heater (a heater attached to an electric cord and plugged into the wall) which has an electric element that gets red hot, follow the manufacturer's instructions in its use. Space heaters are dangerous unless used carefully, and they can start a fire if they are knocked over. These heaters should not be left burning when you leave the house or go to sleep. Every winter, several Americans die from house fires started in this way.

Car Fires

Do not smoke near a gasoline (petroleum) pump and

never smoke when the hood of the car is open. It is a good idea to carry an automobile fire extinguisher in your car, but if you see smoke escaping from any part of the car, get the occupants out and stand clear. Use your extinguisher only if the fire is a small one and you think it is safe to do so, but remember, a car can become a ball of fire very quickly. If you have the proper automobile insurance, you will be paid out the value of your car, so do not risk your life trying to save your car.

Provisions for Handicapped People

Throughout the United States, public buildings should be equipped for handicapped people, especially those in wheelchairs. You will notice special ramps near stairs, special toilet facilities in rest rooms, and sometimes special entrances to buildings to accommodate wheelchairs. If you take a handicapped person some place, it is wise to check the facilities first, but usually you should have little difficulty.

In parking lots, there are usually special parking places (near the building's entrance) painted in blue with a little sign that looks like a person in a wheel chair. These are for handicapped people. To be able to park a vehicle in these places, one must have a special parking sticker to attach to the car in a designated place. These are available, upon application, to all handicapped persons who need them. Vehicles without proper parking authorization will be ticketed and their owners fined for using these spaces.

School, College, and University Education

For many newcomers and immigrants, child rearing practices in America are frightening, confusing, and surprising. Probably the greatest fear parents from other countries have is that their children and teenagers will become undisciplined and disobedient, will get involved in abuse of alcohol and other drugs, will reject or discard parental guidance, will develop problems of adjustment, or will resemble the stereotype of the American teenager out of control. These fears are common and normal and are shared by most American parents as well! However, it should be comforting to the newcomer to learn that the average American teenager is unlike the stereotype. Most are fine, well-adjusted, responsible, law-abiding young people.

Every newcomer is faced with the dilemma of how to use the pattern of child rearing from the homeland (the only pattern known to the newcomer) in an environment so different from home. Does one try to learn the American pattern somehow or adjust one's own pattern to the American one? This question will have to be answered by each individual.

One of the most apparent differences that many people from Asia, the Middle East, Africa, South, and Central America, notice is the attitude of children and young people to older people in America. Americans, as well as some other Westerners, do not insist on children and young people showing respect to adults in the same way that other cultures do. Newcomer parents are especially shocked at the casual and often rude manner in which American children treat teachers and parents.

You probably will want to teach your children to show respect for elders and teachers in the customary way of your homeland—and that will serve them well. Courtesy is always treasured in the South. However, it probably is best to teach a newcomer child not to overdo courtesy as this will make him or her feel too different from class mates.

Many newcomers feel the American family generally does not emphasize family closeness and the importance of family relationships to the extent that people from many other countries do. This is probably true. The typical American family is extremely busy and stressed as often both parents work at demanding jobs; children and teenagers have many activities to attend when school gets out; and relatives and grandparents often live far away and cannot help with household chores and child rearing.

Newcomers would do well to maintain close family ties after coming to the United States, but this probably will entail more effort than in the homeland. If both parents work, it may be difficult to keep the family close, particularly if you adopt the hectic lifestyle of the United States.

The American teenager is a shock to many newcomers. Many own cars and possess an enormous amount of clothing and luxury items. However, many teenagers do not own cars, and those who do often work after school to pay for them. Teenagers all over the United States work in fast food restaurants, hotels, restaurants, stores, supermarkets, and as babysitters to earn money after school hours. This pays for the possessions they acquire, sometimes to the detriment of their schoolwork.

Many newcomers are not prepared for the manner in which many teenagers rebel against their parents. Teenage rebellion is one of the cultural phenomena of the Western world. In fact, it seems this rebellion is expected and tolerated in the United States, though not encouraged, enjoyed, or endorsed. To understand this tolerance, you need to remember that some of the ideals of Western societies are freedom, individualism, creativity, and independence. In the United States these ideals are especially important, and Americans believe that a child should develop individualism from an early age, which is one reason Americans have been progressive, energetic, creative people, responsible for so many benefits the world enjoys.

Americans believe that one of the ways in which a young person becomes independent is by learning to cope with situations in his or her own way. The emphasis in teenage years shifts from the child's place as a subservient member of the family group taking instructions from the parents to the teenager as an individual who is learning to make responsible decisions about his or her own life. The teenager is encouraged to experiment with many of life's situations, especially social interaction with the opposite sex, but not with sexual intercourse.

You may be confronted with the desire of your older children and teenagers to go out at night and stay out very late. They may even resent telling you where they are going and with whom. Even American parents have a hard time with this kind of situation.

The freedom given to teenagers often results in problems between them and their parents, and teenage rebellion can result. Rebellion is also considered part of the way in which young people separate from their parents so that they can live individual, independent lives; it is considered part of maturing into an adult, but it is not endorsed by everybody as good and desirable.

Once young adults leave high school, they often are not expected to obey their parents any longer. Instead, they are encouraged to take responsibility for themselves and are expected to make their own decisions. Of course, parents may offer advice and may insist on obedience when young adults are still at college. Later, when young people graduate, most still ask their parents for advice.

Often newcomers need professional guidance about how to guide a child or teenagers in a new culture. Bookstores and libraries stock a number of books on bringing up children and teenagers to guide you in this task. There are many reputable books by family counselors that give guidelines for discipline for maintaining close family ties because the ideal of American families, in spite of the emphasis on freedom, individualism, and independence, is still for discipline and love.

Peer Pressure

The immigrant or newcomer to the United States needs to understand the nature and influence of the peer group among young people in high school, college, and in the workplace. The influence of a particular group on a young person is both positive and negative.

The concept of peer group comes from the British tradition of people being equal and is used in terms of age, socio-economic condition, and interests. For most adults, peer groups exist primarily in the workplace, church, or social clubs. Interaction with one's peers usually occurs in those settings, and adults are influenced to only a limited degree by the decisions made by peers. In fact, adults often choose to be friends or associates with people who are quite different from themselves.

This is not the case with young people. They spend enormous amounts of time with their peers—primarily in school. And they do so at a time when fitting in, being like everyone else, and being accepted in a group matter a great deal. The standards and behavior of those around a young person usually influence the young person more than the standards and behavior of parents. The influence of peers reaches its strongest point during the teen years when teenagers are preparing for lives away from their parents and with people of their own age. It is only natural that they would begin to seek peer approval with greater intensity than they seek parental approval, and peer group approval is gained by conforming to the behavior and mannerisms of the group.

Peer groups are not formal organizations—they are actually groups of friends who spend as much free time as possible together, socialize together, and, frequently, share common goals. Each group member feels a commitment of friendship, loyalty, and concern for the other members. The peer group also contributes to the child's developing self-concept and becomes very important, especially during teenage years.

The peer group can be positive when it helps make a young person feel less lonely, isolated, and alone while entering the adult world. It also gives young people an identity and provides support as they become adults because a young person feels accepted as a valuable human being. In American culture, where there are few fixed rules about how young people should behave as they enter adulthood, the peer groups fill the void by guiding their behavior.

If a young person belongs to a peer group that adopts and encourages values the parents endorse, there is usually little cause for concern on the part of the parents. However, if the peer group endorses and encourages behavior and upholds values that are contrary to those of the parents, the group can be disruptive to the home(s) of a member(s) and detrimental to individual members of the group. In these cases, parents and young people get into arguments and, often, bitter fighting. In addition, if an individual becomes overly concerned about pleasing the group to the extent that his or her own needs and desires are cast aside, the peer group can interfere with the development of independence, individualism, intellectual development, and even the emotional development of a teenager.

Once a child or teenager becomes friends with a circle of schoolmates, that group will grow in importance and can be the source of conflict as the child gets older. For example, the group will tend to dictate when he or she will return home in the evenings after a party or group activity. This time may not be acceptable to you. You will then have to help your teenager come to terms with the group while obeying you at the same time. Sometimes this struggle will call for the help of a counselor able to help newcomers and their children.

Often the negative influence of peers will lead to a confrontation between child and parents. The parents often confront the teenager about his or her behavior and that of his or her friends; resentment continues to build as the teenager resists the parents and clings to the peers. Then, because the child is afraid to leave the group and risk being alone, he or she will often rebel against the parents.

Newcomer parents need to realize that it is extremely difficult in American society for young people to withstand the influence of peer groups. Friends are very important during these years, and once young people become members of a circle of friends, each feels obligated to participate in the group behavior. Newcomer parents need to know as much as possible about their children's friends and peer groups. The most serious problem with friends and peer groups is that some promote the use of alcohol and other drugs. Unfortunately it is almost impossible to choose the peer group for one's child, but by careful selection of schools, churches, and neighborhoods, it is possible to have a little control over their choice. Local residents will be able to guide you in the selection of a school where your children will find positive peer groups.

Schools that are strict about the use of alcohol and other drugs and that punish violence at school usually have some control over the behavior of students. Newcomers may feel free to interview the counselors at a prospective school about discipline and problems with drugs and alcohol before registering a child in that school. The economic status of a neighborhood is not an indicator of a drug problem or vice versa. Generally, the tougher the discipline and the more definite the policy of the school regarding use of alcohol and drugs, the less likely the appearance of drug-promoting peer groups.

Another problem the parents of newcomers face is the fact that newcomer children are sometimes not accepted in any group. This is a problem for newcomer teenagers more than young children. Younger children are usually more open to newcomer children as they have not yet formed the long-time friendships that teenagers have, nor are they as aware of the differences in individuals.

While the young people already in groups will usually be polite, friendly, and helpful to newcomers, they may not always accept them into the group as full-fledged members. It can be devastating for a newcomer to realize that he or she may have few or no friends and not be part of a group. The newcomer parent will need to be supportive and understanding in a situation like this and may need to reassure the child that not being part of a group may even have advantages.

Parents may need to organize times of fun and recreation over the weekend with a child to help him or her adjust. Also, a counselor at the school can give suggestions on how newcomer young people can adjust to the new life or recommend professional people who can give guidance.

Newcomers may consider getting to know the parents of

children or teenagers in the same class as their children. Also, inviting other children or teenagers home to spend time with your children may help.

Though this section has dealt with the difficulties teenagers and children sometimes face, it is entirely possible that a group of young people and children will be eager to make friends with newcomers. Also, it is important to point out that the vast majority of young people in the South are fine young people with high goals and good values and are taught to be polite and gracious to strangers.

Tuition Costs

Throughout the United States, elementary and secondary education is provided free for all young people, regardless of sex, race, ethnic background, religion, culture, or national origin. Textbooks are free in most public school systems. By law, every child has to attend school until he or she graduates, reaches a certain age (which may differ from state to state), or receives special permission to quit school. Unfortunately, in the South, too many young people, especially those from inner city neighborhoods and very rural areas, drop out of school before graduating.

Each state has many school systems that are independent and run by local people. However, each state also has statewide guidelines for such components such as textbooks and required studies. The money to pay for public schools comes from taxes—primarily from the local community and the state. Certain programs in public schools are supported by funds from the federal government.

Private elementary and secondary schools charge tuition fees for educational programs that are sometimes, though not always, considered superior to those of public school systems. Private institutions are not guaranteed government funding, and they often incorporate religious instruction or other topics not included in the public school system.

Newcomers moving to the United States should consider the local school system in deciding where within a given city or area to live. Currently, where a child attends school depends on where the family lives, and school districts differ in terms of quality of education, safety, and extracurricular activities. The local board of education should be able to supply you with specific information about schools in your area.

General Information about Schools

Enrolling your Child in School

Try to enroll your child in school as soon as possible after you arrive in the United States or as as soon as he or she reaches the appropriate age. In the United States, children between certain ages are required by law to attend school regularly. Your local school board can tell you the age at which your child must be enrolled in school.

When going to enroll your child in school, take your child's visa or green card, immunization record, dental records, a birth certificate, and passport. You may be asked for proof of legal custody of the child if you are not the natural parent.

Attendance at School

Children are expected to attend school regularly and may miss school only for important reasons. These include illness, death in the family, religious holidays, school holidays, and such circumstances as bad weather. If your child must miss school for any reason, you should give a written and signed explanatory letter to the child to take to school on the first day the child goes back to school. The letter should explain the reason the child's absence. If you need your child to leave school early for an important appointment, the child should take a written and signed note from you to the teacher requesting this absence. Many schools require that parents sign a document in the school office when they take children out of school before dismissal time.

Should it be necessary for your child to miss school for several days when school is in session, you should contact the school to make arrangements to get the class assignments so your child will be able to keep up with his or her schoolwork. If your child is ill, however, do not expect him or her to be able to complete all assignments during the time of illness.

Progress Reports (often called Report Cards)

Every few months, the school will send you a report of your child's progress at school. Usually grades (marks) are given for each subject studied by your child, and if your child is not progressing satisfactorily, the report will indicate this.

If you are unhappy about the information on the report, you may request a meeting with your child's teacher or teachers. Teachers are usually cooperative and friendly and welcome discussions with parents of the children they teach, so do not hesitate to approach the teacher. You should not act angry in any way or be abusive when talking with your child's teacher. Teachers, like other Americans, resent rudeness and angry confrontations.

From time to time, schools schedule regular parent-teacher meetings to afford an opportunity for parents to be involved in the education of their children and to get acquainted with the teachers. You should try to attend these meetings, but if that is not possible, you should call and schedule a meeting with teachers at a different time.

Grades

Children younger than six years go to kindergarten, where they are prepared for school but are not subjected to academic pressure. This is called grade K. They then go to elementary or grammar school, where they usually progress from grades one through six. After grade six (or, sometimes, four), they go to a middle or junior high school until the eighth or ninth grade. In some school systems, children go directly from elementary school to high school. At the tenth grade, they go to high school, where they are known as sophomores in the tenth grade, juniors in the eleventh grade, and seniors in the twelfth grade.

Academic Calendar

In the South, the academic year starts in late August or early September and the period from August to December or early January is called the fall semester. At Christmas, schools and colleges have a few days of vacation and resume early in January. In the middle of the spring semester (which often begins in February), many states have a few days vacation called spring break in late March or sometimes early April. During this time many college students who can afford a trip try to go to the beach or some other vacation place. Sometimes these vacations can be a time of anxiety for parents as some (but definitely not all) young people go on drinking sprees that sometimes lead to tragedy.

In May or early June, colleges and schools close for the academic year and hold graduation ceremonies, also called commencement. For graduation, students who are graduating send cards to their close friends and relatives announcing the ceremony. This is not an invitation to attend the ceremony, unless the young person specifically requests your presence. Most people receiving such an announcement send a gift to the graduate.

Many high schools and colleges have a summer school during the three-month summer recess. During this time, students may take courses they have not yet taken, or they may take courses to make up for academic deficiencies they accrued throughout the year.

School Times

Children go to school five days a week, Monday through Friday. In the South, schools usually start at eight o'clock in the morning and close at three o'clock in the afternoon. Many high school clubs and sports activities take place after the schools dismiss students at three o'clock.

School students may purchase lunch in the school cafeteria or bring their lunches from home and eat them in the cafeteria during the designated lunch hour (usually anywhere between 10 a.m. and 1:00 p.m.). During the lunch break, teachers eat with students and supervise the behavior of the students.

Some schools offer supervised programs for children whose parents must drop them off before eight o'clock or cannot pick them up until after three o'clock. Should your schedule require that your child be at school before or after the regular hours, find out if your child's school offers a supervised program. If not, you will need to make arrangements for your child to spend that time elsewhere.

Choices

At both high school and college, students are given choices of courses they can take in addition to the required courses determined by the institution. This gives young people a varied and interesting academic experience that is designed to enrich their lives. In high schools, counselors help young people select courses to meet academic requirements and the personal interests of individuals.

Standard of Education

At the time of this writing, education in the public schools across the United States is considered to be poor. The government has appointed commissions to study the problem and find solutions.

It seems generally accepted that the average public school is not providing America's school children with a sufficient education, especially in the areas of science, mathematics, and written skills. Adding to the problem of inadequate education is the problem of illiteracy, which some put at 25 percent of the population. While some of these are individuals who did not attend school, some have graduated from high school without having mastered basic skills. Others are individuals who are literate in a language other than English and are considered illiterate because of their inability to read and write English.

Although this is a gloomy picture, one needs to remember that there is everything from the very best schools in the world to some of the poorest schools—and everything in between. Not every school is bad.

If you want your child to go to a public school, which is free, you will have no choice where you child goes. The child will have to attend the school in the area in which he or she lives. Thus, before you decide where to live permanently (whether you rent or buy a property), make sure you find out from reliable people what the school system is like in the areas in which you would like to live. Currently, Congress is considering legislation that would give parents greater choice in selecting the schools their children attend.

Generally, the more expensive areas of a county have the best schools, partly because the school system has more money. This enables the schools to have smaller classes, and teachers are sometimes paid more, resulting in easier recruitment of better teachers. Also, affluent parents tend to have higher expectations of their children to achieve. However, some of the excellent schools are in middle-class suburbs. Recently there has been a move to upgrade the quality of education in poor areas as well.

You will need to find out several aspects of the school to which your children would be assigned in a specific area: what type of discipline is practiced in that school; what sort of scores does the school achieve on the national standardized tests; what are the sports programs like; what extramural activities are offered?

Most newcomers accept the fact that the United States has many of the world's finest universities. The standard of education in the South varies from one college to another; on the one end of the scale, one finds some of the finest universities in the nation and, on the other, some of the poorest.

Throughout the United States, organizations exist to evaluate the standard of education offered by colleges and universities. In the South, the Southern Association of Schools and Colleges evaluates universities and colleges, and those that meet its high standards are approved and receive accreditation. One should not attend any college or university that does not have official accreditation.

Academic Grades

Students are evaluated on their projects, assignments, homework, and the tests they are given at school. For excellent work, they receive an evaluation called an A grade; for good work, a B; for satisfactory work, a C; and poor work gets a D. If work is totally unsatisfactory, an F is given, denoting a failing grade. This grading system is used in most Southern schools, although some teachers are reluctant to fail any child.

School Clothes

Public schools and universities do not require students to wear uniforms. High schools usually have guidelines about how to dress for school attendance, but college students use their own discretion about dressing.

Young people from other parts of the U.S.A. have expressed surprise at young people's greater emphasis on clothes in the South. However, most students dress casually when they go to classes. It is not uncommon to see shorts and tee shirts worn by girls and boys alike to classes at some colleges. Jeans and tee shirts are the standard uniform of college students in the South at the time of this writing.

Transportation

Usually free busses are provided for public school students who live beyond a certain distance from the schools they attend. In rural areas especially, children may be assigned to schools a great distance from their homes and have to spend a lot of time on the busses. However, children in urban areas may also have to ride school busses for extended periods of time.

Bussing has come to mean the transporting of children from one community to another in order to integrate the schools racially. If you do not want your child to spend a long time on a school bus, be sure to find out whether the area you are considering is a bussing zone. At the time of this writing, bussing is being considered a failure in its attempt to improve the quality of schooling for all children, and alternatives are being investigated.

Philosophy of Education

Americans believe that the school system in a democracy should prepare every student to become a responsible citizen capable of participating in the political system. Education should, therefore, teach a child to reason and should provide useful skills enabling him or her to live in a modern, industrialized society. Information that is practical and useful is considered most important.

Most American educators believe in educating the whole child, which means that teachers should pay attention to the mental, physical, intellectual, and emotional needs of their students. The development of a positive self-concept (how a student feels and thinks about himself or herself) is as much a concern to a teacher as is the subject material that the child learns. American teachers believe that how a child learns is as important as what the child learns. Therefore, the atmosphere in which the child learns and the relationship between the teacher and the child are extremely important. A good teacher never does anything to humiliate or embarrass a student for fear of damaging his or her self-concept.

At all levels of education, the student is regarded as a human being whose potential the teacher is helping to develop. Independence and individualism are encouraged, and an individual search for knowledge is rewarded. The teacher's function is to help a student think logically and creatively more than merely to teach a student facts. Teachers train the student to interpret facts and information correctly and to find the relationship between facts in the totality of life. To develop this capacity in a student, research papers and other projects that encourage independent study are used.

The idea that people learn best by "doing" explains the practical nature of teaching and learning in American schools. In good schools, students are encouraged to discover facts for themselves, practice skills they have learned, research topics, and then come to class prepared to discuss them to improve their reasoning and speaking ability. Many American students are very articulate and self-assured.

This philosophy of education has helped to develop many characteristics of the American personality, namely the tendency to be practical and functional rather than philosophical, the ability to meet challenges no matter how difficult, the desire to improve and change existing conditions (no matter how good they may seem today), to seek new frontiers of knowledge and skills, and to test oneself against difficulties and problems.

Discipline

One aspect of public elementary and high school education that some newcomers, especially from non-Western countries, often find disturbing is their perception of the lack of discipline and order in some American schools.

Educators in the United States believe that students' creativity and self-concepts are improved if they learn in a relaxed, happy environment. Too strict an atmosphere and too much regimentation, they feel, stifles the creativity and curiosity of students, so discipline tends to be minimal or just enough to keep order in many American schools.

Teachers are expected to find their own ways of disciplining students in their classes. Generally, they are not allowed to use corporal punishment, which means they cannot use any physical methods, such as beating or spanking. If they do, parents may sue them and the school.

Students are encouraged to obey their teachers, but they are also encouraged to question their teachers and examine authority. Unfortunately this has often led to disrespect for teachers, and many teachers find it impossible to teach in some American public schools.

Although this is a gloomy picture, one needs to remember that there is everything from the best of schools in the world to some of the poorest, and there is everything in between. Not every school is excellent, nor is every school bad. In the South, problems of discipline are especially bad in the inner city schools of large cities. If newcomers are selective about the schools they choose for their children, they probably will be satisfied.

Problems of discipline tend to disappear when high schools students go to college or university. Classes tend to be more structured, and students are expected to work hard for tests and examinations. Sometimes colleges have disciplinary problems on the campus, but these are usually after classes have been dismissed.

Violence

From time to time one hears and reads about violence in high schools (but not in colleges) in the South. Occasionally a student may attack a teacher, but the most common violence is fighting between or among students and between members of gangs. These are isolated reports and should not be considered the rule.

Before selecting a school for your children, you may want to know if there have been any incidents of violence in the school. Usually the local people will be able to tell you what reputation a particular school has in this regard.

Social Activities after School Hours

Because the whole child is being educated, Americans expect high school and college to provide fun for their children. Social life appears to be more important to children and young people than is the content they are learning. Peer groups develop, and many social activities develop from groups and friendships at school.

Southern schools, like most schools in the United States, have many activities after three o'clock in the afternoon. There are meetings of academic societies, social organizations, and sports meetings and practices. Many high schools and colleges have some or all of the following team sports: football, basketball, baseball, track, tennis, and swimming. Some institutions also have athletic activities and other sports.

Many institutions, especially those that have a football team, have a marching band that performs at the football games. There is often a dance line made up of girls who dress in distinctive costumes and perform dances at the half-time break at ball games. In addition, there are usually cheerleaders who are also dressed in colorful clothes and who encourage the teams' supporters during the game.

In some schools, social and academic clubs exist for the benefit of students. The counselor at your high school can give you information about these and other organizations and societies that provide opportunities for newcomer teenagers to meet friends with similar interests.

These groups may be athletic and sports organizations, which enable students with sports interests to pursue these; academic clubs, centered around school subjects in which students are interested; service clubs, which use students' time and talents as volunteers in worthy causes; honor clubs, which admit students to an exclusive society based on the grades they achieve in specific academic areas; and music and art clubs that are open to talented young people. These organizations and clubs provide an excellent opportunity for newcomer young people to pursue specific interests and make friends. At organized school functions in the South, alcohol and drug use is prohibited.

Football games are among the most important social events of the high school student's life. Most Friday nights, the high school's football team either plays in the school's own stadium or goes to another high school stadium. The fans attend the game whenever possible.

One of the occasions young Southerners enjoy dressing

formally for is the prom. At the end of the high school year, the juniors and seniors go to a prom, which is a party at which there is a band, food, and dancing. Sometimes the party is held on the school property, other times, in an off-campus location.

The girls are dressed in lavish, gorgeous dresses, and the boys rent tuxedos for the occasion. The students go to the prom in couples. The young man has to arrange to get the girl to the ballroom (often in an expensive car); give her a floral corsage, and be her partner for the evening, which usually incorporates a dance and dinner. The socio-economic status of the young couple determines how lavish the exercise will be.

After the dance has ended (usually around midnight), many of the students go to a restaurant for breakfast in the early hours of the morning. Many young people do not go to bed at all until the next morning and to stay up all night seems part of the occasion. To newcomers, this ritual appears to be an initiation rite!

Prom night causes considerable concern to parents and teachers. While alcohol is usually forbidden on the school property, students go elsewhere for alcohol after the function has ended. Many young people have been killed in drinking and driving accidents. In recent years, various organizations have made suggestions for confronting the problem, and many lives have presumably been saved as a result.

Alcohol and Other Drugs at School and College

One of the most important issues influencing your choice of a school is whether or not that school has a problem with alcohol and/or other drugs, and, if so, what steps are being taken to deal with the problem. Reputedly, drug dealers have students in some elementary and secondary schools who distribute drugs to students. Not all schools have this problem, but many schools in all types of neighborhoods do have a problem with drug abuse and drug distribution. This problem is especially prevalent in inner city schools. Drug abuse is one of the reasons there is sometimes violence in schools.

In recent years, the use and abuse of alcohol and other drugs among children and teenagers in the United States has attracted the attention of lawmakers, parents, health professionals, mental health workers, educators, and many others.

In most states in the United States, the legal age at which young adults may drink alcohol is twenty-one years. Very few states permit drinking of alcohol at a younger age. There is no age at which the use of illegal drugs becomes legal. Unfortunately, one of the ways American young people mimic adult behavior is by drinking and getting drunk. Alcohol is the drug most frequently abused by American young people, as it is the easiest and cheapest drug to obtain, in spite of the fact that it is illegal for stores to sell alcohol to people below the legal drinking age. Even children in elementary school are victims of alcohol abuse. This applies to both male and female, but more often to males.

At many parties, young people are challenged to get drunk, and they are embarrassed and afraid of not participating and being like their friends. American young people have a great fear of being thought chicken (cowardly), so peer pressure often wins in the matter of drinking and getting drunk. In some peer groups, drugs are added to the challenge, further complicating the problems of newcomers who are confronted with this new phenomenon.

Drinking and drunkenness cause a great deal of difficulty in the lives of American young people. Death by accident is the largest killer of young people in the United States, and a great number of these deaths are alcohol related.

Currently one of the greatest concerns for all Americans is the illegal drug problem. Thousands of Americans and some foreigners in the United States become wealthy by importing, manufacturing, and retailing drugs all over the country. Young people are not the only victims, but they are a growing population of drug users and abusers. Newcomers will only have to be in the United States a short while and listen to the news for a few weeks to become aware of the enormity of the drug problem in this country.

The possession, sale, or use of some drugs is forbidden by law. These include heroin, marijuana, PCP (called angel dust), and cocaine (or any of its derivatives such as crack). Certain controlled substances are drugs that may be taken legally when prescribed by a medical doctor but whose use is forbidden by persons who do not obtain them legally. Illegal drugs are sold by drug dealers of all ages, including students. These local dealers are usually supplied by a network of illegal drug smugglers and distributors.

In order to become familiar with the dangers facing their young people, newcomer parents are urged to read about drugs, attend seminars and lectures, and attend any event available that gives information about drug abuse. Parents are encouraged to learn how to warn their children and teenagers about drugs and to discuss these issues with their children so that they do not go into schools and colleges unprepared to face this problem and become a victim of a drug dealer, called a "pusher".

Parents also need to learn how to recognize the symptoms of a child who is taking drugs. This is important because the parent should seek medical and psychological help for the addicted young person or child as soon as possible.

Newcomer children and teenagers of high school and college age must develop a strategy for resisting peer pressure that entices them to use illegal drugs and alcohol. However, the majority of America's young people are not drug addicts or drunks. One study in Alabama, reported in the Birmingham News, July 2, 1989, indicated that children and young people who are involved in useful church and civic activities tend to be less vulnerable to drug and alcohol use and abuse. The report concludes that one way to fight chemical abuse is to get young people involved in activities that raise their self-esteem and make them feel needed and useful.

Newcomers of all ages should also know that alcoholic beverages come in many unusual forms in the United States. "Cocktail", "bloody Mary", and other unusual names are all alcoholic drinks that are potent and should not be purchased by anyone under twenty-one years of age. Many alcoholic drinks often look like soft drinks as they are bright colored, and have fancy names and prices. Fruit juices with alcohol are sometimes sold in grocery stores. Wine has a higher alcoholic content than in many other countries, and it is rarely, if ever, served with water.

If you are offered a drink or see a beverage on a menu in

a restaurant or on the shelves of a grocery store, feel free to ask about the ingredients. Happily most people all over the United States are cooperative and pleased to answer questions honestly posed by a newcomer.

Sometimes young people will put alcohol in a nonalcoholic drink for a friend and will not admit to doing this. This is to make the friend drunk and an object of ridicule. Newcomer young people should be aware of this possibility when with other young people.

There are many young people newcomers can choose for friends who do not partake of drugs or alcohol. Many young people who attend churches, synagogues, mosques, or other places of worship do not drink alcohol at all or do not abuse alcohol and get drunk as this is against their principles.

Many young people are killed each year while driving under the influence of alcohol. A young person does not have to be obviously drunk for his or her driving ability to be affected. Driving ability is affected before a teenager gets obviously drunk. Newcomer teenagers and young adults need to be aware of this danger and need to feel at ease about refusing to get into a car with a driver who has been drinking. Many American young people are doing this nowadays, so do not feel uncomfortable if you have reason to believe the driver has been drinking and you do not want to ride in the same car with him or her.

Many parents and high school students enter into an agreement (promoted by an organization called SADD— Students Against Drunk Driving) that if ever the teenager has been drinking, he or she will phone home and request a lift home. No questions will be asked, nor will the episode be discussed till the next day. This organization aims to prevent accidents and deaths attributable to drunken driving.

Newcomers who have problems with alcohol and/or drugs or who have problems with friends trying to pressure them into participating can call one of the many counseling services in most Southern cities for help. Often the mental health society will be able to make a referral to somebody qualified to help.

Throughout the United States, there are drug and alcohol rehabilitation programs especially for the many young people, some of them in their teens, who are addicted. Unfortunately, the problem is so great at present that there are not enough of these facilities for all those needing treatment. Many institutions have waiting lists of young substance abusers needing professional help.

Currently, the government and the private sector are investigating ways of halting the drug traffic and trying to solve this enormous problem. It is beyond the scope of this book to deal with this problem, but the newcomer is urged to be aware of it.

Private Elementary and High Schools

All over the South, there are private schools; some excellent, some good, some bad, and some average. A great number of these private schools are run by churches. These schools charge tuition fees and can vary considerably from one to another and from public schools in general. Here again, you will need to find out the strengths and weaknesses of the schools. The standard of education is not necessarily higher in a private school than in a public one.

They usually have stricter discipline, have fewer problems with alcohol and other drugs, and have fewer violent acts on school property. Some private schools require students to wear school uniforms.

There is often no bus service offered to students at a private school, so parents are responsible for getting their children to school.

Technical Schools

Throughout the South, technical high schools are available for students who do not wish to pursue strictly academic subjects but wish to be trained in various trades, clerical services, computer operating, interior design, upholstery, automobile mechanics, bricklaying, carpentry, and so on. Students who complete these courses generally do not go to university, as they usually do not have the academic background for college courses.

At the end of this training, young people are prepared for good jobs. Artisans, or blue collar workers as they are sometimes called, often earn large incomes in the United States. They may join trade unions that protect their interests and negotiate with employers for good wages, good fringe benefits, and working conditions.

College and University

College education in the United States is not free, but financial aid and a program of student loans mean that most eligible young people can attend college. State colleges and universities (operated by state governments) are usually less expensive than private universities, and community schools are generally the least expensive. High school counselors can give students the facts about the various colleges and universities.

Most students get part-time employment while they attend college, often as waiters, fast food clerks, sales clerks in stores, and cashiers. Work is also available to students on college campuses. Even students whose families are financially comfortable often choose to work while in college. This gives the students a sense of individualism and independence and allows them to afford such luxuries as their own cars.

College attendance is encouraged in the United States. During the junior or senior year of high school, students take the SAT (Scholastic Aptitude Test) or the ACT (American College Test). These tests are given nationally, and different colleges and universities require different scores for admission. Under this system, most students who are interested in college meet the admission requirements for some institution. Grades earned in high school are also considered by college admissions committees. At least half of all high school students go on to college, although only about 25 percent actually finish college.

While a student is in college, the parents sometimes help to pay the tuition fees and other expenses if they can afford to do so. However, after college, the young person is expected to be financially self-supporting. At this stage, he or she may marry and take on the responsibilities of a family.

Most Southern young people live in dormitories on the campus of the college they attend. Most Americans believe that a valuable part of the college experience is living with other students and learning to relate to other people. Many immigrants do not share this view and have their college-age children living at home. Students who live on campus can often pay for their meals at the beginning of each academic term and eat in the college cafeteria.

Students usually choose one major and a minor or two majors depending on their interests and career goals. They confer with their academic advisors throughout their academic careers in order to take the correct courses for their degree programs. All colleges have certain required courses that all students must take and pass in order to graduate; the balance of coursework comprises the major and minor.

Social Life at Colleges and Universities

Some Southern universities are known as party schools, a term indicating that students place great value on parties. Alcohol consumption and attendant woes have caused many groups to reconsider the nature of parties on some campuses, and, it seems, students are currently developing more responsible attitudes toward alcohol consumption.

Greek societies are very popular on Southern campuses and are called fraternities (societies of male students) and sororities (societies of female students). They are called Greek societies because their names are written in Greek letters. These are exclusive campus groups that admit students on the basis of predetermined criteria, and members pay dues. Although these criteria are kept secret, they generally involve grade point averages, high school honors, appearance, popularity, social skills, and, in some cases, family background and status.

Interested students apply for membership in Greek societies and then endure a gruelling period of activity called "rush", which can last for several weeks. During "rush", members of the society observe the applicants in several situations, particularly social ones. At the end of this time, students chosen by the group for membership receive an invitation or bid to join.

The end of "rush" is a time of celebration or despair, depending on whether or not the student is accepted into the society of his or her choice. Many parents have to comfort rejected and crushed young people after "rush" is over.

The popularity of Greek societies fluctuates and many students do not consider such membership important. Many other campus groups offer opportunities for membership, often with less emphasis on social status. These organizations include academic honor societies (which admit students on the basis of academic achievements only), service societies (which admit students on the basis of several criteria, including the desire to serve the community), social societies, and special interest clubs (which are often organized around certain academic majors or hobbies). Most of these organizations have a membership fee and regular fees.

Students who do not wish to belong to expensive social organizations may belong to **service societies**. These provide a way for students to serve less-fortunate people in the community while being part of a peer group, with its social benefits, at the same time. Newcomer students are likely to feel comfortable in these groups as the members are often friendly, service-oriented young people.

Academic organizations are formed on the basis of academic interests, and all students with the minimum grade point average are free to join. Programs for these meetings focus on the subjects in which the students are interested, and field trips or visits to places of special interest may also be offered. Newcomer students with strong academic interests in specific areas may find these clubs worthwhile.

Special interest clubs exist on many campuses. These are formed around interests ranging from dramatics to chess, from bicycling to environmental issues. Membership is usually open to all students who share the common interest.

Religious organizations are present on many campuses, including those that have no denominational affiliation. These groups provide a setting within which students can meet other students who share their religious beliefs. Usually these societies welcome all students, especially international students, regardless of their beliefs, and there are no academic or social requirements for membership. Sometimes they arrange special events especially for newcomers.

Some campus organizations cater to newcomers in specific ways, and some have special programs for international students. Many campuses even have a special organization for international students. Some colleges have paid staff members who are specifically trained to help students, and newcomers may feel free to solicit the help of these people.

Graduate Students

American graduate students expect to spend several years studying and doing research to earn their degrees. Most graduate students have to rely on scholarships, loans, and student stipends they receive for assisting professors with research and teaching introductory undergraduate courses. Many take part-time work for some hours each day and during weekends. Unless parents make liberal financial contributions or students have their own private money, most graduate students anticipate that these years will be difficult financially, and they plan carefully to live on a small amount of money. Married students commonly take turns, allowing one spouse to complete graduate school while the other supports the family. Once the first spouse completes graduate school, the roles are reversed.

Graduate students tend to live what is known as the graduate student lifestyle. They live in inexpensive apartments as close to the university as possible. These apartments are usually small and are often shabby and in noisy neighborhoods. Whether the apartments are furnished by the landlords or the students, the furniture tends to be old and somewhat shabby or dilapidated.

Newcomers in graduate school should not be disappointed or embarrassed by living in circumstances that are difficult and devoid of luxury and inferior to those in their homelands. If you plan to live in a university's graduate student housing, expect to find the apartment basic and unattractive. If you wish to make any changes to the place, first obtain the permission of the university's housing authority as one is usually not permitted to change anything except the arrangement of the furniture. Of course, you may add extra items of furniture or appliances, provided they do not cause any damage.

Students often try to save money by shopping at discount stores, thrift stores, yard sales, and flea markets (see page 108) for household items and clothes. Some universities operate loan closets through which international students can borrow such items as baby cribs, beds, and dishes for the duration of their enrollment.

Entertainment for graduate students often consists of free programs, concerts, and movies on the college campus. Most cities have parks where students can go for picnics, and many communities have free entertainment from time to time throughout the year.

As a general rule, Americans (apart from family members and close friends) do not give students and graduate students sympathy or monetary gifts. It is considered a privilege to be a student, and suffering economic hardship is part of a temporary lifestyle. Also, the education gained is expected to lead to a better life later, making the sacrifices for that education bearable. It should also be remembered that Americans believe people should learn to be independent and to achieve their own goals with as little help as possible from others. This does not mean that Americans are hard-hearted. Many international students have found American friends very generous with many different kinds of help when they have had problems and have asked for help.

The graduate student lifestyle is generally quite stressful. Most students have to earn money, teach, study, do research, prepare a thesis or dissertation, maintain friendships, sometimes maintain marriages, and serve parental roles. There is not much time for leisure or recreation, and students have to learn to relax and avoid becoming "burned out", the term for emotional and psychological exhaustion. Counselors are available at most universities to help students with such problems, and international students should feel free to make use of the counseling services, regardless of the nature of their problems.

Appearance and Hygiene

Personal Hygiene

The American idea of personal hygiene may seem strange to some newcomers as it differs substantially from the standards of personal hygiene in many other countries. The importance placed on personal hygiene is evident from the numerous T.V. commercials about personal products. It is important for newcomers to understand American personal hygiene, as newcomers sometimes offend Americans with body odors, especially at work.

Most Americans shower or take a bath every day. American women are expected to shave the hair from their legs and under their arms and to use deodorant/antiperspirants in their armpits. Most women also dab perfume behind their ears, on the pulse of the wrist, and on the bend of the elbow. Men also use deodorants, and some use perfume. Unlike in some places in the world, the odor of perspiration is not considered appealing or sexy in the United States, so do use an antiperspirant and deodorant. (This will be a single product and can be found in any drug store and grocery store.)

Teeth generally are brushed at least twice a day: in the morning before work and again at bedtime. This practice is recommended by dentists all over the world. Having particles of food lodged between teeth is definitely unacceptable, hence the container of toothpicks in many restaurants. It is debatable whether these may be used in public, although one sees it often enough. It is considered better to use a toothpick in public (very discreetly behind a cupped hand) than to have offending particles of food visible in one's teeth.

In addition to using a toothbrush with toothpaste every day, American dentists recommend using dental floss. This is a piece of string made for cleaning between teeth and is used before or after brushing the teeth. A word of caution: The use of dental floss in public is totally unacceptable and offensive.

Bad breath is called halitosis and is offensive. If halitosis remains a problem after brushing and flossing teeth, Americans are advised to see a doctor or a dentist as it could be related to a health problem. Mouthwashes are often used for clean breath.

In this country, people try to keep their nails and hands scrupulously clean. For those who work with machinery or do outdoor work, it is understood that this rule cannot be observed always. Even then, hands are supposed to be kept as clean as possible. Women's nails are usually filed into an oval shape, and the nail length is a personal preference. Sometimes women's nails are painted with either a transparent or a colored polish. Men's nails are kept clipped very short and are kept clean but are not colored.

Appearance

Generally the way an individual looks is important in the United States, and good-looking people are believed to be more successful in business than plain-looking people. Most people in the South try to dress and groom themselves appropriately for every occasion.

The appearance of youth is desirable, and many middle-aged people feel sad about getting older and so strive to maintain a "youthful attitude and appearance." Carefully applied cosmetics can make most people look more attractive and younger, so the cosmetic industry in this country is extremely lucrative. This is one reason older women often appear to be younger than they really are, a surprise to many newcomers.

Everywhere in the United Sates, clean, shiny hair for both sexes, is considered a sign of good grooming. Hair need not be stylishly set or as they say in the South "fixed" at all times, but it should be clean.

Sometimes men who are going bald will have small wigs made to fit their heads. Although this is not common, this is an accepted way of attempting to look younger. A few men will dye their grey hair. Sometimes women also wear wigs, and many dye their gray hair other colors. American women change their hair coloring to suit their tastes.

Newcomers should find out from their colleagues what type of dress is expected in their workplace. Every vocation, profession, and place of employment has its own dress code, and it is best to ask the boss at the outset of your employment about what is expected. If you desire promotion and professional advancement, you should dress in accordance with the image your company wants to project.

Americans are not hide-bound and rigid about their standards of dress, as people have freedom to dress as they please. This is why newcomers are often shocked to see men and women of all ages, weights, shapes, and sizes looking terrible in shorts. (Shorts, for casual occasions, are acceptable for women of all ages, weights, and shapes in the United States.)

Casual dressing is almost a uniform: tee shirts (or blouses and shirts) and jeans (or slacks) with casual or tennis shoes (or athletic shoes). Informal dressing is acceptable on the street, going to the movies, eating out at a casual restaurant, casually dropping in on friends, visiting family, mowing the lawn, cleaning your home, going to sports events (except important football games when people usually dress up). Jeans or slacks or skirts with a more dressy blouse or shirt substituting for the tee-shirt can be worn almost anywhere, some church services included.

As in any culture, one indicates one's respect for other individuals and an event by how one dresses. However, Southerners are not going to ostracize you because of your clothes, because they are usually understanding where foreigners are concerned. If you come from a country which has a distinctive national dress, you may wear that to both casual and formal occasions, because Southerners usually enjoy observing the dress of other countries.

Depending on the event and situation, short dresses for women and jackets and ties for men are acceptable in the evenings for entertainment and social occasions.   Formal wear usually means long or short evening dresses for women and evening jackets or tuxedos for men.   If you are invited out, it is best to find out from your host or hostess how you should dress.

Some Southerners have clothes for the four seasons of the year.   Summer clothing is light with bright colors, often with white shoes and accessories. Often sleeves are short, sandals and shorts are worn and cotton is a favorite fabric.   White shoes are popular in the daytime and are worn with formal evening gowns in the evening.

Winter clothing is usually made from fabrics of warm, lightweight wool and synthetic blends in dark and warm colors.   In the fall (the autumn), clothes are of lightweight fabric with long sleeves.   In the spring, people wear light, bright colors of fabric neither as light as in summer nor as warm as in winter.

Traditionally, after Labor Day people no longer wear light or pastel colored clothing or shoes, except for white blouses and shirts, which are worn all year round.   Most of the time the weather dictates the type of clothes people wear in this part of the United States, and people usually wear what is comfortable.

Southerners wash their clothes often, probably because of the climate.   Usually underwear clothing is worn only once and then washed.   Outer wear is sometimes worn several times before being washed, but most men wash a shirt after each wearing.   Men's and women's suits, slacks, and skirts that are not washable are dry cleaned frequently.   Most Americans feel that clothes develop an odor after being worn too often without being washed or cleaned.   This is valid in the summer when one tends to perspire, and newcomers are advised to wash their clothes frequently.

Laundromats are to be found in most towns and cities in the South for use by people who do not have washers and dryers in their own homes.   They are available to the general public for a fee.   As a hygiene precaution, you can wash the inside of the washing machine with strong liquid washing soap or chlorine bleach before placing your clothes in the machine.

Obesity and Diet

Probably over half of Americans are overweight in varying degrees, a fact most newcomers quickly observe. This is attributable to a diet that is high in fats, sugars, and salt. In the South, much food is fried or flavored with fat.

You will see many television commercials about diets, dieting, and exercising, indicating the serious concern people have about their weight problems. Many Americans are on restricted diets and exercise regimens to lose weight as obesity is considered detrimental to good health, appearance, and longevity.

Many Americans can afford to eat well and have jobs that do not offer much opportunity for exercise. The possession of cars also limits the amount of exercise most people get. It is therefore easy for Americans to put on weight, and many newcomers have found that the good food and lack of exercise can add pounds on them, too.

Generally, Americans hate being overweight, and some people—especially women and teenage girls—suffer from eating disorders. These disorders can become health- or even life-threatening and often require psychiatric treatment. Even those who do not suffer from eating disorders often eat carefully to control their weight, passing up foods they enjoy rather than risking gaining weight.

Smoking

In recent years medical science has demonstrated the health dangers of smoking. Americans all over the United States have become aware of the risks of smoking and also of the risks of inhaling other people's smoke. Smoking is no longer "fashionable" or chic. Various educational programs emphasizing the health hazards of smoking are constantly being implemented, many geared for young people as they are the most vulnerable group in terms of starting to smoke. Many people are giving up smoking, and many organizations offer programs to assist those who desire to quit.

Newcomers should be aware of the fact that smoking is only permitted in designated areas in most public buildings, such as restaurants, cinemas, stores, public waiting rooms, and reception areas and places of business and entertainment. In some buildings, smoking is not permitted because of fire and health hazards.

Smoking is not permitted on airline flights of less than two hours within the continental United States. Failure to comply can result in being charged and fined. On most busses, one may not smoke at all. Busses on long journeys stop frequently for passengers to get refreshments, and smokers are expected to make use of these stops.

Many hotels, though not all, have rooms for nonsmokers. If you do not like the odor in most American hotel rooms, you may request a nonsmoking room.

Newcomers who smoke should be sensitive to the current negative attitudes of health-conscious Americans toward smokers. The odor of cigarettes, and especially cigar and pipe tobacco, offends many people. In a private home, one should always ask the host or hostess for permission to smoke. Newcomers should not smoke anywhere unless they are sure that smoking is permitted; otherwise, they may be subject to stares, comments, or commands intended to put an end to their smoking.

The information in this section is relevant to all parts of the United States, not just the South.

Transportation

Most large cities in the South have some form of public transportation, but generally it is considered inadequate. Most people in the South have to have their own transportation unless they live within walking distance of their schools, workplaces, and stores.

Southerners love their cars and often both husband and wife own a car. Very often even the teenage children will have their own cars.

The roads on the whole are extremely good in the South and one may travel from the East to the West on a network of interstates that link all the major cities and towns.

Bus companies link some towns and cities in the South. These companies are well-run and offer fast and safe transportation for a relatively low fare, and provide an opportunity to view the beautiful scenery of the South.

Most Southern towns are within a few driving hours of an **airport**. All the large towns and cities have airports; some like Atlanta, Dallas, Houston, and Miami have international airports. Air travel in the South, and the rest of the United States, is safe, efficient, and comfortable. Large, national airlines serve the South, as do small, regional airlines. Airlines are competitive in their prices so one should always phone as many airlines as possible to get the best price for an air ticket. A travel agent can also be asked to find the best price for an air fare. Sometimes planes do not keep their schedules, so bear this in mind when booking flights for important meetings.

Apart from the few cities like Atlanta that have underground suburban **train services**, in the South there are few train services like those in Northern cities. However, there are railroad (train) companies that link cities by rail and provide freight and passenger services. It is possible to go great distances by train, all over the United States. This is an excellent method of seeing the incredible beauty of the South and the rest of the United States. However, train and bus fares are not always lower than air fares, and the service is infrequent.

If you expect friends and relatives to visit you, you might like to advise them to check United States air, bus, and train fares with their travel agents in their homelands. It is often cheaper to buy tourist tickets outside of the United States than to pay for them within the borders of the United States. Sometimes transportation companies offer tourists package deals for traveling in the United States at low costs.

Leasing an Automobile (Car)

If you are going to be in the United States for just a short while, you may wish to lease (rent) a car instead of buying one. The car rental business is very competitive, so shop around for the best price. You will find the numbers of rental companies in the Yellow Pages of your telephone directory under "Automobiles."

When you consider renting a car, you should decide what car to lease based on your answers to the following questions. For how long will you need a car? How large a car will you need—compact, medium-sized, or large? How many miles does each car get from a gallon of gas (petrol)? What do you need in the car—radio, air conditioning, cellular phone, reclining seats, extra space for large loads? What is the hourly, daily, weekly, or monthly rate? Who pays for the cost of repairs if the car is damaged while you have it? How will you pay for the lease of the car—check, credit card, or cash?

Before signing a lease (contract), you need to find out whether you or the company pays for repairs should the car break down while you are using it and what procedures to follow in the event of a breakdown. Also, what type of insurance does the leasing company offer? Do you need to pay for insurance over and above the cost of the lease? If the car is not insured, will you have to insure it? If so, you will need to know the cost of insurance in order to determine the actual cost of leasing the car.

Be sure you drive only with full insurance. In the event of an accident, the proper insurance will cover your medical expenses, as well as those of other people hurt in the accident. Also be sure the car has collision insurance that covers damage to the leased car and to other cars or property damaged in an accident. If your leased car is not adequately insured, you could find yourself liable for repairing or replacing the car.

You will need a valid driver's license, your passport, and possibly a credit card for long- and short-term leases. For long-term leases, you may also need to furnish details about your credit, employment, and possibly mortgage history, as well as other information required by the individual leasing company.

Be careful to read the fine print (small type) on the lease and understand it fully before you sign. If you are not confident about your understanding of English, get a trusted American friend (or a lawyer) to help you interpret the lease.

The larger rental companies have national toll-free telephone numbers that can be obtained from Directory Assistance. (See telephone directory for the number)

Owning and Driving a Car

Buying a Car

There are two ways of buying cars in the United States. One can either buy a new car or used (second-hand) car from a dealer or directly from the owner. Buying a used car is always risky as even an honest seller may not be aware of flaws in the engine. Few used cars have warranties.

If you buy a used car, employ an experienced and recommended mechanic to go with you to check it (unless you have a good knowledge of the mechanics of cars yourself); otherwise you may buy a car which is unreliable, even if it looks perfect. The mechanic will check essential parts of the car and will sometimes recommend that the car be put through a type of automobile x-ray machine that ought to reveal some hidden problems. This check-up can be fairly expensive, but in the long run is worth it. However, it is impossible to get a flawless used car and one should expect to have some trouble once a car has done more than 50,000 miles.

Books can be bought (or found in most libraries) that publish the "list" price of a used car. These books are published regularly and contain the car's name and the year in which it was manufactured and give the retail and wholesale price of that car in a given month. Usually one can purchase a used car for less than the "list" price, not more. Some banks will tell you over the phone what the current list price is. The knowledge of the list price can enable one to negotiate for a good price with the seller of a car.

Magazines like *Consumer Reports* give information about the strengths and weaknesses of each type of car. Points for consideration when purchasing a car are: How large or small should the car be? How big a payment can one afford to make each month? How many miles can the car go on one gallon of gasoline (petrol)? Does the car have re-sale value? (Currently, Japanese cars have higher re-sale values than cars manufactured in other countries, including the United States.) Is the engine in good condition? Are the brakes working properly? What reputation for reliability does the brand of car have? Many of these questions can be answered in an issue of the consumer guide magazines available in many libraries and bookstores.

When considering the price of a car one should also check the car to see if any parts need replacing, if repairs need to be made to the body of the car and whether the tires are in good condition. For instance, if one has to buy new tires, or if a windshield needs replacing, the buyer will have an immediate expense on top of the price of the car.

When you buy a car, make sure you understand the terms and conditions of the sale, especially if you are making a monthly payment. Employ an advisor to help you if necessary, especially if you are still learning English. Often a car dealer will charge a higher interest rate than a bank charges, so it is a good idea to check the rates at both the dealer and a bank before you decide on taking a loan.

After you have bought a car, ask the seller to demon-strate how to use the controls. Do not drive away in a car without knowing how the lights turn on, how the gears work, how the wind shield wipers start and stop, how to operate the blinkers, and how to operate the radio. Learn how to park the car and always put the gears in the "park" position in addition to using the hand brake to keep the car from moving itself from the parked position in your absence. (Many acci-dents have occurred due to cars not being properly parked.)

Insurance

Do not operate a motor vehicle without adequate insur-ance. If you are preparing to purchase a new or used car, check on the cost of liability insurance before making your decision. Most Southern states legally require every driver to have liability insurance to pay the medical and hospital costs of any injured people, as well as the repair of any cars dam-aged in an accident in which you were at fault. If you have no insurance, the injured person can sue you for everything you have. You must have information regarding your insur-ance policy with you when you drive, and most insurance companies supply their customers with small cards contain-ing the necessary information. Keep this in your glove compartment.

You may also wish to purchase collision and comprehen-sive insurance that pays for damage to your car through accident, theft, or fire. An automobile association can provide information about insurance. If you have difficulty in getting insurance, as many foreign nationals do, call an agent at a local branch of the American Automobile Association. That agent can put you in touch with an insurance company expe-rienced in dealing with foreign nationals. Automobile insurance is very complicated, and it is important to get an insurance agent who can explain the complexities of insur-ance to you. Payment rates are based on age, sex, driving record, and experience, as well as the type of automobile insured. As a foreign national, you should expect to pay quite high premiums (payments).

License

Newcomers should get a valid state driver's license as soon as possible. Anyone driving without a license or driving with a learner's license (without a licensed driver in the car) can be charged with a felony. Such a driver involved in an accident, especially if somebody else is hurt or killed, is in serious trouble and could receive a prison sentence.

If you have an international license, obtain a local license to avoid problems with police, especially in the event of an accident. An international license is valid only for short-term visitors. A local license is also a good means of identification. Anyone sixteen years old or older may apply for a driver's license, which is obtained from the local Motor Vehicle Department of the Highway Department, the telephone number of which is found in the government (blue) pages of the local telephone directory. Call this department and make an appointment to get a license. At the Highway Department, a Driver's Manual is available that describes the signs and rules of the road. This book contains the material on which you will be given a written or oral test which has to be completed successfully before a license is issued. Newcomers should never drive a car anywhere in the United States without studying a driver's guide.

If you have never driven before, you must get a learner's license or permit before you take driving lessons. Otherwise, you could be breaking the law. Be sure that the person teaching you to drive holds a valid driver's license as your learner's license is valid only when you are driving with a licensed driver in the vehicle.

Once you have completed your driving lessons, as a test of your driving ability, an examining officer will ask you to drive him at his instruction. A licensed driver must accompany you when you go to the Motor Vehicle Department since you are never allowed to drive alone while unlicensed or with only a learner's permit.

A license must be kept with you whenever you drive as your license must be available immediately should a policeman ask you to produce it. If you are ever in an automobile accident, whether it was your fault or not, you will be asked to produce your driver's license. Be sure to have your address changed on your license when you move from one location to another.

Make sure you know when your driver's license expires

and have it renewed a few weeks before the expiration date; otherwise you may have to be tested again before it is re-issued. It is a criminal offense to drive a car with an expired license.

Do not assume that the road signs in your homeland have the same meaning in the United States. Usually all the states in the United States have the same road rules and signs, but there are exceptions. For instance, in some states you may make a right hand turn at a red traffic light provided there are no other cars on the road, but there are states that do not permit this turn. If you are uncertain about this rule in another state, do not turn right when the light is red.

License Plate

You must register your vehicle in the city where you live, usually at the town or county courthouse. After you have registered your vehicle and paid the appropriate fees, you will be given a license plate (tag) to attach to the back of your car. (Some states issue two tags, and one must be placed on the front of the vehicle, the other on the back.) Tags must be renewed annually, and the issuing agency sends notification at the time renewal is due.

If you buy a new or used car from a car dealer, the sales-person can help you apply for the tag. Be sure this is handled promptly.

You will also need a "title of ownership" for your vehicle in order to register it. Make sure you receive this when you buy a car. Keep this proof of ownership in a safe place. If you sell your car—or should your car be stolen—you will need to prove that you own the car.

Keeping Your Car Roadworthy

Keeping your car in good condition is essential for it will save you time and money. Immediately after buying a car find a reliable mechanic, recommended by a friend or col-league, and ask him to guide you in maintaining your car.

In some Southern states you need to have your car checked at a state agency for roadworthiness at regular inter-vals. If you have never owned a car before, or you know nothing about maintaining a car, you need to have a mechanic check it for you every six months for your own and others' safety.   An owner's manual available at the car dealer's shop can advise owners about maintaining cars.

Usually a car needs an oil change every 3,000 miles, and a "tune-up" every 9,000 miles.   You will also need to have your steering and brakes checked regularly every 6,000 miles.   Any good mechanic can do these checks for you. Before you have maintenance or repair work done on your car find out what the work will cost.   You may want to find out what mechanics charge for repairs as prices vary from one shop to another.

Newcomers from countries with mild climates may not know about anti-freeze, a liquid poured into the car's radiator to prevent the engine from freezing in the winter.   Freon must be used in the air conditioning system in the summer. A mechanic will demonstrate the use of antifreeze and freon (which must be stored out of the reach of children and pets as they are extremely poisonous and ingestion usually is lethal.)

Tires need to be kept filled with air.   A service station attendant can guide you about how much air to have in your particular tires.   Check your tires frequently to see that they are always in good condition as worn tires can contribute to skidding, blow-outs and accidents.   Wheels should be aligned properly by a serviceman specializing in this service.

Stations where gasoline fuel is purchased provide many of these services: oil checks, air for tires, windshield wipers, antifreeze, and freon.

Road Signs and Traffic Lanes

All over the United States, one drives on the right hand side of the road.   A solid line, often yellow or white, indicates where the middle of the road is.   One should never drive on the left of a solid lane, even to pass another car when one thinks it's safe.   One may pass a car when there is a broken line that looks like long, thin rectangular marks in a straight line painted on the road.

Most American drivers are courteous and considerate of

others on the road and expect courtesy from everyone else. One should not cut in front of other drivers, nor should one drive without giving signals.

Unlike in some places in the world, it is important to drive in traffic lanes. A driver's guidebook will describe and explain the signs on streets, but a few extra comments are appropriate. In some Southern cities and towns, road signs or instructions are also painted on the street. These signs are sometimes hard to read in the day time and almost impossible to read at night, so one needs to pay special attention when driving. Sometimes "Stop" signs are painted on the road instead of on a board or pole on the side of the road. One common road sign is a bent arrow in one lane that indicates the direction the driver must take when in that lane. If you find yourself in a "turning lane" you have to turn whether you want to or not. You must go on down the road and try to retrace your steps after you have made the turn.

Some streets are "one-way streets," and they are marked by signs saying or indicating (with international symbols) "do not enter" or by arrows pointing in the direction traffic may go. Make sure you recognize this sign as you could have a head-on collision if you drive in the wrong direction on a one-way street.

Also pay attention to the placement of traffic lights at intersections. In some instances, traffic lights hang from wires in the center of the road, sometimes higher than one would expect. In some places, traffic lights are on poles beside the road.

Membership in an Automobile Association

For a small fee, automobile associations offer such services as providing assistance if your car breaks down, giving advice on planning a trip, and supplying information on hotels and other accommodations. You can also get travel literature and maps with guidance about routes to take on a trip. Most automobile associations are listed in the yellow pages of the phone book.

What to Do after an Accident

If you collide with another vehicle or are hit by somebody else's vehicle, immediately stop your car where the impact occurred and turn off your ignition. If you are unhurt, see whether anybody is hurt and, if so, ask someone to call the ambulance and the police. Wait at the site of the accident; never leave the scene of an accident until a policeman gives you permission to depart.

Avoid arguing, apologizing, or discussing the accident with people involved. A representative of the law will decide who is at fault. Do not allow anybody to persuade you to move your vehicle. The police will instruct you what to do after they arrive.

If somebody is hurt, assist if you know what to do; otherwise leave the victim alone, unless there is something obvious you can do to make the injured person more comfortable. If the person is bleeding you may press your hand, preferably covered with a clean cloth, tightly over the wound to try to stop the blood flow—if there is nobody nearby who is trained in first aid.

There are two reasons for being cautious about helping an injured accident victim, especially if you know nothing about first aid: your help could make the injury worse and, secondly, you could be sued for aggravating the injury. Usually an accident draws a crowd of onlookers and you can appeal to the crowd for somebody skilled in first aid.

When the police arrive, you will have to produce your driver's license and give your current address. If your address is different from that reflected on your driver's license, give your current address. You will also be required to give the officer investigating the accident the name and telephone number of the agency which has your car insurance. You and the driver of the other vehicle involved in the accident should exchange the names and addresses of the insurance companies holding insurance for the vehicles involved. It is a very serious offense to give incorrect information to the police.

Driving Record

Obey the rules of the road and do not exceed the speed limit. Every few miles, you will notice signs along the road giving the speed limits. Stick to these limits, otherwise you may be stopped by a policeman or state trooper for speeding. This usually involves a fine and a notation against your name on a central computer.

If a police car follows you with its lights flashing, pull over to the shoulder of the road and stop. Stay in your car and keep your hands visible on the steering wheel to show that you are not holding a weapon. The officer will get out of his or her car and tell you what offense you have committed. Officers usually have equipment that monitors your speed, and they may stop you for speeding. They may also stop you for reckless driving. If you feel you need to explain your driving, do so politely. Do not argue with law officers, nor be abusive to them.

You should try to avoid acquiring tickets for any traffic violations. A central computerized system keeps check of your offenses and when you have a certain number, your license is noted and after too many violations, your license can be revoked. Too many traffic violations cause your insurance rate to go up or, worse, the insurance company could cancel your insurance. This is especially true if you are cited for drunken driving.

Driving under the Influence of Alcohol

Driving while under the influence of alcohol is an extremely serious offense in the United States. The penalty for someone caught "driving under the influence" (DUI) depends on the jury and judge trying the case and the law of the state in which the crime has occurred. If someone is killed in an accident the drunken driver may be charged with murder. Blood tests are given to determine the alcohol level in the blood, coordination tests are given, and breathalyzers test the breath of a suspected drunken driver at the time of the accident.

Never drink any alcohol if you have to drive a vehicle. If

you have had too much to drink, get a taxi or ask somebody to take you home. Be aware that alcoholic products in the United States may not be the same as those in your country. It is thought that only one alcoholic drink is enough to affect one's driving ability immediately after having the drink. One does not have to be drunk to be under the influence of alcohol at the wheel of a car.

Newcomers should know that at a reception or party, a beverage called "punch" may be served that may or may not contain alcohol. Feel free to check whether or not the punch has alcohol as one can unknowingly get drunk and then have the dilemma of getting home without having an accident. If you do not wish to drink alcohol it is quite acceptable to refuse it, and your host will generally not be offended as there are many people in the South who, for religious and other reasons, never drink any alcohol. You may ask for a drink such as Coca-Cola or a fruit juice by asking for a "soft" drink, which does not contain alcohol. "Hard liquor" is the term for an alcoholic drink with a high alcoholic content and includes drinks such as whiskey, brandy, gin, etc.

There is some discussion about having laws against driving under the influence of drugs, especially "recreation" drugs such as marijuana, crack, cocaine, heroin, and others. Some medications taken for illness cause a drowsy effect and make it hazardous to drive a car while taking them. Usually labels on these will warn consumers of these risks. Prescription drugs that have this effect should carry similar labels. Pharmacists are helpful in the South and are willing to discuss the hazards of taking medicine, so feel free to ask them about the effects of medication.

Seat Belts

Some states have laws that require you to wear seat belts; others do not. Often at the state line (the boundary between states) there is a sign that tells you if there is a seat belt law. Statistically you have a much better chance of survival in an accident if you are wearing a seat belt than if you do not; therefore the use of seat belts is highly recommended, even when no law requires it.

A child from newborn up to the age of three years should always be secured in a baby or child car seat for their own safety. In most, if not all, states this is a law. If you fail to comply you can expect to be punished if caught by a policeman or state trooper. Children older than three years should be secured by seat belts for their safety, too.

What to Do if Your Car Breaks Down on the Highway

If your car breaks down, park it well off the road, turn on your hazard lights, and raise the hood of the car. Carry a sign that requests passing motorists to call the police for you and place this in the inside of the back window so that passersby can see it. (These signs can be bought in many general or automotive parts stores.) Then lock all your doors and do not get out of your car unless the police are with you. Unfortunately you have to be cautious about people approaching you when you break down as they may be criminals.

If you see somebody who has broken down on the highway it is courteous for you to inform the nearest police station of the breakdown and its location. The highway patrol will then be informed by radio and will offer assistance to the person who needs help. You should note, however, that some Americans are careless about the use of signs asking for help. Sun screens (cardboard sheets designed to block the sun while a car is parked) sometimes carry messages about needing help. It is not uncommon for this message to appear in the windshield of parked cars when no help is needed. If you see this message in the windshield of a car in a parking lot or parking space along a city street, it is likely that the car owner does not need assistance.

Pedestrians

You need to be constantly on the alert for pedestrians because a vehicle driver is held responsible for harm to a pedestrian, even if the pedestrian is at fault. This is especially true if the pedestrian is a child. While keeping your eyes on the road, be sure to notice the sides of the road for pedestrians. You will be in great trouble if you hit a pedestrian, especially if the person dies.

Pedestrian crossings are parallel lines painted several feet apart across the street. Sometimes they are in the middle of city blocks; other times they are at red lights. Whenever a person steps into one of the pedestrian crossings, motorists are expected to stop to allow that person to cross the street. Driving cautiously and slowly enough to stop at short notice is a good rule of thumb for driving in a town or city as it gives you time to stop suddenly and also enables you to read the road signs.

It is important that you observe the slow speed limits posted on signs in the vicinity of schools. It is an extremely serious offense to injure or kill a child anywhere in America.

Drivers need to drive with special care when motorcyclists and bicyclists are on the road. These people have equal rights on the roads as vehicle drivers but may sometimes be difficult to see.

School Busses

All over the United States, you will notice golden yellow school busses driving children to or from school between about 7 a.m. and 4 p.m. The bus ride is free, and all children may ride the bus if they attend a public school and live a certain distance from that school. Usually there are several points at which the bus will pick up and deliver children in every neighborhood.

If you are driving behind a school bus, you must stop when the bus flashes its lights and stops. You wait until the bus moves forward before you move. You may not pass a stationary school bus. You will notice two red flaps that look like stop signs protruding from the front and back of the bus when children are alighting or exiting the bus. No car may be moving when the bus stops, and even cars travelling in opposite directions have to stop. This law is in effect to give children safety when crossing the road after they get off the bus. Anyone injuring or killing a child in the area of a school bus is in very serious trouble.

Lock Your Car

There are thousands of cars stolen in the United States each year, and the South is not exempt. Insurance companies encourage drivers to lock all car doors when the car is not being used as this discourages, but does not stop, car thieves. Always take your keys out of the ignition when you get out of your car as keys left in the car are an invitation to thieves, and then lock all the doors. Place all valuables and personal items in the locked trunk of your car as any items in the body of the car may encourage thieves to break the car windows to steal your belongings.

Hitchhikers

You may notice people standing on the side of the roads with a small bag asking for a ride. These people are called "hitchhikers" and while some are fine people who would not do anyone harm, it is not recommended that you give such people lifts in your car. Many well-meaning motorists have been robbed or killed by hitchhikers. Also, many hitchhikers have been killed by people picking them up. In some states it is illegal to hitchhike or to give hitchhikers a ride.

Going on a Trip

The United States has many wonderful interstate highways which allow one to travel at a relatively fast speed. There are perimeter roads in many major cities which enable one to change interstate highways quickly and to bypass the towns and cities. Unfortunately, interstates do not usually include the most scenic routes. If you wish to see villages, towns and cities more clearly, choose a route that goes through them. Such routes, however, are often only two-lane highways that slow down one's progress and may sometimes include dangerous roads.

The numerous automobile associations can give you information about planning a trip, provide up-to-date road maps and provide information about hotels. Bookstores and other businesses also sell maps of the United States.

If you plan to go anywhere in the United States in the summer months, it is a good idea to plan your trip carefully and make reservations for hotels in advance. This is especially important if you travel just before or on public holidays. Many tourist attractions close after Labor Day, the first Monday in September, especially in areas of the United States outside the South. Automobile associations have literature which can give you information regarding the times tourist attractions are open.

In the South, you will find many fast food stores open at all hours of the day and night in most towns and cities, but in some rural places few or no food stores or pharmacists are open late at night. It is a good idea to take medicines, some food, and beverages with you, especially if you travel with children.

Some health insurance companies stipulate procedures that should be followed when receiving emergency medical attention on a trip. Should you need to go to an emergency room while you are on a trip, you may need to pay cash or write a check for the services and then seek reimbursement from your insurance company upon your return. A credit card is useful in this situation. Some hospitals will bill the insurance company.

It is not recommended that you carry a lot of cash on you on a trip for fear of losing it to robbers or by accident. Carry enough cash on you to cover your gas and food expenses in case you purchase these at places which do not accept credit cards.

Some hotels will not take cash unless you have some form of identification like a credit card and/or a driver's license. These and other hotels prefer credit cards as this gives them some way of keeping track of people who steal hotel property.

You can use some major credit cards to draw cash from banks along your route if you have the sort of card that enables you to do this. Entrance fees to tourist attractions throughout the United States like museums, amusement parks, etc. all require cash and do not accept credit cards.

Another safe way of taking money on a trip is to buy

"Traveler's Checks" from your bank. You can use these checks as cash on your trip. They are safer than cash, because they can be replaced if you lose them.. Ask the bank clerk to explain clearly how to use traveler's checks and how to have them replaced if they should get lost.

The Harvard Student Agencies at Harvard University (Thayer Hall B, Cambridge, Massachusetts 02138) publishes a book called Let's Go: USA. The Budget Guide to the USA. This book describes the tourist attractions of all fifty states and lists lodgings available at budget prices. Information on this book can be obtained from St. Martin's Press, 175 Fifth Avenue, New York, New York 10010.

Employment

In the United States, the philosophies and practices of management, organization, and performance differ from one organization to another. Thus newcomers should not assume that there is a standard policy all employers follow in the United States.

An organization has specific goals and a specific job that has to be done, and the best person is chosen to do that job. In return for acceptable performance, a wage or salary is paid according to the value of the job to the employer. Employees may also receive "fringe benefits," and a safe working environment, as well as other benefits of employment as stipulated by law. But there is no agreement that the employer will take care of an employee in a personal sense: that he will provide housing, friends, or fun at work. Some companies do provide sports, day care facilities, exercise facilities, and other social and recreational facilities for use outside of work hours, but these are not required by law and are not available for all employees.

An employer expects an employee to be efficient and competent, polite and courteous to supervisors, colleagues, and the public, to be honest in all matters, punctual, responsible and reliable, loyal while employed, appropriately behaved and dressed, and cooperative with other employees. If the employee fails to produce the quality or quantity of work required, the employer is required to warn the employee of his dissatisfaction. If several warnings fail to produce results, the employer may dismiss the employee. There is no sense of loyalty to an employee who does not perform satisfactorily.

An employee may terminate his or her employment if he

or she dislikes the work, feels the pay is inadequate, dislikes the working conditions or the people at work, or if another job with higher pay is offered to him or her. An employee is not expected to have loyalty to an organization if another job is offered to him or her with better conditions and pay.

Some companies will arrange social events or give bonuses especially at Christmas time to express appreciation to employees for work well done. Others provide incentives and rewards for motivating employees to do good work. However, these expressions are left to the discretion of the organization. Governmental agencies are usually forbidden by law to offer bonuses, so many government employees do not enjoy these rewards.

Some organizations employ counselors in their personnel departments to help employees with personal difficulties and problems related to employment. Most large companies provide health insurance and some form of disability insurance.

Job Description and Salary

Usually when an employer interviews a potential employee, the "job description" will be discussed. This is a detailed description of the work and duties expected of an employee and should always be in writing. Every applicant should find out exactly what the job description and salary are before accepting a job. This avoids confusion later. Job descriptions may change as companies expand or change and job descriptions often have to be renegotiated.

Your pay check will be less than the amount you are actually being paid due to deductions. Some of these—such as those for taxes and for social security (see an explanation of this in the chapter on national concerns). Other deductions may be made to cover your health insurance, retirement benefits, and contributions you make to charitable agencies.

Fringe Benefits

Fringe benefits are usually available to full-time employees, although some companies do provide limited fringe benefits to temporary or part-time staff. These usually include: (1) health insurance, which will pay a percentage or all of a doctor's bills, a hospital's bills, and sometimes, but not always, a percentage of medicines; (2) retirement benefits, which provide pensions when employees are too old to work; (3) vacation and sick leave; (4) life insurance; and, (5) sometimes disability insurance. Some companies offer additional benefits not listed above.

Usually employees have to contribute part of the premium for health insurance, and the employer pays part of the premium. Not all companies offer this benefit, and sometimes employees have to arrange their own medical insurance.

Retirement benefits differ from one employer to another. Some companies pay a monthly contribution for employees, and some pay part of the contribution with the employee paying the other part. Both employers and employees have to pay into the Social Security fund, a government fund from which benefits are paid to employees upon retirement.

Most employers give employees two weeks of vacation per year. Some employers reward long service or important employees with more paid vacation time. In addition, employees get paid public vacation days like Christmas, Thanksgiving, etc. Most employers also have to give full-time employees paid time off for illness. The amount of time available for sick leave differs from one company to another. Usually employers allow employees to take vacation time for serious illness or death and funerals in the immediate family. This leave is sometimes given without pay, or it can be taken as paid vacation. Some companies allow employees to take extra time for vacation without pay if such leave is considered in the interests of the employee and employer.

Large companies often give life and disability insurance (for employees who are medically unable to work) as fringe benefits. An amount is deducted from the employee's paycheck to cover part of the premium for this insurance with the balance being paid by the company, or the company may pay the full insurance premium for the employee.

Many employers distribute a handbook that explains benefits such as vacation privileges, medical insurance, disability insurance, etc., as well as the rules and expectations of the company. If you do not get such a book, ask your supervisor to give you a written statement about your benefits so that you will not have any confusion. Most employers will be happy to do this, especially if you explain that English is not your native language and that verbal explanations are sometimes difficult to remember.

Southerners and other Americans generally are kind people, but they do expect a lot from their employees. At the same time, they are usually willing to help their employees in whatever way possible, provided the employee is honest with them.

Understand the Rules

Before being interviewed for a job, it is best to find out as much as possible about the company for which you wish to work. Usually somebody in the community can tell you something about it, and most companies or organizations have some literature that describes their goals and services. Dress neatly and appropriately when you go for an interview. You should also appear enthusiastic about the organization and the position for which you are applying.

When you are hired, make sure you understand the rules of your organization, even if you are employed only part-time. Find out exactly what is expected of you. If you come from a non-Western country, this is especially important as there may be differences in the expectations of employers in this country from those in your homeland.

You need to find out who your immediate supervisor (boss) is and what your relationship to other people in the organization is. You also need to have a clear understanding of what work your boss wants you to do and how, when, and where it should be done. You need to know what the dress code of your organization is; when and where breaks and lunch times should be taken and for how long; what time you should arrive and when you should leave; and when and how vacations should be scheduled.

Punctuality

Most American firms expect their employees to arrive on time, and some companies have time clocks that register the time you arrive and leave. The hours logged in on these time clocks are used to determine how much you will be paid if you are hourly paid. Employers frown on employees who are not punctual, especially those who are habitually late. Similarly, employees are expected to be punctual about observing lunch hours and breaks.

Taking Time Off

Employees should not go home before departure time or leave the premises of their employment without the permission of their supervisors. Many companies do not pay for the time an employee is not working. This applies to time taken off to do personal business. Many employers expect their employees to do personal business on their lunch breaks, after work, or on their vacation. If personal business cannot be done at these times, the problem should be explained to the supervisor, and permission for time off should be obtained. Usually supervisors are understanding and helpful in these situations, but it is possible that you may not be paid for the time you take off, especially if you are hourly paid. Generally, Americans get less vacation time than workers in other industrialized nations.

Time may be taken off for medical reasons, and some companies will take this time out of your sick vacation time. Others will give you this time off with pay or will give you unpaid leave for this purpose. Become familiar with your employer's policy regarding sick leave. If you have children, you should also find out if you can take sick leave to care for a sick child. When you are sick and cannot go to work, phone your supervisor early in the morning every day you are to be absent. Otherwise, you may be "fired" for neglecting your job.

Behavior at Work

While at work, employees are expected to work at their assignments, even in the absence of their supervisors. Because many tasks cannot be checked by superiors, workers are expected to do accurate work at all times. They should not spend much time conversing with other employees, nor should they attend to personal business like writing private letters, talking on the phones to friends, transacting private business, or working at chores that should be done at home, unless their supervisors give them permission to do so. You should not do any work, paid or unpaid, for people other than your employers at your place of employment. Such behavior can be interpreted as theft of an employer's time.

Employees should not use equipment, stationery, office supplies, or anything that belongs to the employer for themselves without permission. Some companies allow employees to use supplies; others consider unauthorized use of such as theft.

Attitudes at Work

Employees are expected to be polite and courteous to the public they serve, their supervisors, and co-workers, who are called colleagues. Employees are expected to obey their supervisors and perform a task exactly as requested by them. However, if an employee is asked to perform an illegal task or to perform a task illegally, he or she should seek advice from a lawyer. Employers and employees can be indicted and charged for breaking a law.

Americans, especially bosses, like everybody to look happy and be enthusiastic, so they prefer employees to be smiling, cheerful people who are cooperative and friendly. It is important to have good relationships with co-workers, to cooperate with them, and to help them when necessary.

Employees are expected to try to prevent personal and family problems from adversely influencing their performance at work. Sometimes, it is expected that employees inform supervisors, in confidence, of an extraordinarily stressful circumstance in their private lives if it could interfere with the employee's performance at work, so the supervisor can make allowance for the employee and adjust the work load to help him.

Decorations in the Office

If you wish to decorate your office, you should do so more or less in the style of others in the organization, but newcomers should discuss decorations with their supervisors first. The more important the person in an organization, the more elaborately is the office decorated. Often an office has a desk, a few chairs, a telephone, reading lamps, some pictures on the wall, sometimes certificates or degrees earned, maybe a coffee maker, and often colored photographs of the official's spouse and children. Photographs of family members should not be overdone. Photographs in offices in the South are usually of living people and do not indicate that the relative is deceased, as is the case in some countries.

Moonlighting

Many Americans "moonlight," which means they go to another job after they have finished working a full day at their primary job. If you feel you cannot live on the salary you earn from your primary job and wish to have a second job, you need to find out if your employer permits employees to work at another job also. Some companies allow this, but some do not. If your employer allows it, you should not accept a second position in a company that is a competitor of your primary employer.

Procedures for Terminating Employment

Employees should find out what procedures their employers have for terminating employment. Some procedures for termination are prescribed by law if an employer wishes to terminate an employee. Usually these consist of warnings by the employer and discussions of the causes of dissatisfaction with the employee. After time has been given for the employee to improve but no improvement has occurred, terminating procedures are put into effect; these are known as "firing."

While employers must usually meet certain guidelines in order to terminate an employee, an employee may resign anytime he or she chooses. People usually resign when they find better-paying work, positions they prefer to their present ones, or when they are unhappy in their present ones. It is courteous and customary to give written, advance notice of your resignation from any position. You should find out how much advance notice you need to give if you wish to resign. This procedure is usually described in the employment contract.

If a written resignation is required, a letter stating the last day you wish to work is necessary. In addition, you should thank the employer for the opportunity of employment given you and express your appreciation for the experience you have gained. You may state the reasons for your resignation, but you may refrain if you wish and may simply state that you have taken other employment. One should avoid being abusive or rude when resigning, even if one's supervisor has been annoying, because you may wish to return to the employer for work in the future, or you may need written or verbal references from the employer. Often a new employer (with the applicant's consent) will consult with the current employer about a potential employee before making a selection.

One should not resign one job before definitely getting other employment. In the United States, it is much easier to get a job if you are employed than if you are unemployed.

E.E.O.C.
(Equal Employment Opportunity Commission)

This is an agency established by the United States (federal) government for the protection of workers. This agency investigates complaints of discrimination in any form, employment practices, working conditions and the working environment, terminations, etc. The agency will reprimand or bring charges against an employer considered to have broken the law in respect to treatment of employees. There is usually no cost to the employee for this service.

Trade Unions

In the United States, trade unions exist to protect the rights of employees who are employed in skilled jobs like electricians, welders, mechanics, technicians of all descriptions, some clerical workers, factory employees, musicians, etc. Trade unions have power to negotiate with employers over wages, fringe benefits, and the conditions of employment. They also act on behalf of their members if any exploitation of workers and unfair or unlawful practices are reported. Sometimes unions will ask their members to "strike," which means they refuse to go to work until satisfactory negotiations are completed.

The largest trade unions have powerful lobbying groups in Washington, where the federal government does its business. The unions' lobbyists will discuss proposed bills to be brought before the representatives and senators in Congress and will try to persuade them to vote in the interests of the unions.

Some jobs require that the worker belong to a specific union. If you apply for a job that requires union membership, you may need to join that union and arrange to pay the monthly or yearly membership fees in order to hold that position of employment.

Newcomer Supervisors

If you are a newcomer and have a supervisory position or any other position that requires you to give instructions to co-workers, you probably will benefit from an understanding of how Southern workers like to be treated. This is especially important if you work with women and come from a country in which women are considered inferior to men in the workplace.

Southern people expect to be greeted in a friendly manner each day, requested to perform tasks in a polite, considerate manner, and thanked when a task is completed. The fact that an employee gets paid for performing an assignment does not remove the necessity for expressing appreciation. If an employee does extra work or work outside of regular hours, he or she expects some expression of appreciation. Southern people also appreciate receiving compliments when they have completed a task well or have exceeded the expectations of an employer. Some Southern employers are generous about complimenting their staff members; others are not.

There are several ways in which institutions show appreciation to employees. Many workplaces observe "appreciation days" such as "Employee of the Month Day," "Secretary's Day," "Boss' Day," or "Awards Day" on which employees are honored for length of service, etc. On these occasions, the administrators and supervisors of institutions express appreciation in a suitable manner. A gift, flowers, plants, dinners, or luncheons are examples of expressions of appreciation to co-workers who make the workplace efficient and pleasant.

At Christmas time and on birthdays, some people recognize their co-workers in a similar manner. Often supervisors will give their employees gifts; others will only give their secretaries gifts. These expressions are not obligatory; they are left to the discretion of the people involved.

In general, Southern women, and for that matter, all American women, in the workplace do not appreciate being spoken to in a paternalistic or a condescending manner. Women employees do not perceive themselves as servants or inferior to men in their workplace and resent being given orders in an abrupt, impolite manner. In their relationships with their supervisors, women perceive themselves as co-workers or members of a team. They expect to be treated kindly, courteously, and appreciatively, even if they are paid salaries.

Although the ideal has not yet been fully achieved, the goal of American women is that they will be perceived and remunerated as the equals of men in the economic sector. The male newcomer who looks upon a female co-worker as inferior, even if her position is ranked lower than his in status, is inviting a troubled relationship. A newcomer, in our opinion, should never appear dictatorial and demanding to any Southern employee.

 Seldom do Southern employees articulate their expectations of an employer or a supervisor. This makes it difficult for newcomers but no less important to learn what the employee and employer expectations are. Usually the personnel director of your institution will be able to help you relate to employees effectively.

It is important for newcomers whose native language is not English to realize that American employees do not always understand a foreign accent, idiom, or sense of humor. One needs to give **instructions** very clearly and politely to avoid confusion and mistakes.

A newcomer should avoid giving the impression that employees who have communication problems with him or her are unintelligent, uncooperative, or incompetent for misunderstanding instructions. If newcomers gain a reputation for being unpopular, impolite, or unreasonable bosses, they will have problems eliciting pleasant cooperation from co-workers and employees or getting promoted.

Americans and Work

Work is very important to Americans, and most take pride in their work. Americans are expected to be dedicated workers, prepared to work long, hard hours. Americans (and most other Westerners) tend to evaluate each other by the jobs they do, so it is common to hear people ask each other what they "do" for a living when they are first introduced.

Today, perhaps more than ever, Americans love to work and expect great rewards both material and emotional from their occupations. Most Americans, therefore, want their jobs to be interesting, rewarding, and, if possible, challenging and even entertaining.

Americans work long hours. The average American works about forty hours a week, but many (or most) professionals work much longer hours; many work more than sixty hours per week. Some people feel many Americans are now too work-conscious and are neglecting their homes, spouses, and children. Competitive organizations place much stress on their employees, as they are very demanding, and rarely give them more than two or three weeks of paid vacation. Most Americans are considered "stressed" at work—and often at home—as they try to balance the many demands placed on them.

While many workers do enjoy their work, some do not. And while many professions and jobs are fun and rewarding, many are not. To compensate for boring, unsatisfying jobs many Americans devote time to hobbies, to forming friendships, and to social, religious, civic, sports, and political activities.

Social Situations and What to Do When...

Every newcomer is faced with social situations that are confusing. This section attempts to deal with some of the ones you are most likely to encounter.

Public Behavior

Anger

Most Southerners do not approve of talking too loudly in public, pushing people out of one's way, or bumping against others, except by accident when it is obligatory to apologize by saying "excuse me." They are not comfortable about expressing anger, even in a civilized way, and especially in public. They frown on public displays of anger, verbal or physical. Of course, this does not imply that violence does not happen; it certainly does. But friends and family members are expected to argue or fight in the privacy of their own homes. Similarly, sarcastic and hurtful remarks addressed to others in public are considered to be in poor taste.

Speaking in a Foreign Language

One should never speak in a foreign language in the presence of people who do not understand that language. This rule can be broken if the conversation takes places out of the hearing of English speakers or when an explanation has to be made to somebody who has only limited or no knowledge of English.

Coughing, Sneezing, and Burping

When one coughs or sneezes, one should turn one's head away from other people and cover the mouth with either one's fist or a hand holding a handkerchief. Southerners do not blow their noses in front of other people, unless this cannot be avoided. They usually go to a rest room for this purpose. Nowhere in the United States does one burp in public. When this is unavoidable, one should always say "excuse me" afterwards. Burping after a meal is not considered a compliment to the cook!

Interrupting

Southerners do not approve of interrupting somebody else's conversation; if they need to talk to somebody already engaged in a conversation, they wait until the speakers pause, excuse themselves, and then proceed with their statement. The only time one should burst in on a conversation is when there is an emergency.

Boasting

It is considered bad manners in the South to talk about oneself or one's own achievements or those of one's family too much. If one talks about oneself at all, it has to be done very discreetly and usually in response to a question. However, if asked a direct question about these things, one may respond honestly, but one is not supposed to make anyone feel inferior by exalting oneself.

Visiting Friends

In most parts of the United States, most people prefer friends to phone to inquire whether or not a visit would be convenient. This does not mean that one cannot stop for a moment at a friend's home to deliver or collect something, but a phone call gives the host or hostess time to tidy the home and himself or herself. Should one drop in like this, one should not stay too long to avoid interrupting the friend's schedule. This is not a hard and fast rule, however.

When visiting friends, one should arrive about five to ten minutes after the time stated in the invitation. It is considered inconvenient to arrive before the time for which one has been invited, but one should not arrive more than ten minutes late. One should be sensitive about leaving a friend's home, too. Usually an hour or two after a meal, it is appropriate to leave. It is wise to ask the host or hostess what time one should leave when the invitation is first extended. There is no hard and fast rule, but if the host or hostess seems to be tired, it is time to leave!

When visiting friends, one should offer to help with the kitchen chores after a meal, even though the hostess often declines the offer. When one arrives, it is also customary to offer to help the hostess with last-minute meal preparations, but the offer is usually declined.

Visiting Sick Friends

Southerners are concerned about their friends and family members who are in the hospital and usually try to visit them at least once while they are there. One should visit sick friends during the hospital visiting hours and should not take children to a hospital. Visiting hours are expected to be observed, and if one has to visit outside of visiting hours, the permission of the head nurse on the floor should always be obtained before entering a patient's room.

Often people will take sick friends a gift of flowers, plants, or fruit. When one visits a sick friend, one should be cheerful, and visits to the hospital should be brief, maybe just fifteen minutes. Do not sit on the patient's bed or make noise in the patient's room or in the hospital hallways.

If one cannot visit a sick friend in the hospital or if the friend is sick at home, one can send a **"get well"** card. Employers, professors, and friends all appreciate receiving cards when they are sick, but do not expect to receive a thank you note for your card. Close friends and relatives take food to the home where someone is sick.

Queuing or Standing in Line

It is quite common to stand in line (or a queue) at amusement parks, fast food stores, movies, theaters, airports, stores, etc. One should always take a position at the end of the line and should never sneak into a space ahead of others, for this is considered very bad manners. In some places, a little machine dispenses numbered tickets. Since customers are served in numerical order, there is no need to stand in line in these places. Unfortunately these machines are not always available.

Borrowing

At times it may be necessary to borrow friends' goods. Southerners are generally happy to lend friends their possessions but they expect these to be returned promptly and in good repair. If a borrowed item is broken, the owner usually appreciates an apology and an offer to have it replaced or repaired.

Making and Keeping Appointments

Americans are very conscious of time and they hate wasting time; they are very busy at their places of employment and have schedules they need to follow each day. Often business people are too busy to be interrupted, so if one needs to see somebody at his or her place of employment, it is polite to make an appointment through the secretary first. One generally asks the secretary how much time is available for the appointment, and it is important to arrive and leave punctually. Sometimes the business person cannot keep the appointment punctually, so you may have to wait a few minutes in the waiting area before your appointment begins. You are expected to understand that this delay is unavoidable, but you should never be late for an appointment as this is considered bad manners. Doctors are notorious for keeping patients waiting.

Questions One Should Never Ask

Newcomers need to know that while one can ask a Southerner or any American most questions, there are certain questions that should not be asked.

It is impolite to ask questions about people's financial savings, or investments. One should not ask questions about anybody's sex life or practices. Some people do not like being asked what religion they follow or to which political party they belong. One may ask what work they do, where they grew up, what schools or universities they attended, if their parents are still living, if they have children and grandchildren, where they live, and what food, sports, hobbies, music, books, and movies they enjoy.

In addition, the following topics should be avoided:

Age: Americans do not ask each other their ages. It is only permissible to ask the age of a child or young person up till about the age of fifteen years. When people are over eighty, they are sometimes happy to be asked their ages and are proud to respond, especially if they look younger than they are and are in good health.

Weight: In the United States, people are sensitive and embarrassed about being overweight. One should never ask anyone what he or she weighs. Nor should one ask an overweight person why he or she does not lose weight. In fact, one should never make any comment about anybody's weight—over or under weight.

Salaries and Prices: Most Americans do not like to discuss their salaries or wages with friends, unless they have a specific reason, and they do not like being asked what they earn. Many employers ask their employees never to discuss their salaries with other employees.

Sometimes Americans will volunteer the price of a recently purchased item, but unless one is talking to a relative or very close friend, one should not ask the price directly. This includes the price of a home, car, clothes, jewelry, appliances, and furniture, etc. One may ask general questions about prices but not about a specific item. For example, you may ask what the price of refrigerators is, but not the cost of one in a friend's home. Sometimes Americans will boast about the price they paid for some item, especially if they got a bargain.

Illness: Some Southerners are embarrassed about some illnesses, especially those pertaining to elimination or sexual functions. This is hard to believe considering the numerous television commercials for laxatives! For example, if a woman has had a hysterectomy, sometimes the husband is vague about the nature of her surgery. If somebody tells you that he or she or a relative is ill but does not name the illness, it is best not to ask specific questions. Express sympathy by saying something like: "I am sorry to hear that and I hope your spouse's illness is not serious and that he or she improves quickly." Generally, you should not ask too many details about an illness. Bowel movements and bladder functions are not considered polite conversation topics in the South, and one speaks of going to "the bathroom," "the restroom," "the little boys' room," or the "little girls' room" when referring to these activities.

Bereavement: When somebody dies, one should sympathize with the bereaved family members by simply saying that one feels sorry that the death has occurred. Unless the bereaved person volunteers details about the death, one should not ask questions, especially if the death resulted from AIDS, suicide, or murder or involved alcohol or other drugs. One question is usually valid: Is there anything I can do to help?

Family Problems: When somebody goes through a crisis such as losing a job, suicide, murder, losing money, divorce, imprisonment, or such, you should not ask for details. Often the family members experiencing the crisis will want to speak about the situation and may volunteer information and share details, but friends (except family and close friends) should not ask questions about the crisis. You should, however, let the friend know that you are sorry about the sad circumstance and that you would like to help if possible. This can be done either verbally or by way of a short written note or greeting card sent through the mail.

Topics to Avoid

Certain topics arouse extreme emotions in Americans, particularly when a group includes individuals of differing opinions. These include such nationally topical issues as abortion and gun ownership. You will see protestors and demonstrators near clinics that perform abortion, and individuals and groups on both sides of the issue often hold rallies in public places. Although the issue of gun ownership does not attract demonstrators to gun stores, it, too, is a controversial issue.

In some parts of the country, activists demonstrate on behalf of "animal rights." These groups often gather at research institutions or fur stores. However, most Americans are not strongly opinionated on this issue.

Compliments

Southerners are often quick to compliment people because it is considered good manners to do so. One may be complimented on one's appearance, clothes, achievements, possessions, children, and a variety of other things. There is no need to be embarrassed or to deny the compliment; you need only say "thank you."

If a Southerner pats one on the arm or strokes a child's head, this should be considered a compliment. It is definitely not an insult, as is the case in some countries. In the South, newcomers can generally assume that any personal interaction between themselves and Southerners is without malice or rudeness. If one feels insulted, it is probably a misinterpretation of Southern culture because Southerners will rarely deliberately insult anyone.

Refusing Food

If somebody offers you food you do not like, you may say something like "no thank you, I am not yet used to all the wonderful food here." You may wish to explain that you are slowly getting used to American food and that you hope to enjoy everything in time. You do not have to eat food you dislike; Americans are not easily offended by a simple explanation. If you do want something, say yes when the first offer is made. Americans will take your answer literally and will not continue to make the offer once you refuse.

When to Say Good Morning (or Afternoon or Evening), Hello and Hi!

People over forty in the South are more formal and traditional than younger people whom many newcomers find uncomfortably casual. As a broad guide, it would be considered polite to say "good morning (afternoon or evening)" or "hello" to older people and people one does not know well. "Hi" is the least formal way of greeting people and is often used when greeting young people and close friends of any age.

Impolite Statements

Generally one does not make insulting statements to another person face to face. For instance, one should never tell anyone that he or she is a "liar," even if one knows that person is lying. A statement like this is considered very bad manners and could result in your being sued, especially if you are incorrect in your statement. If one has to respond, one should say something vague like: "I did not understand you to mean that" or "that is not how I see the situation." Similarly, one should not say someone is "drunk" for the same reasons. One may say "to me, that person seemed to be drunk."

One should not criticize another person's behavior anywhere in the Western world unless invited to do so. If one is asked for advice, one may give it, but advice or criticism is seldom welcomed, except in unusual circumstances, when it is requested.

When a friend tells you about future plans and past or present actions, you should show much interest but not ask personal questions. For instance, if your friend who already has two cars tells you he is buying a third, your response should simply be something like: "I am glad about this for you" or "That is interesting and I am happy you are able to do this" or "I hope your plans work out." One should never make comments like "Why are you so extravagant?" or "You really do not need to do this." Furthermore, one should not give one's opinion about whether you think this action is good or bad.

Social Situations

If you are **given a gift** by a Southerner you should accept it and thank the giver, adding that you like the gift, that you are glad to have it, and that you appreciate the warm feelings the gift represents. It is customary in the United States to open the gift in the presence of the giver whenever possible. One should not refuse to accept a gift, nor should one say that the gift is not necessary or not needed, unless there is some definite reason to believe the gift is given as a trap or an obligation. In this case, the gift should be politely refused. Generally, Southerners are generous and wish to help newcomers with gifts, especially when they are settling in.

When **somebody says something nice** about you, try not to get embarrassed. Just say "thank you." You may also feel free to say nice things about Southerners; they will appreciate sincere comments.

When **somebody invites you for a meal** or to visit their homes, just say "thank you" and ask when and what time they have in mind, if you wish to accept the invitation. You should not tell your friends that they do not need to entertain you. If you cannot or do not wish to accept the invitation, just say "thank you" and explain that you are unable to accept. You do not need to explain your reasons for refusing. Do not ask your friend why you are being invited, because he or she may be embarrassed or confused by this question. If you need to know, simply ask "is this invitation for a special occasion?" You may offer to bring a dish of food, but this is not expected of you.

When **being introduced** to another person take the right hand of that person, if it is held out, and shake it once up and down. Usually men shake hands when being introduced or when seeing each other after a separation. If a woman extends her right hand to greet you, then you shake her hand, but do not extend your hand first if you are a man. In the South a woman determines whose hand she will shake. Usually women do not shake each others' hands except in a formal or business situation. One need only say "I am pleased to meet you" or "It is so nice to meet you."

When somebody says **"thank you"** for something you have done, you may respond by saying "you're welcome." In the South when one thanks somebody else, one should say "thank you" and add "I appreciate it." Many people omit the "thank you" and just say "I appreciate it." Many Southerners under the age of forty use "appreciate it" more than "thank you." At the end of a social time with friends, one usually says "I enjoyed it"when saying good-bye.

In the 1990s, **when interacting with people over forty-five** in the South, one should be more polite than when communicating with younger people who are usually very informal and casual.

When **receiving instructions** at work, school, or elsewhere, one need not feel embarrassed if one does not understand. Ask questions until you do understand. Southerners use the expressions "feel free to ..." or "do not hesitate to call me ..." by which they invite one to ask for further help.

If you need directions about **finding some place**, inside a building or outdoors, do not hesitate to ask. Most Southerners are happy to help and will give you direct and honest answers. If they don't know how to direct you, they will usually tell you to ask somebody else. Rarely will anybody in the United States play a joke on a newcomer by giving wrong answers to a question.

If you find people do not understand you **when you speak English**, keep little cards and a small pen in your pocket. Write the word you wish to make understood on the card and show this to the person with whom you are talking. This will save a lot of time and confusion. When **trying to find an item** in a store write the item on a card and show it to a clerk who will then be able to direct you to it.

Occasionally somebody will laugh or smile when you pronounce a word differently from the way it is pronounced in the South. This is usually done in a friendly way and is not meant to humiliate you. The best way to handle this is to laugh and then afterwards ask that person to explain how the word should be pronounced. As a newcomer, remember that many of your actions and attitudes are as humorous to Southerners as theirs are to you!

Expressing Appreciation and Saying "Thank You"

Correctly expressing thanks and appreciation is very important. Southerners expect a short written thank you on small notes for gifts, entertainment, or favors. **Thank you notes** are supposed to be hand-written on nice writing paper or a card. The note should thank the giver and describe the gift or event. In addition, some comment should be made to indicate that the gift or event was appreciated.

A thank you note should always be written when gifts have been received for weddings, baby, and bridal showers, birthday parties, or receptions and "teas" or other events that have been given in one's honor. If one receives a birthday or Christmas gift from a close friend or relative, a thank you note is not necessary if you open the gift in front of the giver and express thanks immediately. In some instances, a phone call to express thanks is in order, especially if thanks are being expressed for an evening's entertainment or a meal. Usually a thank you note needs to be mailed within a week of having received the favor.

If you are **invited to a restaurant** and your host pays for you or you go to a home for dinner, it is always a good idea to phone the next day to thank your host, especially if your host or hostess is an older person. This is not absolutely essential, but recommended.

If you are **invited to spend a week-end or to have dinner in the home** of an acquaintance for the first time, you may take take a small gift: flowers, fruit, chocolate, a book, or something useful from your home country. Your Southern host or hostess will not expect a gift, so you need not feel obligated to take anything, although a gift is appreciated. You should compliment your friends on their home and the good food they served.

It is best not to give gifts of food from your home country to Southerners unless you are sure that they really do enjoy it. Something you think tastes wonderful does not necessarily appeal to Americans, just as you may not enjoy all American foods. Before giving treasured articles from your homeland, make sure these are enjoyed by Southerners because not all Southerners like items from other cultures on their persons or in their homes, unless, of course, the articles have already been accepted as part of American decorating.

Southerners appreciate a **gift as a way of expressing thanks**, but keep the gift rather small in monetary value so that your Southern friend will not feel that you are trying to "repay" him or her. Also, you don't want your friend to feel obligated to return a gift to you.

Many Southerners express appreciation to friends by inviting them to have dinner either in their homes or at a restaurant. But, of course, you would never do this to a public official (government officer or employee) in exchange for a favor.

Southerners enjoy sending **greeting cards** for Christmas, birthdays, Easter, illnesses, graduation, trips, and just to keep in touch. Generally, you need not write thank you letters or make phone calls for greeting cards, unless they contain a gift. You do not even need to phone to thank the sender, but, you may, if you wish, thank the sender if you should see him or her shortly after receiving the card.

Usually at Christmas, cards are reciprocated by friends, and the general rule is that you send cards to all your friends, acquaintances, and business associates to whom you would not feel obligated to give a gift. Many people keep a list, sometimes only mentally, of those who sent them cards and then return the favor the following Christmas, but thank you letters or cards are not deemed necessary. It is not obligatory to send Christmas cards. This is entirely a voluntary gesture and if one cannot afford to send cards, do not send any.

Birthday cards are extremely popular in the United States and often take the place of presents between acquaintances and distant relatives. Cards to acknowledge and celebrate other happy occasions—the birth of a baby, graduation from high school or college, weddings, and anniversaries—are also sent by many Americans to their friends and families.

Bribes and Gifts

In the United States, it is customary to **exchange gifts** on special occasions like birthdays and Christmas with family members, friends, relatives, teachers, colleagues, and other associates. But offering gifts to any law enforcement agent (policeman, state trooper, etc.), politician, government employee, or other public employee as gifts for favors is considered a serious crime (known as bribery) in the United States and is punishable by law.

Some newcomers come from countries where it is acceptable to give gifts to somebody in authority in return for a favor. But in the United States, one should never offer any public official a gift for doing something for one, nor should one offer to do a favor in return for help received. Obviously, bribery takes place in the United States, but, even so, it is considered illegal.

Employees are not permitted to receive gifts from contractors or business associates for arranging to obtain contracts or business for them. This is known as a "kickback" and is considered a bribe. Newcomers in employment should be careful not to accept gifts that could be considered bribes.

It is acceptable to give small gifts of appreciation to people one pays for services or who have already rendered services to one without pay (but who are not public officials). Christmas is a good time to do this. For instance, school children often take their teachers small gifts at Christmas time, and employers and employees often exchange gifts. Sometimes only the employers or supervisors will give gifts to their staff members without expecting gifts in return.

Sometimes, though not often, people give gifts of appreciation to neighbors, friends, colleagues, or teachers for help received, especially if the help was given without charge. Such gifts should not be expensive; Southerners appreciate the thought the gift conveys and do not give many gifts as tokens of appreciation, so they do not expect gifts from others. Southerners do not feel comfortable about accepting expensive gifts from people other than family members, as they do not like feeling under any obligation to people. Usually, a generously worded thank you note is all that is necessary for favors received. A trusted friend will be willing to guide you if you are in doubt.

Introductions, Greetings, and the Use of Titles

Each country has different customs about how to meet and greet people, initially and after absences, and how to behave in the presence of the opposite sex. Much of this discussion in this section does not apply to other regions of the United States and deals specifically with Southern customs.

When **friends meet** each other **after an absence**, short or long, the men generally shake hands. Sometimes Southern men will pat each other on the shoulder, if they are close friends, as a gesture of warmth and friendship. In some cases, though not often, a father and son might put their arms around each others' shoulders in an embrace. Sometimes this might happen between friends when they are overjoyed.

Men are reserved in physical contact with other men and do not kiss each other on the cheeks or lips, nor do they ever walk down a street holding hands. Generally, if they do hold hands, it indicates that the men have a homosexual relationship or that they are just doing something unusual as a prank.

It is different with women. Southern women will show their affection for each other by hugging each other warmly when meeting after an absence. They might even kiss each other on the cheeks, but seldom on the lips. Women do not generally walk hand in hand, except in rare instances, such as a mother and small daughter, friends meeting after a long absence, or women in a lesbian relationship.

Southern men and women freely express their pleasure when meeting each other. It is common for Southern men to hug other men's wives when greeting them. Generally kissing on the lips is considered a sign of a relationship involving some commitment of two people, but recently it is becoming a little more acceptable for men and women not married to each other to kiss on the lips when they meet in public. Such expressions of friendship are considered proper if they take place in front of the spouses of the people concerned or in public. If physical contact takes place in private, this is considered unacceptable and is a symptom of marital infidelity.

Often people hug or kiss **when parting** after a social evening or situation. However, there are no rules about this, and many people have no form of physical contact when they say goodbye to each other.

When Southerners talk to each other **while standing up**, they generally stand about two to three feet away from each other. Southerners often touch each other on the shoulder or arm when they talk. Men should never touch any sexual area of a woman's body in public (or in private without her permission), and a woman tends to refrain from touching a man in the same way. However, when men and women flirt, many kinds of light touching are practiced by both men and women, but this is usually subtle, and newcomers unaccustomed to the culture of the South are advised not to imitate this behavior.

Americans have the reputation for being informal people

who love titles but do not enjoy **using titles**. This stereotype is misleading in the South, and newcomers have to learn when to use a title and when to refrain because Southerners are a little more traditional and formal than many other Americans.

Sometimes, younger Southerners are less formal about using their own titles or calling others by their titles. They generally use only first names from the time they are introduced to each other and often do not even tell each other that they have titles. People over forty-five years of age in the South are more traditional and more formal and tend to use titles more than young people.

In a **social setting**, people are introduced to each other by their first names (Christian names) announced first and then their last names (surnames). For example, you may be introduced to Anne White and Henry Black at a party, and you may call them by their first names.

In a **business or professional situation**, you will most likely be introduced to somebody with the mention of their titles and full names. For instance, you might be introduced to Dr. Anne White and Professor Henry Black. You should call them Dr. White and Professor Black until they invite you to call them by their first names.

Generally, the higher up the hierarchy in an organization a man or woman is, the less likely one is to call him or her by their first name, unless and until, one is given permission by that person to do this. It is also common at the time of this writing for employees to call their supervisors by their title and their last names. For example, a college professor may be called Dr. or Professor White by his or her secretary and the students, unless the administration of that college wants to create a casual atmosphere. Similarly, a nurse working with doctors is likely to call the doctor by his medical title and his last name, unless invited to do otherwise.

One is generally on safe Southern ground when one uses a title. This avoids being considered too familiar or "pushy." The usual titles are: "Mister" (Mr.) for a man over twelve years of age, "Miss" for a young lady over twelve who is not married, although many young women prefer being called "Ms." (pronounced "miz") as this is a title which does not indicate whether the female is married or not. "Missus" (Mrs.) is the title given a married women of any age. "Doctor" is used when addressing a medical doctor (physician) or a person who has earned an academic doctorate.

"Professor" is the title a teacher in a university or college is given. There are three levels of professors in the United States: assistant professor, the most junior professor who gets paid the least; associate professor, the professor who has more experience and, usually a doctoral degree (though there are exceptions); and full professor, one who has a doctoral degree and several years experience and service in an academic setting. There are a very few academic fields in which one cannot earn a doctorate and one uses the title "professor" regardless of the type of professor. However, it is more usual to refer to a professor as "Doctor" than "Professor", if he or she has a doctorate. Some university teachers are called instructors, especially if they do not have doctorates.

There are few other professions and fields of business where one uses titles. For example, one does not refer to a president of a commercial or industrial organization as "President Black," though this might happen occasionally. Nor does one refer to the manager of a departmental store as "Manager White." In these cases one can say "Mr. Black, President of the Holiday Organization".

In the South, parents often teach their children to have respect and affection for older people by giving them titles. For instance, it is common for small children and young people to refer affectionately to an older lady as "Miz Ann" (not Mrs. White or Ann) or an older man as "Mr. Eric" (not Mr. Black or Eric).

In conclusion, if you are ever in doubt about how to address a Southerner, use the title you know. If this is not acceptable to him or her, you will be invited to call your acquaintance by his or her first name, and you will not have offended anybody. Whenever you are invited to use a first name, you should always do so. However, a newcomer need not be too concerned about these matters as most Southerners are understanding about differences in cultures.

Invitations

One can receive invitations in two ways in America: a friend or acquaintance can either speak to you in person or over the phone and invite you to an event or you can receive a printed card with all the details through the mail. Usually more formal invitations are received through the mail.

In the South when couples make arrangements for social occasions, the wives usually get together to discuss the details, as married men do not usually invite friends for dinner or to a restaurant. Unmarried people have no rules about who does the inviting.

Invitations can be for showers, weddings, birthday parties, receptions, dinners, luncheons, banquets, and parties. Usually the card will tell you who is giving the event, where, when, and at what time it takes place. At the bottom of the card you may find the letters printed "R.S.V.P". This is an abbreviation of the French "respondez s'il vous plait" which simply means "please reply." Sometimes a little card is included in the envelope with the invitation, and on this you should indicate whether or not you will be attending and then return it through the mail to the person inviting you. Sometimes you will be expected to give your reply over the phone.

Often the invitation card will simply say: "Regrets only." This means that if you wish to attend the event, you need not reply to the invitation and the host or hostess will assume that you are coming, but if you do not choose to attend, you should phone the host or hostess as soon as possible and decline.

Once you have stated that you are attending a function, you should make every effort to attend because your host has paid for refreshments for you. If you are prevented at the very last minute from attending, you should phone your host as soon as possible and apologize for the unforeseen circumstance preventing you from attending the event.

Sometimes the invitation card will tell you what to wear to the occasion. If you are to be semi-formally dressed, for example, a business suit for men and a semi-formal short dress and stockings for women are appropriate. Formal wear, tuxedos for men and long formal ball gowns, is seldom required in the South and usually is clearly stated on the printed invitation when it is. If in doubt about how to dress, call the hostess and ask.

Friends sometimes invite people to their homes for cook-outs, suppers or dessert, and they will suggest informal wear. This means men should dress casually in slacks, shirt, and no tie; women should wear blouses and skirts or slacks or informal dresses.

The guiding rule in the South about most things is: when in doubt, ask! This is especially true when you are in doubt about whether an invitation includes your children or not. Do not take children unless you are sure they are included in the invitation.

Holidays

The most important holidays that virtually all Americans celebrate are Christmas (December 25), New Year's Day (January 1), Thanksgiving (last Thursday in November), Independence Day (July 4), Labor Day (first Monday in September), and Memorial Day (last Monday in May). Businesses and some stores close for these holidays, although many department and other stores take advantage of the holidays and have sales. Generally, employers like to give their employees these days as paid vacations to celebrate with their families.

Some special days are observed that are not paid holidays. These include birthdays of some past presidents and other famous Americans, as well as Veterans' Day, Mother's Day, Father's Day, sometimes Memorial Day, Halloween, and Easter.

Christmas
This season in December is considered one of the most important celebrations in the Christian calendar because it celebrates the birth of Jesus. However, it has become a national holiday in the United States and is also observed as a time of gift-giving by many who are not Christians. It is becoming increasingly a secular, as well as religious, holiday.

In the South, most Christian churches spend the month

of December celebrating Christmas. Christmas music and hymns, called carols, are sung in Sunday schools and churches. The emphasis of the services is one of joy and gratitude, and there is a great deal of music. Many churches and organizations have musical concerts and plays with Christmas themes.

After Thanksgiving in November, some people decorate their homes for Christmas with holly wreaths, candles, bouquets of green branches from trees, bunches of ribbon, Christmas ornaments and a Christmas tree. The tree is a triangular-shaped green tree, real or artificial, which is decorated with colored balls, streamers, tiny electric lights and small ornaments in a variety of shapes. Sometimes artificial trees are colored white.

Gifts are part of the Christmas tradition in most Western countries, based on the Christian belief that God gave his son Jesus as a gift to the world. In the South, brightly colored gifts with pretty bows are placed under the tree for friends and relatives. These gifts are usually distributed sometime on Christmas Day or Christmas Eve, depending on the preference of the family.

One of the stories of Christmas, based on a centuries-old event in Europe, which young children are taught, is that of Santa Claus (in England called "Father Christmas"). He is portrayed as a good and happy old man with a large stomach, white hair, and a long white beard, who wears a red suit, and rides along the streets of towns and cities on a sleigh drawn by nine strong reindeer. On Christmas Eve, he loads his sleigh with toys, goes down the chimney stacks of the homes, and leaves the gifts under the Christmas trees or in gaily colored stockings that are hung on the mantels of many American homes. On Christmas Day, children open their gifts when they wake up in the morning.

Most families meet with relatives and close friends for dinner sometime around midday or at night on Christmas, day, though some families have their dinner on the night before Christmas. Dinner in the South usually consists of roast turkey with dressing (a dish made from cornmeal and celery), baked ham, sometimes with a sweet glaze, sweet potatoes, and many different vegetables. For dessert many people eat pumpkin pie and/or pecan pie with whipped cream or ice cream, and many other fancy pies.

Decorations for Christmas are usually colored red and dark green with silver or gold highlights.

Many places of employment have special parties for their employees. Some employees receive gifts or bonuses that are usually cash gifts.

Airplanes, busses, some trains, and highways are full at Christmas time as many people try to go home for Christmas. Make reservations early if you plan to make a trip at this time of year. Christmas is essentially a family time in the United States and family members travel great distances to be together.

Many people have parties at Christmas, and many serve alcohol. There is always a problem of drinking and driving over the Christmas and New Year holidays. In some Southern cities, taxi drivers offer free service to people who have drunk too much alcohol. Newcomers need to be aware of this danger over the Christmas and New Year holidays.

Easter

Easter is the most important festival of the Christian Church and is observed on a Sunday in either March or April each year. There are seldom any paid holidays associated with Easter, although some companies give employees the Friday before Easter as a vacation day. Unlike Europe and the British Commonwealth, Good Friday is not observed as a religious holiday in the South, and only a few churches offer Good Friday services. Some churches observe a Maundy service on the Thursday night before Easter.

Christians believe that Jesus Christ, the Son of God, died after being nailed to a wooden cross on the Friday before Easter. After Jesus died, he was buried in a stone tomb, but he came back to life again on Sunday, talked with his followers, proving that he is God, alive forever. For this reason, Easter is the most important and happiest celebration for Christians everywhere in the world. Jesus' return to life is called the "resurrection".

On Easter Sunday churches are usually decorated with white "Easter lilies," often in memory of a deceased relative.

The service is usually joyous, with lively music. The sermon is generally encouraging and focuses on the Christian's belief in the immortality and cleansing of the soul.

Easter is also celebrated with nonreligious symbolism. Some people give each other chocolate Easter eggs or hen's eggs that are boiled and dyed bright colors. Children enjoy Easter egg hunts, where adults hide Easter eggs in the yard or in the house. The children are expected to "hunt" and keep the eggs they find. Many schools and children's organizations arrange a "hunt" either a few days before Easter Sunday or on Easter Sunday itself. The eggs symbolize the "new life" of the resurrection of Jesus Christ.

Many people celebrate with a dinner on Easter Sunday. Often this is a family affair, and married children with their children visit grandparents, or family members meet in the home of one of the brothers or sisters. Sometimes each family member brings a "covered dish," which is food brought in a dish with a lid, which can be reheated at the host's house.

Easter is the time of the year when most people try to get new summer clothes. Few people wear hats to church on Easter Sunday anymore, but years ago women would go to church with a new "Easter bonnet," and sometimes little Southern girls still wear Easter bonnets.

The colors for Easter decorations are white and green for religious worship and purple and yellow for Easter eggs and home decorations.

Thanksgiving

In 1620 a group of English settlers, called Pilgrims, arrived on the coast of Massachusetts, after trying to reach Virginia, but having been blown off course. Although they tried to farm, a severe winter brought crop failures. Many of the settlers died, but those who survived were taught by a tribe of native American Indians to farm and to prepare native vegetables. At the end of the summer, after the crops had been harvested, the Pilgrims and Indians met together to celebrate their survival. They cooked a dinner of wild turkey, pumpkin, corn and other indigenous food. At the celebration, the Pilgrims thanked God for supplying their physical needs and thanked the Indians for introducing them to new methods of survival.

Today, Americans observe the fourth Thursday of November as a day for remembering the goodness of God and the blessing of family and friends. In the South, people get together in families and have a meal together, usually at noon or in the afternoon. The meal consists of food resembling the food eaten by the original observers of Thanksgiving: turkey, corn, sweet potato and other seasonal vegetables. For dessert they eat pumpkin pie with cream or ice cream.

Thanksgiving decorations are colored in orange, brown, yellow, and dark green. Indian corn and a variety of squashes are often used to decorate the home and workplace for Thanksgiving.

Memorial Day

On the last Monday of May, Memorial Day pays tribute to the Americans killed in all the wars in which the United States has been involved. This holiday is not a paid holiday for many people in the South, but some people who get this vacation day celebrate it with picnics and cookouts as the spring weather is usually pleasant. Some people attend services and parades to honor Americans killed in past wars. The American flag is often seen displayed in the streets and outside some private homes.

Labor Day

Labor Day, the first Monday in September, celebrates the birth of the Labor movement, which began about a hundred years ago in the United States. Today, Labor Day honors all working Americans. As it is the last holiday during warm weather, many people go on picnics or go out of town for a long weekend vacation before children and students start a new academic year. The state parks across the nation are usually heavily reserved for Labor Day weekend, and accommodation at the beaches is equally full.

After Labor Day, many resorts, tourist attractions and outdoor vacation facilities close in the Northern states of America. Because the winters are mild in the South, many attractions stay open after Labor Day. If you are planning a trip outside the South after Labor Day, check to be sure that the places you wish to visit will be open.

Veterans' Day

Although school children have a holiday on November 11, not many working people in the South get this holiday, unless they work for the government. On Veterans' Day, the people of the United States honor their servicemen in the Army, Air Force, and the Navy who served in any of the wars waged by the United States. Most cities in the South have parades of veterans, servicemen and others. Many American flags can be seen in streets and outside buildings.

Independence Day

July 4 marks the American colonies' declaration of independence from England in 1776 and the subsequent creation of the United States of America. This is a happy holiday, and, because it is in the summer, many Southerners celebrate out of doors with a cookout. The favorite food for July the Fourth is "barbecue." This is thinly sliced pork or beef with an orange-colored spicy sauce. Vegetables and salads are served with the meal. The dessert is often homemade ice cream and cake.

All over the country, there are parades in the streets with marching bands playing loud music. At night firework displays are featured in many Southern towns and cities, and people take their families to strategic places to view the fireworks. One of the hazards of this holiday is that people, often children, get hurt by falling firecrackers.

The colors for decorations for this holiday are red, white, and blue, the colors of the American flag. The American flag is flown in many streets and outside some homes.

Halloween

Halloween is observed on the last day of October and is neither a paid holiday nor a religious one. On this day, people pretend that mischievous goblins, devils, witches, and evil spirits are loose in the world trying to terrify humans. Children dress up in costumes and go from door to door "trick or treating," which is really asking people for treats of candy. If they do not get a treat, they threaten the inhabitants of the house with a "trick" (mischief), though the trick is seldom ever delivered.

In recent years, the practice of letting children go from

door to door in a neighborhood has lost its popularity because several incidents of malice and cruelty to children have been reported. Candy has been contaminated with poison and dangerous objects (like razor blades). Newcomers should not allow children to go "trick or treating" without adult supervision and protection. Candy should not be eaten till an adult has inspected it for tampering. In the past, some large city hospitals have offered to X-ray Halloween candy before children eat it to see if dangerous objects are in the candy treats.

A few adults dress in costumes for work on Halloween, and some people have parties at Halloween to which guests wear fancy costumes. The decoration colors for Halloween are orange and black. Often a home will display an orange hollowed out pumpkin with a candle inside as a decoration. This is called a "Jack-o-Lantern". Many Christians do not approve of this holiday.

April Fool's Day

On the first day of April, people sometimes play mild tricks on their friends. The trick should not be dangerous or cause any real unhappiness and is not meant as an insult. Usually the trickster confesses to the prank and everyone enjoys the joke.

This is not a holiday and is no longer observed very much in the South. But newcomers should be aware of the possibility of having a trick played on them in case they feel confused, foolish, or insulted.

Valentine's Day

Valentine's day is observed in February 14. It is not a holiday, but it is a special occasion for many Americans who give gifts or send cards (called valentines) to those they love in a special way. Dating and married couples usually exchange valentines, and it is not unusual for elementary school children to exchange valentines with each of their classmates. (When school children exchange valentines, each usually gives one to the teacher, but the teacher does not usually give valentines to the children.)

Parties

In the South, when somebody has a **birthday,** often family or friends, or both, will arrange a party. The party could be elaborate and include a meal or may be simple with a birthday cake and drinks. One does not plan, nor give, one's own birthday party as is the custom in some cultures. At a party there is usually a decorated cake, often with the words "Happy Birthday" with the name of the person written on the top of the cake. Sometimes there is also one candle for each year of the person's life. The candles are blown out by the person celebrating the birthday before the cake is cut. While blowing out the candles, the person makes a wish for something pleasant.

Usually those invited to a birthday party will bring a gift for the person honored. Gifts given by friends do not have to be expensive, but the family of the birthday person will spend whatever they can afford on a gift.

Christmas parties are very popular in the South. Often this is the only time during the year that some people see acquaintances. These parties can be elaborate or simple, ranging from a buffet or "sit down" supper to a reception called an "open house." If you are invited to one of these, you do not need to take a Christmas gift, as it is not customary to take the hostess a gift every time you are invited to a party or a meal. However, if you wish to take a gift, it should only be something useful and inexpensive and should be given to the hostess at the door as you enter the party. Usually gifts of Christmas food treats are the most appreciated.

Some people give **Halloween parties** and ask guests to come in "fancy dress." Guests are expected to dress in some costume related to ghosts, and famous, or infamous people. Newcomers should inquire from a host exactly what is expected when an invitation to such a party is received.

Sometimes, though not often, people give **graduation parties**. Usually guests bring gifts suitable for young people entering the work force or going to college. Again, gifts need not be expensive, unless the host is a close friend or relative.

When invited to a **football party**, one does not take a gift. However, it is appreciated by the hostess if one offers to bring a food dish as a contribution for the meal. One can always offer to bring some food or drink when invited to a meal, regardless of the occasion.

Children's birthday parties are popular. Often they are held at home and consist of simple foods like cake and ice cream, cookies and candy with soft drinks. Sometimes these parties are given at some restaurant, fast food place, amusement or entertainment center. It is customary to take a gift to a child's birthday party of either a book, toy, or clothing. You should arrive on time and leave when the first group of mothers and children leave.

Young people enjoy parties over the **weekends**. There need not be any occasion for the party, and the food served is often very simple. Young people like loud music and the opportunity to talk, watch movies or television, and, sometimes, to dance. At these parties, alcohol may or may not be served. It is polite, when invited to a party, to ask what contribution of food one can bring. Often the time when the party starts and ends is not clearly stated, so you may wish to ask specifically when you are expected to arrive and leave. Only casual clothing is worn to these informal parties.

Baby showers are parties held for pregnant women. Guests bring gifts that will be useful once the baby is born. Pink gifts are considered to be for little girls, and blue is the color for boys. (Often when the baby is born, couples will tie a large blue or pink bow to their mailbox or the door of their home to announce the birth and sex of the baby.)

Housewarming parties are given by friends of a couple who move into a new house. Gifts of houseware are usually taken to the couple.

Special Mention

Three American customs merit special discussion. Behavior surrounding dating, weddings, and funerals is likely to differ considerably from that of your homeland. Here are some general guidelines for conduct on these occasions.

Dating

Dating is the term used to describe the process by which a man and woman get to select and then get to know each other before they marry. This process is necessary as parents and family do not arrange marriages. Usually dating involves the man (or boy) asking the woman (or girl) to spend time together alone for one of two reasons: to enjoy the company of each other or to get to know each other with the possible goal of marriage.

Usually a boy invites a girl he finds attractive to spend some time with him. He invites her to have dinner in a restaurant, to go to a movie, a sports event, concert, or the theatre, etc. The boy pays all the expenses and provides transportation unless the couple have an arrangement to "go dutch," which means that each person pays for himself or herself. This option is not practiced widely in the South, and most dating expenses are paid by the boy.

The boy will go to the girl's home and pick her up, take her to the selected event, and then take her back to her home. If the girl is young and lives with her parents, Southern parents appreciate meeting the young man before the date. The boy should inform the parents of the time he intends bringing the girl (known as his "date") home. Many parents have time limits for their young daughters to be out at night, and the girl will usually tell the boy what this time is. When meeting the girl's parents, the boy should be polite and should assure them he'll abide by their rules. Many young people live in apartments of their own or share apartments with friends after they leave school or college. In this case, the parents are not considered when people go out on a date.

In all cases, the boy is expected to discuss with the girl the details about the date. Ideally, the girl should then say whether or not she can accept the invitation. Sometimes Southern girls will tell a boy that they cannot go on a date because they are "busy." This can either mean that the girl does not wish to date the boy or that she has another engagement but would like him to ask her again. This refusal is usually more subtle than most newcomers can understand. For a newcomer, it is best to be honest with a Southern (or any American) girl and ask whether she would really like to go out later or not.

Newcomer boys who find that girls are not keen to go out on a date with them should not have their feelings hurt. A girl may have several reasons for not wanting to go on a date with a newcomer. She may be nervous or feel ill-equipped to handle a cultural or racial difference and, therefore, does not wish to become acquainted. She may be too busy with a hectic schedule, or she may already have a "boyfriend," which means that she is dating a boy "seriously" and exclusively.

When two people decide they like each other well enough to date frequently, with a view to marriage, they call their relationship exclusive or serious. In this relationship they do not have a marital commitment, but they have an understanding that they will not date other people of the opposite sex, unless this is agreed upon by both parties. People who try to date others who are seriously dating or are married, can expect to be rejected.

Americans have a reputation in other countries for being willing to have sexual intercourse with almost everyone, whether they are married to that person or not. This stereotype also gives the impression that the majority of Americans finish almost every social date with sexual intercourse. The movies certainly give one this impression. The statistics, which are repeatedly being updated, unfortunately seem to indicate that probably half, or maybe even a little more than half, of all American teenagers are sexually active by their mid or late teens. Among older single people, there are also many who engage in sexual activity without being married. Probably half of all married people, at some time in their married lives, have a sexual experience with somebody to whom they are not married. However, the majority of Americans disapprove of this practice. Teenage pregnancy is strongly disapproved of and there is constant discussion about how to prevent this from happening.

Many Americans do not have sexual relationships outside of marriage. Newcomers, therefore, should never assume that an American boy or girl who dates them will be expecting some sort of sexual activity or is willing to end each date with sex.

There are many reasons why some American males and females do not practice indiscriminate sex. Many people are afraid of contracting AIDS. Other people feel that there is too much instability in a relationship when sexual behavior takes place before marriage or that they are not ready for sexual expression. Still others, especially those with religious convictions (and many Southern young people are religious), believe that sexual intercourse before or outside of marriage is morally wrong.

Some Advice to Newcomer Males about Dating

Newcomers should remember that going on a date can be extremely expensive as most events or places to which one would take a middle-class American girl are fairly expensive. If you feel you would like to get to know a girl better, but you do not have much to spend on her, you can invite her to have a cup of coffee or soft drink. Snack bars on most university campuses are an ideal place for this suggestion. You will then have the opportunity for conversation, and this will give you an idea of what the girl is like without your having to spend a great deal of money. Also, this is a useful and convenient place to meet, one that does not involve premature obligations on the part of either. Remember, however, to avoid personal questions (see page 194). It is best to ask her to tell you something about herself and what she enjoys doing, but always to let her decide what she will tell you. If several of these meetings go well, you might like to follow this up with an invitation to something more interesting.

If you plan to invite a girl out who is still at school or who is living with her parents, you should be sure to go to her home, meet her parents, tell them where you are going, and what time you will be returning with their daughter. Remember, some parents are not accustomed to newcomers, especially people from different cultures. They need to be reassured that you are a decent, respectful, and reliable man. Be sure to bring the girl home at the time you have said. If for some unavoidable reason, you are going to be late, urge the girl to phone her parents to tell them of the delay. Although many American girls do not treat their parents as considerately as this, parents will respect and trust you, if you insist on this consideration. Most newcomer boys are used to treating older people this way, and it probably will be natural for you to do this, anyway.

Newcomers should behave politely when dating a Southern girl, especially on the first date. Do not try to engage in any sexual activity. If you have moral principles that prevent you from engaging in sexual activity, do not feel that your date will frown on you. Simply explain, if you have to, that this is not part of your lifestyle. Usually a Southern girl will respect this point of view.

As a newcomer boy, you will also have to be on your guard against being exploited by an American girl. Be careful that you are not manipulated into spending a lot of money (which you may not have) or into a sexual encounter you do not want. It is always acceptable to say no when asked or nagged to do something you do not wish to do, but say "no" politely.

You should not get drunk or inebriated when out on a date. If you are driving, it is your responsibility to get your date home safely. Drunkenness can cause your date embarrassment and can lead you to act in a way you would disapprove of, when sober. Also you could say, do, or promise things you would regret later.

It is a good idea to speak to an American boy or girl for advice about dating, especially if you have met somebody in particular that you would like to get to know better. If possible, ask your friends to tell you something about the girl you find attractive before you ask her for a date. They may be able to tell you something about her personality, character, and willingness to date a newcomer.

Help for a Newcomer Girl

If an American boy asks you to go out on a date with him, be cautious. If you do not know anything about the boy, try to find out something about him from other girls. If you know a boy you trust, ask him about this boy. You need to be on your guard against a boy who may wish to take you out in order to have casual sexual relationships with you or to take advantage of you in other ways, especially if you are not familiar with the local culture. You also need to be careful that you are not dating somebody who will take you into illicit drug or other illegal activities.

If you are invited out, you should ask several questions: what time you will be picked up, whether others will be going also; where you are going; what time you will be brought home; whether you are "going dutch" and if so, how much money you should bring, and how you should dress.

Newcomer girls often come from cultures where premarital sex is not permitted. If this is the code in your culture, or is your religious and moral belief, simply explain this to the boy if you feel he is making sexual advances to you. He will understand; he has had this explained to him by American girls.

As a woman in America, you do not have to obey somebody just because he is a man. You always have the right to choose what you wish to do, where you want to go, what you wish to eat, and with whom. As long as you are polite, you may say "no" to anything you do not wish to do.

To All Newcomers

Do not be afraid of telling Southerners, girls and boys, that you do not understand something they are saying or doing. You do need to explain to them why you are confused by some action or word as they are just as unfamiliar with your culture as you are with theirs. In America, you do not have to do anything that conflicts with your morals, but remember to be polite. Fortunately Americans, not just Southerners, are understanding about the differences in culture, provided these are explained to them.

To Newcomer Parents

Newcomer parents are understandably nervous about their young people dating in the United States—few countries in the world give their young people so much freedom.

This freedom is the result of many things. There is much more money in this country for young people to earn and spend; young people are able to have their own cars or drive the family car; the culture encourages independence from an early age; respect for adults and older people is no longer strongly encouraged; peer groups are a powerful force and are encouraged in the culture (see page 130) and "dating" is an activity highly encouraged by the culture. In a sense, it has to be, because adults do not choose marriage partners for young people.

Some newcomers who are only temporarily in the United States are able to forbid their children from dating, but those who are permanently here have problems when they try to forbid this practice. Generally Southerners allow their daughters to date a boy when the girls are somewhere between fourteen and sixteen years of age. This varies from family to family. Each family has the responsibility of establishing its own rules for dating behavior. Individual families decide where a daughter may go for a date, with whom, for how long, what times of the day and night, and at what time the young couple should return.

Newcomer parents should consult with Southern neighbors and find out what happens in their neighborhood. The guidance counselor at the school your children attend will also be able to give you information and guidance about how to set rules for your children when dating. You may decide not to allow your children to date until they are adults. If your children abide by your authority, all is well. If they become resentful about your decision, you will need to find a way of explaining your reasons for not letting them follow the general pattern in this country, and try to help them deal with their feelings of being treated "differently" from American young people.

Newcomer parents may wish to encourage their children to go out in groups rather than with one young person exclusively. However, peer groups also have potential dangers. See page 130 for information on peer groups.

It is the privilege of newcomer parents to make rules about dating and to enforce them. Parents will need to meet the young people their children are dating, will want to know where they are going, with whom, when they expect to return home, and whether or not alcohol or drugs will be involved in the date. If this is the case, parents will be able to refuse permission for the date. Even though in their home culture parents do not usually discuss sexual subjects with their teenage children, newcomer parents should be acquainted with behavior on dates and should discuss sexual behavior with their teenage children and should state their views and desires with regard to this behavior. Even if it is embarrassing for parents to discuss these subjects, it is important to warn teenagers about the possibility of pregnancy and sexually transmitted diseases, especially AIDS. (See page 244 for information on AIDS and other STDs.)

Interracial Dating

Some Southern young people and their parents may feel greatly disturbed at the thought of dating somebody from another racial group. This may be because of prejudice or because of fear of what a person of another racial group is like, or it may stem from a fear of the culture from which the different person comes or because of uncertainty about how to behave with somebody of another racial group.

A newcomer of a different race may want to discover what the attitudes of a particular person are about this type of dating before actually inviting the person for a date. This can be discovered by asking general questions about this topic, without directly saying that you would like to date him or her. Or you may ask somebody acquainted with the person to whom you are attracted what the person's attitudes are.

Newcomers who are refused a date on the grounds of racial factors should understand that interracial dating is not widespread in the South, and, therefore, some young people may be uncertain about somebody racially different. In most cities, interracial dating is tolerated, although sometimes surprised glances or intolerant stares may be directed at an interracial couple who are dating or already married.

Dating and intermarriage between white Southerners and Oriental people is becoming more and more obvious and acceptable. Few such couples are viewed with much surprise currently in the South, and many Southern families are eager to adopt Oriental children.

Double and Group Dates

Double dating is fairly popular in the South. In this situation, two boys date two girls, but it is understood that each boy has one of the girls as his partner for the evening. It is common to see four people in restaurants or social events.

This form of dating provides the opportunity of getting to know another person to whom one is attracted without two people having to keep conversation bright and entertaining all the time. It also gives a couple the opportunity of seeing how the other functions in a group setting. Sometimes more than four people go out together, for all the reasons mentioned above. Of course, the couples pay for themselves or go "dutch", unless somebody is treating the whole group.

Weddings

Southern weddings are much like weddings in the rest of the United States, and even in the rest of the Western world. Probably the only difference between a Southern wedding is the number of receptions, luncheons, showers, "coffees," and "teas" given by friends and relatives to honor the bride prior to the wedding date.

Once the couple agrees on a wedding date, the engagement is announced. At this time, the girl receives a diamond ring, which is often, though not always, selected by the girl and the boy together. This ring is worn on the third finger of the girl's left hand and is sometimes given to the girl as a surprise at some romantic event, even if the girl has selected her ring.

Once the date has been firmly set, the couple begins planning for the wedding. Usually the parents allow the couple to decide on all the details for the wedding, but the girl's parents pay the bills and make suggestions about the arrangements. About a month before the wedding, the engagement notice appears in the local newspaper. The notice includes the names of the couple, their parents' names, and, usually, a picture of the girl.

The wedding festivities start many weeks or months before the marriage, depending on the number of friends the families have and the social status of the families. These festivities include showers, teas, and receptions. Because a number of guidebooks are available for planning and conducting weddings, only an overview is presented here.

Bridal Teas

The bridal tea, not to be confused with a bridal shower, is given for a bride by her mother's best friend and other friends who wish to share the expense. This is usually a rather formal occasion and gives the bride, her mother, her grandmother, and her bridesmaids the opportunity to meet her friends. Gifts are brought by guests, opened by the engaged girl or a bridesmaid, and are displayed in the hostess' home. Guests may come and leave as they wish within the time limits described on the invitation.

Some brides do not have "teas." Instead close friends of the mother of the bride will give the bride a "reception" in place of the "tea." A reception is similar to a tea except that gifts are not given.

Showers
Most brides have a friend or friends who give her showers. Guests are requested to bring gifts, sometimes of a specific type. Guests are expected to arrive when the shower starts and to leave when it ends unless an excuse is offered to the hostess in advance. The bride-to-be opens her gifts in the presence of her friends, and then refreshments are served.

Some brides-to-be have so many showers, dinners, and receptions before the wedding date that they feel exhausted. If your children wish to marry in the Southern tradition, be prepared for the pre-wedding festivities to last at least a month.

Bachelor Party
The night before the wedding, friends of the engaged boy meet to give him a party (a "stag" party) in a home, a club, or any suitable place. His fiancé is not supposed to attend this party, which sometimes unfortunately turns into a wild affair with questionable behavior and drinking. However, probably most parties are merely happy, decent parties to help the prospective bridegroom bid farewell to bachelorhood.

Bridesmaids' Luncheon
If the wedding is in the afternoon or evening, a member of the bride's family gives a luncheon for her and her bridesmaids at a suitable place in appreciation for the work the bridesmaids have done for the wedding. This may be a breakfast if the wedding takes place in the morning. If these times are not suitable, the luncheon can be held at any other time and date.

The Wedding Party
The wedding party consists of the bridal couple, the parents on both sides, the grandparents, the groomsmen,

bridesmaids, the best man, and the maid of honor (usually the bride's sister or closest friend). A small wedding may have only one bridesmaid; a large one can have eight or more. Usually there is a groomsman for each bridesmaid. In the South, the bridegroom often asks his father (regardless of his age) to be his best man; however another relative or close friend can also be the best man.

Sometimes the wedding party may also have one or two small children. The girl is called a flower girl and the boy, a ring bearer. The boy sometimes carries a small pillow on which the rings are placed. The bridesmaids are the brides attendants and are usually relatives or close friends; the groomsmen are the groom's attendants and escorts for the bridesmaids and are usually relatives or close friends of the groom.

Wedding Clothes

The bridesmaids are expected to pay for their outfits, and the groomsmen usually pay to rent their clothes, called tuxedos. In traditional weddings, the bride wears a long white dress and a veil of net on her head. She carries a bouquet of flowers. The bridesmaids usually wear long or short dresses the color of the bride's choice and style. They also carry bouquets of flowers.

The mothers and grandmothers of the bridal couple wear either long dresses or short elegant dresses of their choice, often with long sleeves. On their left shoulders, they usually wear small bouquets of flowers called corsages.

The bridegroom, best man, and groomsmen generally wear tuxedos that are usually black suits with a white shirt, a large belt under the jacket, and a rather fancy tie. Sometimes, though not often, the men will wear regular business suits. Each man in the party wears a flower called a boutonniere on his left lapel.

Wedding Locale

The wedding ceremony can take place in a church, a judge's office in the courthouse, a garden, or living room. Usually the ceremony in a Protestant church takes 15 to 30 minutes; ceremonies are a little longer in a Jewish synagogue and a Roman Catholic church. Except at the courthouse, there is usually music at the ceremony, an exchange of vows, and sometimes, though infrequently, a short sermon. The form of the ceremony differs from denomination to denomination.

Wedding Rehearsal

The night before the wedding, the wedding party rehearses where the event will take place. After the rehearsal, very close friends and family join the bridal party for a dinner at a restaurant, hotel, or club, and the expense is borne by the bridegroom's family.

The Ceremony

Guests invited to a wedding arrive at least ten minutes before the service takes place. If the ceremony is in a church, guests wait in the foyer for an attendant to seat them. Wedding music plays while the guests are being seated. The bridegroom, his best man, and sometimes the groomsmen stand at the front of the church waiting on the bride and her party. The parents of the bride and groom are seated last. After the guests are all seated, the organist plays music of the bride's choice, at which point the mother of the bride stands. This is a signal to the congregation to stand. The bride's party then enters the church. Usually the flower girl and page boy lead the way, followed by the bridesmaids and, finally, the bride.

The wedding party all stand in the front of the church, which is usually decorated with lit candles, green plants, and, sometimes, flowers. The ceremony is performed according to the preferences of the couple and the guidelines of the denomination and officiating minister. Vows are made by the couple to love and care for each other, and to live together as man and wife. The bride and groom give each other rings as a symbol of marriage and these are worn on the third finger of the left hand.

After the ceremony, the wedding party leaves the church in much the same way as it entered. The guests then leave, and the photographer then takes many photographs of the party.

Reception

After the ceremony there is usually a reception. This can

be simple or grand, depending on the wishes and financial position of the bride and bridegroom and their parents. At the reception, guests stand in line to sign the guest book and to congratulate the wedding party. If the reception consists of only light refreshments, guests may leave the reception after having refreshments. However, if the reception is a meal, everyone should stay until the reception is over.

You may take a wedding present to the reception (if you have not already presented the couple with a gift). The gift is usually something that can be used in the couple's new home. Food is not usually a gift, and food should not be taken to a wedding reception.

After the reception, the bride and groom change their clothes, and guests gather around them as they proceed to the vehicle taking them to their honeymoon. The bride will then throw her bouquet or a substitute bouquet into the crowd, and the girl who catches it is predicted to be the next bride. It is traditional to "mess up" the vehicle in which the bridal party will travel by writing words such as "Just Married" on the car with toothpaste, shaving cream, etc. and tying tin cans to the back bumper.

The Honeymoon

Most couples still go away for a honeymoon—a vacation designed to give the couple an opportunity to get away alone together. Because so few young people can afford a long honeymoon (the couple pay the expenses of the honeymoon), this vacation is seldom long these days. The destination is usually not kept a great secret as is the case in some places.

Cost of Weddings

Weddings in the United States are usually paid for by the bride's parents and can cost from a few hundred dollars for a small, simple wedding to thousands of dollars for a large, elaborate one. Costs include such items as the invitations, clothes, flowers, photographer, candelabras, reception food, appreciation gifts to the members of the wedding party, and rental cost of the locale. The rehearsal dinner, the bride's bouquet, the boutonnieres, corsages, and the rehearsal dinner are paid for by the bridegroom and his family.

Most bookstores stock guide books on wedding arrangements. These are useful for newcomers who wish to have a Southern wedding. Usually churches have their own guidelines for weddings taking place in their sanctuaries, and newcomers should consult the chosen church for information.

Some people prefer to have a nonreligious wedding ceremony, or a "civil" wedding, so they choose to have a judge perform the ceremony, often in a courthouse. All weddings must be legally conducted in the United States, and must be performed by individuals authorized by the state to do so.

Funerals

After death, the corpse is taken from the hospital or home where the death occurred to a "funeral home." This is usually a beautifully decorated building with a calm atmosphere. At the funeral home, a mortician prepares the body by embalming it, dressing it in clothes chosen by the family, applying cosmetics to the face, and combing the hair. The body is then placed in a decorated coffin, usually lined with white satin material. The lid of the coffin is usually left open so mourners can view the body, and the coffin with the body is placed in one of the rooms of the funeral home.

Usually friends send wreaths of fresh or silk flowers to decorate the room. If you know the family or the deceased person, you are expected to go to the funeral home at an announced time to express sympathy to the family. "I am sorry about your loved one" or "Please accept my sincere sympathy" are appropriate remarks to make to the family.

One does not go to the home of the bereaved family unless they are close friends. At the funeral home, be sure to sign the visitors' book so the family will remember your visit.

The funeral ceremony is usually held in a church to which the deceased belonged or in a room at the funeral home. The ceremony, called a funeral service, is often conducted by a minister of religion and often begins with a prayer. The body is placed at the front of the church or room, along with the wreaths of flowers sent by relatives and friends. The minister may also read from the Bible and may give a short talk in which he speaks comfortingly to the family and friends. Someone who knows the deceased well will often give a speech in which the good character of the deceased is mentioned.

After the service in the church, the family and friends go to a cemetery where a grave has been prepared, usually about six feet deep. Only rarely do Southerners cremate (burn) a body. The family and friends gather around the open grave, the minister prays, then the coffin is lowered into the grave, thus ending the service. The family and close friends often go to a relative's home to have refreshments after the funeral.

In some cases, families have only graveside services. These are held at the grave site without preliminary church services.

Southerners do expect their friends and relatives to make the effort to be with them at the time of a relative's death, and friends and family members travel great distances to attend funerals. Most employers understand this aspect of the South and are happy to give employees time off to attend a funeral, though sometimes one has to work to make up the time. If one did not know the person who has died well enough to attend the funeral, but well enough to acknowledge the death, one may send a sympathy card instead.

Some Southerners, especially those of Irish descent, observe a "wake." Family members take turns sitting in a room with the body from the time it is prepared for burial until time for the funeral. This practice is no longer very common, however.

Old Age
and
Retirement Centers

In a technological society like the United States, old age is not given great status. Sadly, this is because old people (usually called "senior citizens") are not vital for the transmission of skills to the young. Older people no longer achieve and earn much—two important sources of status in American society. In addition, aging leads to death—a process most Americans wish to delay as long as possible.

The United States is definitely a youth-oriented society, so the aging process is dreaded by most Americans. Even at thirty years of age people speak of being "over the hill" (aged), and birthdays that mark the passing of a decade are referred to as "the big three-o" or "the big four-o" (thirtieth or fortieth birthday).

Americans are resourceful, so most adjust to old age satisfactorily, especially those who plan early, both psychologically and financially, for their old age and retirement (which usually takes place between sixty-five and seventy years of age). Generally, the people who find the most enjoyment and fulfillment in retirement are those who stay mentally and physically active, healthy, and involved in social and service projects. Many elderly people volunteer their services to charity organizations.

Financial preparation for retirement is made by most middle-class men and women through deductions from their monthly pay checks to social security and to separate retirement plans available through their places of employment (since social security is not sufficient for most retired Americans).

Unfortunately, many old people have small incomes and find it difficult to make ends meet, although most middle-class retired Americans live comfortably, if not luxuriously. Many take part-time employment to keep them busy and useful, in addition to augmenting their incomes. There is currently considerable concern about the number of aged people living in poverty (and sometimes on the streets) without proper medical care and accommodations.

To alleviate the problem of loneliness suffered by many old people, especially those who live alone, concerned citizens and mental health professionals provide programs, organizations, and clubs that provide services such as providing meals, domestic help, activities for intellectual and social enrichment, and exercise programs, among others. Your local mental health society can supply details about such programs in your community.

Elderly people in the United states have one of the longest life expectancies in the world, and this figure is rising. This group will grow even larger in years to come as the large number of people born shortly after World War II enter old age. Currently, there are more elderly women than men in the United States, and most of them live alone.

Many old people prefer to live in retirement centers or alone because, even in old age, they value their independence and individualism and prefer to pursue their own lives. Many do not wish to live with younger people or to be a burden to their families. Others have no families who are able or willing to take care of them.

There are many varieties of retirement centers that provide different types of accommodations. These can be modest or luxurious and can be purchased or rented. Many provide recreational and medical facilities, and some provide meals. They are licensed by the government and subject to regular inspection.

Provided the living arrangements are chosen in mutual agreement by the elderly people and other family members, Americans do not feel that it is wrong or uncaring for old people to live in retirement homes or centers, especially when the elderly persons need specialized care. Most families maintain contact with their elderly parents and other relatives who live in these homes.

It is true that some Western families, not just American

ones, do not want their aged parents living with them. This is largely because the families are highly stressed and could find it difficult to meet the financial and emotional needs of small children, teenagers, and parents all at the same time. In spite of this, however, many families do have older relatives and parents living with them because this is their choice or because retirement centers are too expensive.

Caution: Immigrants to the United States should plan early in life for retirement. Such planning is complicated, and a licensed, reputable financial counselor should be consulted for advice. Beware of advisors who urge you to invest in risky endeavors and retirement schemes. Be careful, too, of counselors who promise enormous income from limited investment.

National Considerations

Newcomers should be aware of certain aspects of life in the United States regardless of the section of the country where they live. This section addresses the ones most likely to apply to all newcomers.

Change of Time

For six months of the year, from April until the end of October, most sections of the United States have what is called "daylight saving time." This manipulation of the clock puts time ahead by one hour on the first Sunday in April. Consequently, there are more daylight hours in the afternoon and early evening, which means farmers have longer to work in the fields, people have more time for sports, travel, and other activities after work.

Similarly, in the fall (autumn), the clock is put back an hour on the morning of the last Sunday in October, which means it becomes light earlier in the morning. This enables children to go to school in the daylight in the winter.

Newcomers need to consult the newspapers, the radio, or television in October and April for the exact day on which this change is made to avoid arriving an hour late or early for an appointment. Employers and friends do not feel responsible for informing others of the time change; one is expected to find out from the media when these changes take place.

Time Zones

Because the continental United States is such a large

country, it encompasses four time zones: Eastern, Central, Mountain, and Pacific. During the months when Daylight Savings Time is in effect, these are referred to as Eastern Daylight Time, Central Daylight Time, etc. During the balance of the year, they are known as Eastern Standard Time, Central Standard Time, etc.

The Eastern time zone covers the Eastern United States and includes such cities as New York, Atlanta, and Miami. The Central time zone lies immediately west of the Eastern zone and includes such cities as Chicago, Birmingham, New Orleans, and Dallas. The Mountain zone is west of the Central zone and includes Phoenix and Denver. The Pacific zone runs down the west coast and includes Seattle, Los Angeles, and San Francisco. All zones run from the northern to the southern boundary of the country.

These zones are an hour apart. Thus, when it is 8:00 a.m. in Atlanta, it is 7:00 a.m. in Birmingham, 6:00 a.m. in Denver, and 5:00 a.m. in Los Angeles. Television programs are often broadcast at different times in different zones, and broadcasters frequently announce the minutes before or after the hour without mentioning the hour to allow for the differences in time in various places.

Newcomers need to be aware of these changes in time, especially when planning and going on a trip. Public transportation schedules always list arrival and departure times in the time zones where they will be arriving or departing.

Taxes

Taxes are charges levied by federal, state, and local governments to support the operation of those governments and the services they provide. This material summarizes the most common forms of taxes.

Income taxes are paid by every person with an income above a certain amount, regardless of the source of that income. If you are employed, taxes will usually be deducted each month from your pay check. These deductions will be for federal taxes, as well as for state and local taxes if those are required where you work. If you are not employed and have income from stock, bonds, or other investments, a representative of the Internal Revenue Service can explain how to file quarterly reports.

The amount of income tax paid each month is determined by several factors, including how much is earned. When you begin work, your employer will ask you to complete a form that enables the company to determine the correct amount to be withheld each month. If you later have a baby or if one of your children marries and leaves home, you will need to change the form on file with your employer to assure that the correct amount continues to be deducted.

Each year, the federal government requires everyone who had income during the previous year to file an income report for tax purposes. This form is due no later than April 15 of each year and is handled by the Internal Revenue Service. Failure to disclose income, however it is obtained, is an offense and is punishable by law. Since the form is complicated and changes from year to year, many newcomers employ qualified professionals like Certified Public Accountants or tax specialists to help them complete their tax returns. (Many United States citizens also use the services of these professionals.)

Most states also require income tax filing, and these requirements are similar to the federal ones. You can find additional information concerning income tax requirements for your state at your local library.

Social security is the common name given the federal program providing retirement income, for which taxes are also deducted each pay period for each employed person. (This will be shown on your pay voucher as F.I.C.A.)

Property taxes are local taxes paid by property owners. Homeowners pay these taxes on the assessed value of their homes, and each homeowner receives a tax bill once a year. The bill will state when the tax is due and where it is to be paid.

When a car owner purchases a license tag, a portion of the fee covers the property tax due on that car. The amount of fee that is property tax is noted on the license tag form.

Sales taxes are collected by merchants when you make purchases and are added on to the price of your purchase.

Sales taxes equal a certain percentage of the total price of your purchase. These taxes are levied by most states, many cities, and some counties.

Litigation

In a land where personal liberty and freedoms are cherished, there are numerous laws designed to insure that one person's liberty does not take away or limit the liberty of another person. For instance, one person may not injure, harm, or kill another person in the pursuit of his or her liberty. Consequently, numerous civil laws assure that individuals will not be denied rights and opportunities to which they are entitled.

To curb one individual from harming another, the law allows one person to "sue" another. This simply means that anyone who believes he or she has been harmed psychologically or bodily, had his or her reputation harmed, or had his or her rights threatened in any way may ask a court to intervene and prevent the threatening action from taking place or to punish the offender if the action has taken place. This is called "filing a lawsuit."

There are numerous reasons for which people sue other people. They sue after sustaining injuries in a public, private, or government place through negligence of another; getting hurt through negligence or intent, such as an error made by a doctor, policeman, etc.; being defrauded (cheated) of money or possessions; and having one's reputation harmed by lies or other means.

If the injured party wins the law suit, then the offender is usually required to pay the injured party monetary compensation. Often individuals who are at risk for lawsuits have insurance that provides the money they have to pay as compensation. If an offender has no money, the judge will decide how he or she should make restitution.

Many doctors and employers are sued. Newspaper and television reporters have to avoid printing untrue stories about people and events as they could be sued for damaging the reputation of others. Homeowners could be sued if they keep items in their homes or yards that result in harm to someone. There are literally thousands of instances of action that could result in lawsuits. Some Americans feel that too many individuals are suing others for offenses that are not considered serious enough for such action and that this trend is becoming too time consuming and costly in the United States.

The fear of being sued has resulted in doctors and hospitals having expensive insurance policies, the cost of which is borne by the patients. This is one reason why medical care is so expensive in the United States.

Lawyers

The United States is governed by "laws, not people." This is a protection for ordinary citizens as it means that no person can be indicted, charged, or punished for a misdemeanor, felony, or crime without the protection and benefit of the law. Every case brought before a judge is evaluated by the law, which is the highest authority in the land.

All people, including criminals, are protected by the law and have certain rights. When people break the law, they employ the services of a lawyer, who represents them to assure they receive the just and fair treatment they deserve, even as accused law-breakers and criminals.

Newcomers should consult a lawyer if they ever break any law, because the legal system is too complicated for the average person to understand without help. A good lawyer will defend your rights, plead and argue your case, and represent you before the judge and the jury.

If you feel you have been wronged, harmed, abused, or threatened, a lawyer can give you advice about what action (if any) you should take. Lawyers are also necessary when you are entering into a contract with an individual or organization, especially if large sums of money are involved, such as when one purchases a home or other property.

In the United States, contracts are often extremely complicated and detailed, so consult a contract lawyer before you enter into any business transaction involving a lot of money. Your lawyer will take care of your interests.

Before hiring a lawyer, ask the following questions: Has the lawyer had experience with foreign nationals? What are the fees you will be expected to pay? How will you be expected to pay the lawyer? Will other lawyers also work on your case? How long will the case take to handle? Will you be constantly informed about the progress of your case? How much will a telephone conversation with your lawyer cost? Can you have a limit on the fees charged so that the bill does not exceed your ability to pay?

Although lawyers' fees are expensive, in most cases their services are indispensable. In America, lawyers are specialists, and you need to choose one who specializes in the area in which you need help, and one that is licensed. If you decide you need a lawyer, ask trusted and reliable friends to recommend one to you or call the local lawyers' association (called the Bar Association) for a recommendation.

Business Agreements and Contracts

It is usually worth the money involved to employ the services of a contract lawyer when entering into a business agreement. This will be understood by Southerners, especially if English is not your native tongue.

By far the majority of Southerners and other American business people are honest and straightforward. However, if you are entering into a business agreement or making a contract, you should always make sure that every detail of the agreement (however trivial it seems) is written down on paper to help all parties remember and understand exactly the details of the agreement and to help everyone avoid misinterpreting another's intentions. If you feel embarrassed about doing this, explain that you are a newcomer and don't always understand the complexities of American business customs.

Crime and Violence

Crime and violence are a part of life to which everyone must adjust. Before newcomers arrive in the United States, they are usually familiar with the problem of violence here, and they always ask why. There are no easy answers to this problem, but some suggestions are presented.

The diversity of the heterogeneous population is a factor. There are so many different groups of people with different moral standards, cultures, and values that agreement on behavior is difficult to achieve. When different racial and cultural groups cannot deal with their feelings of fear, threat, resentment, and anger, violence is easily resorted to as an emotional expression. Groups that feel discriminated against or feel their political voice is not being heard also sometimes express their anger in some form of violence.

Organized drug trafficking has become a trade that accounts for a great deal of violence. Under American law, the drug criminals are also entitled to the freedoms and protection guaranteed by the Constitution and the Bill of Rights. This means that they often find loopholes in the law and go undetected and unpunished, leaving them free to commit more violence. Their violence is often deadly as it usually involves guns.

Though the middle class is the country's largest group, America has great extremes of rich and poor. The difference between the middle class and the poor is easily recognized, and, consequently, poor people feel deprived and resentful as they view the "good life" lived by middle-class Americans so glamorously portrayed on television, in the press, and in real life. Sometimes their frustration and hopelessness at not being able to move easily from the poor group to the more affluent middle class gives way to despair and violence. Violence can be used to get "money or goods" (robbery), to settle disputes, or as a form of organized social behavior such as gang violence.

A recent type of violence of great concern in the 1990s is violence for "fun." Some teenager gang members have stated that they find violent confrontations with other groups to be somewhat entertaining. Violence is part of the behavior of some gangs, and the illegal possession of guns by so many makes this "fun" dangerous. Often innocent bystanders are injured or killed by gang activity.

Another concern is the problem that has recently emerged of "drive-by" shootings. People in cars drive on the freeways or streets and randomly shoot through car windows, often killing or hurting people.

Another contributing factor, at present greatly debated, may be the effect of the movies and television when they portray the "culture of the frontier." This is based on the tradition of the pioneers who trekked to the Western part of the continent in covered wagons, far from the protection of the law. These people had to carry weapons (mostly guns) to protect themselves, and their exploits have been glamorized in the popular "cowboy" movies. Modern "cowboys" possibly act out this fantasy in an urban, suburban, and even rural setting. These are usually impressionable people, especially young adults. There is some debate about evidence that criminal gangs imitate this behavior and that young people and children are more apt to be violent after viewing violence on the screen.

Though hotly debated, some people feel that the American belief that all citizens have the "right to bear arms" to defend themselves makes violence more likely. Regardless of the effect of this "right," it is a fact that a large percentage of the population own guns, a right which the National Rifle Association (NRA), a strong lobbying group, protects.

Violence among family members is common, though the majority of Americans are appalled by any type of violence and strongly condemn it. The modern American family is greatly stressed, often has too few financial resources, and has little, or no, guidance about settling family and marital-problems. In a country where so many people own guns, the shooting of a family member during an argument is fairly common. A great national concern at present is the amount of violence, both physical and verbal, inflicted on children. Alcohol abuse also contributes to family violence, as well as to violence on the streets.

Though not researched and proven, there is a theory that Americans are people who do not have adequate cultural patterns from which they can learn how to handle anger constructively. The American culture expects people to be pleasant, friendly, enthusiastic, and cooperative. Anger is, therefore, a taboo subject, and any outward expression of it is frowned upon. The theory holds that when too much anger is suppressed, it explodes in a form of violence, often physical.

The South has some of the most crime-ridden cities in the nation: Miami, Atlanta, Birmingham, Richmond, New Orleans, Houston, Dallas, and others. Newcomers should be aware of this problem and should discover what parts of the city are considered by the natives to be dangerous. Often (but not always), these neighborhoods look neglected, untidy, and littered. Some neighborhoods are not safe even in the daytime. One should not walk around alone in any area without first finding out if the neighborhood is safe. Do not let children walk around alone, nor play outside in the street or your yard, unless you have checked about the safety of the neighborhood.

Before permanently locating in a particular neighborhood, find out how big a problem violence and crime is in that area. One needs to consider two types of crime: robberies resulting from criminals breaking into houses and stealing the occupants belongings (and sometimes injuring the occupants) and assaults by criminals on sidewalks or in parking areas.

Some Americans buy cans of mace (tear gas) for their homes, and some women carry it in their handbags. This practice is debated; some people feel it is wise, others feel it is not a good means of protection. Tear gas can be sprayed into the face of a potential attacker without doing any permanent damage and gives one about ten to fifteen minutes to escape. Tear gas should be kept out of the reach of children and should be carefully used, as it is easy to impair oneself even when using it against an attacker.

Children should be warned not to speak to strangers and not to accept any gifts, including candy, from strangers, unless parents are with them. Sometimes, though not frequently, young children and babies are abducted or kidnapped with horrible consequences. Babies and young children should never be left alone in a yard, a car, or a buggy inside or outside a store.

Never leave young children alone in a house. If you have to leave your older children at home alone, teach them to keep all doors and windows locked; never to open the door to any stranger, however friendly; never to answer the phone giving details about your absence, but rather to say that the parent is occupied and not able to answer the phone, and to offer to take a message.

Some people install alarm systems in their homes. Each system works differently, but generally, when an intruder touches certain areas of the house, an alarm bell rings loudly, waking up the sleeping inhabitants, alerting the neighbors, and, sometimes, even the police. This is usually enough deterrent for the burglars to leave the house.

When you respond to a knock at your door, ask the caller for a name and why he or she needs to see you before opening the door, especially if there is no other adult in the house. If you do not know the caller or cannot be sure he or she is harmless, do not open the door. Many criminals (both male and female) pretend to be in trouble, or they pretend to have goods for sale in order to get into houses or apartments.

At night if you are unfamiliar with a neighborhood, do not drive down side streets, but keep to main, well lighted roads. Always keep your doors locked when driving. If you need directions, stop at a well lighted store or gas station for instructions. You should not stop for strangers when driving; however, should this be unavoidable, keep your car doors locked and speak through a closed or slightly cracked window. Also, keep the car motor running so you can get away quickly if you feel threatened.

Parking lots of shopping malls constitute a real danger to shoppers, usually at night, but sometimes in the daytime. As you approach your car, look underneath it for signs of somebody hiding. At night, look in the back and front seats of the car for a hiding robber. It is wise to carry a tiny flashlight in your pocket or handbag to look in the car before you open the doors.

While walking the streets and malls, be aware of how you are carrying your wallet, purse, or handbag. Keep these as close to your body as possible. Wallets should not be stored in a hip pocket unless the pocket closes securely. However, if you are robbed, it is better to let go of your possessions than to risk losing your life defending them. Pickpockets use many ploys to rob innocent people. Some schemes include asking people for directions to specific places, streets, buildings, etc. and while they are receiving these instructions, they rob the person helping them. Others will tell sad stories of misfortune and ask for a small amount of money and then will rob the person listening to them. However, this does not mean that one should never give help to anyone. Rather, one should always be alert and suspicious.

Beware of people on the street who ask you for money, ask you to lend them money, offer you free gifts, offer to take you some place to get money, ask you to sign anything you do not understand, or try to persuade you to give them your money so they can invest it for you at a high interest rate. Usually such people are crooks, and you could lose your money or be assaulted if you linger around them. Beware also of strangers on the street who tell you they need you to withdraw your money from the bank in order to make more money.

These paragraphs are not meant to scare newcomers. Not every part of the South is considered dangerous enough to call for such drastic measures of protection. The above mentioned situations are extreme examples. Many, maybe most, areas are safe and require very few security measures to be taken. However, by being aware of the possibilities of crime and violence and by taking sensible precautions, one can sometimes avoid being a victim of such crime and violence.

Guns

"Frontier" is a word used to describe the unknown territory on this continent into which the early pioneers moved with their wagons and possessions. Often these pioneers were attacked by lawless people while traveling and after when they settled in their homes. There were few lawmen on the frontier to protect ordinary citizens, and individual settlers had to take care of themselves and their families. They acquired and learned how to use guns for protection. Hence the tradition of carrying guns was born. Today most Americans own guns for hunting, though many carry guns for protection also.

Not just some Southerners, but many Americans, feel it is their constitutional right to own and use guns, and some women carry guns for protection. Today there is considerable controversy about this issue. Some citizens feel guns should not be owned by private citizens, except under unusual circumstances and with a special license, and others feel everyone (except criminals) should have the right to be armed.

Those who carry guns or other dangerous weapons have to carry them in such a manner that they can be seen, unless they have a permit for concealing a weapon. It is an offense to have a gun or weapon concealed. In many states you have to have a license to own a gun. Even states without the license law have certain requirements for those wishing to own guns. These differ from state to state, and from time to time. However, access to guns makes it easy for criminals to have guns and accounts in part for the high incidence of murders during robberies. The presence of guns in homes also contributes to the murders being committed during arguments and fights.

Whether private citizens should own a gun or not is a matter to be decided by the individual, but, those who decide to have one should take lessons on the use and safe storage of guns. A surprisingly high number of children are killed accidentally by guns stored in homes.

Acquiring United States Citizenship

Newcomers who have permanent resident status and are in possession of an alien registration card (the so-called "green card") may apply for citizenship after they have lived in the United States for five years, if they wish. Some newcomers never apply for citizenship, while others are eager to become citizens as soon as possible. There are many reasons for wanting United States citizenship: the desire for a better life, the desire to vote, the desire to have a United States passport, or the legal and political protection of the United States government.

If you desire United States citizenship, you should apply for it at your nearest immigration office. You will receive forms and pages of explanations about what is expected of you. You may need to be sponsored by a U.S. citizen who is a relative or an employer. Your application will be processed, and you will be notified of the date on which you are expected to appear before an immigration official for an interview. During this interview, you will be tested for your fluency in English and knowledge of United States history.

To pass this test, you should be competent in written and spoken English. You will also need to have a considerable knowledge of United Sates history. The Daughters of the American Revolution publish a booklet on American history to help you prepare for the questions you will be asked about United States history. This book is useful as it is concise, factual, and easy to read. The librarian at the local public library should be able to help you acquire this book.

After your interview, you may also be investigated by the Federal Bureau of Investigation and the Central Intelligence Agency. There may be other checks on your general status as a newcomer as well. When all these investigations have been completed to the satisfaction of the Immigration Department, you will be recommended for citizenship. The above-mentioned information was valid at the time of writing; however, check with your local immigration department about current procedure as policies may change.

Visas

Most newcomers have substantial information about visa requirements before entering the United States, so this mention is brief. Immigration visas include the following:

"B" Visas—issued to visitors, **B-1** for business purposes and **B-2** for pleasure. You must not accept employment if you have this type of visa. These visas should be obtained at a United States consulate before you leave your country.

Student Visa or F-1 Visa—issued upon receipt of an I-120 form issued by the school the student plans to attend. This form is to be presented to the U.S. consulate in the student's home country.

"L-1" Inter-company Transfer Visa—issued for up to five years to an employee of a company operating outside the U.S. and bringing foreign employees to work in the U.S.

E Visa—issued to a foreign national who must actively oversee major operations or investments in the U.S.

"**H Visa**"—is negotiated between individual companies and the U.S. Department of Labor.

H-1 Visa—given to a foreign national coming to the U.S. to fill a position that requires expertise and special qualifications.

H-2 Visa—given to a foreign national coming to accept a position for which American workers are in short supply.

H-3 Visa—issued to a trainee brought to the U.S. for training by a company operating outside the U.S.

Please note that the laws regarding visas and the definitions of visas change often, so check with the INS for the latest information (see below for telephone numbers). Do not try to work if you do not have the correct visa; you could risk deportation. Make sure you know when and how to renew your visa. The acquisition of visas is a very complicated process, and the laws change from time to time. Consult the visa specialist at your company or university for assistance and information or call the Immigration and Naturalization Service in Atlanta at 1-404-331-2781 or 1-404-351-5158 or in Dallas at 1-214-767-7769. Please note that these numbers can change after publication, but Directory Assistance can provide updated numbers.

Social Welfare

The provisions and laws for persons in need are constantly changing through legislation at the local level or through Congress. Basically, however, the government of the United States and the local state governments provide limited financial assistance to persons who are disabled or too ill to work. In order to receive aid, individuals must usually meet certain criteria, and some who qualify do not always receive the aid due to limited government funds. While the United States may appear to be very affluent, the number of indigent (poor) citizens continues to increase. A recent report (1991) noted that one American child in five lives in poverty. The following is a discussion of programs that exist to address the most pressing of social issues.

Mothers without husbands can apply for financial assistance for their children. People in need may also apply for food stamps that can be taken to a grocery store (supermarket) and used to purchase food. (There is a small fee for food stamps that must be paid by the recipient.) The government provides some basic housing at low rental rates to those on limited incomes and those receiving government assistance— although there are often waiting lists for some low-income housing facilities. Medical and hospital care ("Medicaid") is provided under certain circumstances for people in need.

The Social Security pension paid to retired persons (or to minor children of deceased workers) is not considered aid to needy people since workers paid into the account prior to retirement or death. Retired persons are also eligible for "Medicare," a program to assist with medical and hospital bills for retirees.

In cities and towns across the country, one may find an agent of the welfare agency called the Department of Human Resources. A representative of this agency can offer advice to anyone with economic needs. There are other agencies newcomers may consult in a crisis. Many churches are willing to help in an emergency, and agencies offering advice and help are listed in the Yellow Pages of the telephone directory. Newcomers should ask colleagues and friends to help them find a suitable agency should they have problems. The people of the United States are compassionate and caring, and nobody need have overwelming problems without the knowledge of the possibility of help, but you are expected to ask or to apply for help. Rarely do Americans infringe on your privacy and give you unasked for assistance. To do so would violate your right to be independent.

If you do apply to a crisis or welfare agency for help, be prepared for their personnel to conduct a check on your situation. This may involve interviewing people who know you both socially and professionally.

Programs Funded by the Government

There are too many projects funded by the federal and local governments to discuss them all. The United States government provides funds for all kinds of research, educational programs, universities, programs to help minorities, handicapped people, disadvantaged people, poor people, projects in other countries (especially those in the less-developed countries of the Developing World), the arts, science, national parks, environmental projects, and many other causes.

Acquired Immune Deficiency Syndrome (AIDS)

Most newcomers are aware of the problem the disease called AIDS has become in the United States. Newcomers should become well acquainted with the nature, course, and symptoms of AIDS, as well as methods of transmission of this disease.

AIDS is a disease caused by a virus that destroys a person's immune system, leaving that individual unable to cope with many varieties of infections and illnesses. The disease is infectious and is transmitted from one affected person to a healthy person through body fluids, such as blood and sexual secretions. Some people believe that saliva may also carry the virus. As of this writing AIDS is invariably fatal.

Literature and other information is provided free to all at the offices of the local health department. The address of this department can be obtained in the local telephone directory. A local hospital or medical society can also put a newcomer in touch with an official who can provide educational materials on how AIDS is spread and how it can be prevented.

Since there is no known cure for AIDS, the prevention of AIDS is of utmost importance.   To date, though treatment alleviates some of the many symptoms, there is no cure. The AIDS virus most dominant in the United States is the Virus I variety. At the present time the Virus II, prevalent in Africa, though already identified in the United States, is not yet as widespread as the Virus I.

In the United States, people most likely to contract the AIDS virus are homosexual men, male and female prostitutes, and intravenous drug users. However, at the present time, the virus is also spreading among the heterosexual population.

There is widespread fear of contracting AIDS, but health

care professionals believe the only way this virus is transmitted is through sexual intercourse, sharing infected needles when injecting drugs, by receiving contaminated blood during a blood transfusion, and by the passing of the infection from a mother to an unborn child. Blood used in transfusions is rigorously tested, so the incidence of contamination by blood transfusion is currently believed to be low. Lately, a few cases of patients being infected by health professionals have been reported, and a number of health-care professionals have been infected by patients.

Because sexual transmission seems to be the most frequent method of transmission, a monogamous relationship with an uninfected person is currently the only real safeguard against acquiring the AIDS virus. Sexual intercourse with prostitutes is highly risky.

In some states, people are required to be tested for AIDS before marriage. It is a good idea to insist that the person one wishes to marry should be tested; otherwise, one can become infected also if the partner is infected.

Health authorities suggest that all individuals with a sexual partner who has the AIDS virus should use condoms when having sexual intercourse. Condoms are available for both men and women. It should be noted, however, that condoms are not total protection against acquiring the disease; they only reduce the risk. Condoms may be purchased in many places, notably in drug stores, pharmacies, and large supermarkets.

Sexually Transmitted Diseases

Newcomers should be warned that though sexual freedom is prevalent in the United States, it carries great risks. In addition to AIDS, other sexually transmitted diseases, sometimes called venereal diseases, include syphilis, gonorrhea, chlamydia, herpes, and other strains of diseases specifically related to promiscuous sexual activity. In some states, before a couple can obtain a marriage license, they must have blood tests to determine the presence or absence of a venereal disease. If the tests are positive, the individuals are encouraged to obtain medical treatment, which in most cases, can alleviate the symptoms, though cannot always cure the disease. This test is important, as venereal disease in the mother can result in severe problems for a newborn infant, and partners need to know the risks of marrying an infected person.

Medical authorities believe that sexually transmitted diseases, including the AIDS virus, are not transmitted by talking or living with an infected individual. Nor is the use of public toilets, drinking fountains, utensils in a restaurant or other public places considered dangerous. These diseases are thought to be transmitted mainly through sexual contact with infected individuals. Prostitutes are among the main carriers of these diseases, and only one contact with an infected prostitute (or other infected individual) can result in contracting a sexually transmitted disease, including AIDS.

Sexual Harassment

At the time of writing, sexual harassment is one of the most debated topics, and many institutions have definite policies about how employees and students should behave toward members of the opposite sex.

Sexual harassment exists when one person tries to persuade another person to do something sexual against his or her wishes. Often fear of losing a job or some benefit, or promises of gaining some benefit, are used in the persuasion. Often a person in a superior position, such as a supervisor, pays sexual attention to a person of inferior position who does not want this attention, but feels that he or she has to accept it to please the superior. Sexual harassment also refers to actions like flirting, inappropriately touching a person of the opposite sex or saying something sexually inappropriate. In many cultures this type of interaction between the sexes is acceptable, but in the United States it is not when it occurs at work, college, or at university.

It is wise for all newcomers, whether they are business people, professionals, or students to find out exactly what the policy is in the institution in which they work and study. Some colleges and universities have strict policies regulating how males and females treat each other. Violating the institutions policies could result in serious trouble, or a lawsuit.

The Final Word: For College, University and Graduate Students Only

Most of this book will be relevant to foreign students at college and university; therefore, students are encouraged to read the whole book. However, this additional information may be especially relevant and helpful to students only.

Homesickness and Loneliness

This is one of the worst problems students face. Read page 69 for a fuller discussion of this topic and for suggestions about how to deal with it. Also, find out from the counselor or advisor to "international" (foreign) students if there are other people from your country at the university or college you are now attending or in your present accommodations. Try to contact them. Usually people from the same country are happy to be friendly to each other.

If you find you are so unhappy that you feel scared and worried, and unable to cope with your daily duties, speak to a doctor about the stress you feel. Also, read the section on depression on page 64.

Although you will be very busy as a student, try to make time for relaxation and plenty of rest. It is also important to eat as well as you can afford to. See page 105 for information about grocery stores.

In order to reduce loneliness, as well as to relax, try to attend the functions the director of the international programs at your institution arranges especially for foreign students. If you do not have a special department for foreign students, find out which functions are arranged for students in order to provide relaxation and an opportunity for mixing with friends.

Often the religious organizations on campus provide activities you may find interesting and helpful. Most of the activities provided by these organizations are free. Often the leaders and students in these organizations are aware of the problems of newcomers and they try to make newcomers feel welcome. You do not need to feel embarrassed about attending their meetings, even if you are of another religion.

The Importance of Earning Good Grades (Marks)

Remember that you should earn the very best grades possible because every grade for every course taken is listed on a permanent record called a "transcript". Admission to a graduate school (including doctoral studies) and, sometimes acceptance for employment, depends on the sort of grades students earn.

Cheating

At all colleges and universities in the United States, cheating is considered an extremely serious offense. Cheating involves copying somebody else's work in an exam, or writing information in a research paper that was taken from another source, such as a journal, paper, etc. or a person without giving that person or source credit. Cheating is also the copying of information from a piece of paper, clothing or even one's body taken into the examination room. Students who get caught cheating can be required to leave the college or university permanently. Ask an advisor or a professor to explain what cheating is if you are not sure what it really involves.

When you take an examination, you are expected to have all the information only in your memory. Be extremely careful that you do not do anything that could give the **appearance** of cheating, even if you are **not** cheating, because it could be hard to prove your innocence.

Complaints

When you are having serious problems and you feel you need to make complaints, remember that you are a visitor and, as such, should behave at all times with courtesy and politeness in your host country.

If you have problems with your employer on campus, your professors or teachers, or conditions in your apartment or room, there is usually a person to whom you can complain.

Should you have problems with your accommodation, speak to your landlord or the director of university housing. Here again, be polite and avoid being demanding. For some students, especially those who have come from wealthy backgrounds in their homelands, living quarters on a university campus may seem inadequate because they usually consist only of basic furnishings and appliances. If you need extra luxuries you will probably have to pay for these yourself as the university usually will not provide additional comforts.

Dealing With Problems With Your Teachers

If you do not understand a lecture, make an appointment to see your professor. Do not feel embarrassed about asking for help; you will be admired for it. Do not be embarrassed about asking questions after the class, or, during the class if you are confused about information presented in class. American students are encouraged to ask questions, so you may also feel free to do so. However, be polite when you ask questions, and never verbally attack your teacher.

If you feel an assignment or a test has not been fairly evaluated or graded, you can feel free to speak to your professor. However, you should not accuse him or her, and you should speak in a very polite manner when you explain your complaint. Explain that you do not understand how you have been evaluated. If you feel your grade is too low, you can ask your teacher to explain how you earned that grade. You should only go to the department head or dean if you feel that you have not been able to solve the problem with your teacher.

If you are having difficulty with understanding the class lectures, the reading material or assignments in any of your courses, speak to your teachers. American professors and teachers are usually sympathetic and can sometimes put you in touch with tutors who can give you help with your studies.

Writing Term Papers and Research Papers

One of the ways in which American students learn is by the "research" method. This method encourages students to discover facts and information for themselves from a variety of sources, including books. The information gathered is organized into a long essay, called a "term or research paper." (See pages 141 & 142 for more information.)

Many foreign students are not accustomed to this method of learning and do not know how to write these papers or "long essays". If you do not know how to write these papers, do **not** be embarrassed, but ask your teacher to explain how to do this research, or ask your teacher to guide you to somebody who can help you. Remember, teachers admire students who ask for help and advice and they also understand that you have come from a different country which may have different methods of instruction.

Learning To Speak English

Most foreign students read English fairly easily. However, many students have difficulty **speaking** English so it is wise to attend classes in conversational English. Make an effort to learn to pronounce English words in the American way so that you will be easily understood.

Many churches in the South have programs that help foreign students with conversational English. These are usually offered free of charge and students are generally warmly welcomed. An advisor in the International Department of your college will be able to put you in touch with some organization that offers courses in conversational English.

If you are a graduate student and have a job teaching students in the United States, you should learn to speak clearly, slowly and without a strong accent. American students get irritated when their teachers speak with such a strong accent that they cannot understand their lectures.

Say What You Mean

See also page 200.

Remember that people in the United States do not usually speak indirectly when they need help. If you need some help or directions from an any American say **exactly** what you mean and what you want. Avoid trying to get people to do things for you without asking in a direct way, or by making them feel guilty if they don't help you. This is called "manipulating" in this country and people resent this.

If you are offered help, refreshments or gifts, all you have to do is accept them. Americans will not understand if you make polite indirect comments that do not indicate clearly that you are accepting what is offered.

Dealing With People With Less Education Than Yourself

Remember that Americans believe that everybody has equal rights and deserves equal respect regardless of their education, or money (economic status). Always be careful to speak respectfully and politely to people with low status jobs and less education than you have, otherwise you will create resentment and anger toward yourself. Sometimes these Americans show hostility to foreigners who, they feel, are enjoying the benefits of education in the United States that they themselves cannot afford.

Be Sure To Have The Correct Visa
See also page 247

At most colleges and universities there is an officer who can explain visa requirements to you if you have any confusion. Do not do any work at all unless you have the correct visa. At the time of writing, the Immigration and Naturalization Service is tracking illegal aliens. You could be deported if you work without the correct visa and you may risk being banned from the United States permanently.

Medical Insurance
See also page 84.

Most colleges and universities want or require foreign students to have medical insurance. It is important for you, and your spouse and children, to participate in your college's insurance plan. See page 84 for further information and warnings.

Taking Care of Your Room or Apartment
You may find that your apartment gets a strange odor. This is often because of the humidity, smoke in the carpet or curtains, and the lack of circulation of fresh air.

The air conditioning cleans the air in the apartment or room only up to a point, but does not remove dust and all odors. Dust will still settle in your carpets, curtains, and furnishings. It is recommended that you vacuum carpets regularly and open windows at least once a week to get clean air circulating. This will help to keep a fresh smell in the apartment. When you open your windows you should cut off your air conditioning. See page 87 for more information regarding air conditioning and page 80, for dealing with cooking odors.

Additional Information

Students are urged to read pages 132, 137, 141, 145, 150, 151, and 153 for more information about life on a college or university campus. The section on "dating", page 216, and "taking trips", page 175, may also be especially interesting to students.

Index